GOD GAVE ME A RHYME

GOD GAVE ME A RHYME

Adventuring With God

by

Pat Harold Carter

iUniverse, Inc.
New York   Bloomington

God Gave Me a Rhyme
Adventuring With God

iUniverse books may be ordered through booksellers or by contacting:

iUniverse
1663 Liberty Drive
Bloomington, IN 47403
www.iuniverse.com
1-800-Authors (1-800-288-4677)

ISBN: 978-1-4401-2453-2 (pbk)
ISBN: 978-1-4401-2455-6 (dj)
ISBN: 978-1-4401-2454-9 (ebk)

Printed in the United States of America

iUniverse rev. date: 3/2/2009

Prologue

We are His workmanship, created in Christ Jesus for good works, which God prepared beforehand that we should walk in them (Eph. 2:10)

We are *God's workmanship.*

The Greek word translated workmanship is *poiema.* "Poem" comes down to us from this word, by way of the Latin word *poema.*

I am God's poem! God wrote it before I was born. Paul says I should take this poem as the map for my life, and "walk in the good works" God has prepared for me. If I do, my future is secure: "We know that God is working all things together for good to those who love the Lord, to those who have been called *according to His purpose*" (Romans 8:28).

I am God's poem. What is a poem? There are two kinds of poetry, lyric and narrative. A lyric poem is short and beautiful, with a songlike quality. Certain people in the Bible are like lyric poems, for example, Simeon and Anna. They appeared very briefly, at the moment of the presentation of the infant Jesus and spoke words of prophecy (Luke 2:22-36). God continues writing lyric poems, for example the beautiful life of a baby who blesses its family for a few days or weeks, then is taken up into heaven.

But most of God's poems are narrative, longer and more complicated than the lyric poem. The lives of Moses, Abraham, and Paul are narrative poems. And so are our lives. Whether we live twenty, fifty, eighty or ninety years, God has written the script for each day.

What makes a poem? A poem has a unique design, a pattern quite different from prose. When we see our lives as a poem written by God, our imagination, anointed by the Holy Spirit and awakened by faith, can discern God's design!

The most touching poems are love poems. The poem God has written for you is a love poem. John exclaims: "Behold what manner of love the Father has bestowed on us that we should be called the sons of God" (1John 3:1). During all of our life, in the good things and the bad, we should grow in our appreciation of God's incredible love for us.

One last thing: a poem may, or may not have rhyme. But rhyme adds special beauty to a poem. That happened in at least one of God's life poems in the Bible: the life of John the Baptist rhymed with the life of Elijah. The way he dressed, the food he ate, the place he lived, the message he proclaimed, was a rhyme of that Old Testament prophet (Malachai 4:5; Matthew 3:1-4; 17:10-13).

A few years ago, in the midst of the worst crisis I had ever faced, I discovered that God had written rhyme into my own life poem, that my life rhymes with the life of Caleb! I'll tell you about that moment of discovery in chapter twenty-eight. (You have my permission to read that chapter now, if you can't wait.) That discovery encouraged me to review my entire life as a reflection of Caleb's life. I was amazed at so many similarities! That's why, in this memoir, Caleb's history forms the background of my own. In the first three chapters I recount the life of Caleb and his family before Caleb was named as one of the twelve spies, showing how his father's life rhymed with my own father's. Though the Bible doesn't supply information about Caleb's father, I imagine how his life must have been, based on what we learn about Caleb later.

I invite you to consider an exciting possibility: *God may have written rhyme into your life poem!* If that sounds illogical to you, remember that a poem speaks, not to reason, but to the heart and the imagination. So as you read my story, suspend logic and free your heart and imagination to hear the whisper of the Holy Spirit.

A Confession

As I wrote this story of my life, I soon bumped into a phenomenon that caused me a lot of frustration: I was obligated to employ a filter. Many times it was impossible to recount some of the most interesting things that happened, because I found myself asking: if I tell it just like it happened,
Will it offend someone?
Will it make someone angry?
Will I lose someone's friendship?
Will I get sued?
So, I used the filter of discretion to:
Censor some of the most titillating events.
Invent fictitious names.

Chapter One
The Birth of a Dream

The day Jephunneh talked with his grandfather Kenaz the dream was born.*

Kenaz was one of the most honored men of the nation of Edom. Named for the founder of the tribe of the Kenizzites, he was well over a hundred years of age. General Kenaz had distinguished himself as a fearless warrior before his retirement thirty years before. He lived now in the magnificent red rock city of Petra, where his grateful king had bequeathed him a palace. Jephunneh's father had spoken to him frequently of the great honor he had inherited as a member of the tribe of the Kenizzites.

On Jephunneh's twelfth birthday, Kenaz invited his grandson to spend the day with him. Little Jephunneh listened with awe as the general recounted the story of his tribe: "My son, the Kennizzites are one of the oldest of the tribes of Edom. More than seven hundred years ago the God Yahveh spoke of us when He made his pact with Abraham."

"And who is the God Yahveh, Grandfather? And Abraham?"

His eyebrows raised, General Kenaz answered, "I'm sorry to hear that your father has not told you about our God Yahveh and our Father Abraham!"

He spent the rest of the afternoon describing for his grandson Abraham's encounter with the one true God. And how Abraham's grandson Esau, nicknamed Edom, had been born in the beautiful hill country of Hebron, some fifty miles to the northeast of Seir. The eldest of twins, Edom was in line to receive the family inheritance from his wealthy father, Isaac. But his brother Jacob stole his birthright. This treason evoked in the heart of Edom a hatred that he passed on to his children. Later, he migrated to the land of the Kennizzites. Through the centuries the descendents of Kenaz and of Edom had intermarried. Now, most of the Kenizzites, though proud of their tribal heritage, considered themselves a part of the nation of Edom. And they had acquired from the Edomites, not only the knowledge of the true God, and a loyalty to their adopted grandfather Esau, but also an intense hatred for the descendents of Jacob,

"Grandfather," asked Jephunneh, "do the descendents of Jacob still live in Hebron?"

"No, my son, centuries ago, because of a great drought, Jacob took his family to live in Egypt. They have been there ever since. For some generations they were favored by the Pharoah, but now, for hundreds of years, they have lived in slavery."

"Have you ever met any of the descendents of Jacob?"

"No my little son, and I regret it. It is too late now for me, but I hope some day you will be able to do so. They are now called the Israelites. And may you, with the help of Yahveh, put an end to this senseless hatred that has infected our souls for more than four hundred years.

"And what of our ancestral home, Hebron?"

"A sad story, Jephunneh. Our beloved homeland is occupied by a fierce people known as the Canaanites. I have always dreamed of visiting the tombs of my ancestors, Abraham and Isaac, but it has been impossible."

"Is there no hope we may one day recover our homeland?"

"I'm afraid not. The Cannanites are a powerful people, with walled cities and iron chariots. I once led an army against them, but we were too few and too poorly armed to overcome them."

That night, back in his bed, little Jephunneh had a hard time going to sleep. His mind churned with the stories his grandfather had told him. Grandfather Kenaz was right, it was foolish to continue nourishing a hatred because of something that happened hundreds of years before. For the first time in his life, Jephunneh prayed to the God of his ancestors. And asked Him for the opportunity to fulfill the wish of his grandfather: that he might someday befriend his cousins, the Israelites. And what of Hebron, where his ancestors were buried? His grandfather had described it as a green, fruitful heaven on earth, in striking contrast to the rocky, arid country of Edom.

Finally Jephunneh went to sleep, and dreamed of visiting Hebron. And strangely, his companions in that visit were his Israelite cousins. He awoke with the conviction that Yahveh had given him that dream. One day he would meet his cousins. And one day he would have a home in Hebron!

One moonlit night an hour before sunup sixteen-year-old James Alec, the boy who one day would become my father, crawled out the bedroom window of his family's farmhouse and disappeared into the woods. The eldest of eight children, he was fed up with the hard scrabble life on his father's backwoods farm in South Louisiana. James' life should have been better. His grandfather had been a surveyor and itinerant preacher. He bought up, at twenty-five cents an acre, much of the land he surveyed, and left his eldest son several thousand of those acres. But his spoiled offspring never learned the virtue of hard work. He dedicated himself to begetting children and hunting deer. His wife, a refined Methodist lady, spent her time nurturing the children and cooking mush for her husband's kennel of hungry deer dogs.

The time had come to venture out and see if the world didn't have something better to offer!

James walked to the railroad, waited until a freight train stopped at a water tank to refuel its steam locomotive, and hopped into a boxcar. He rode as far as Port Arthur, Texas, jumped down and wandered the streets until he came to the shipyards. A big freighter was tied up at the dock. Summing up his courage he went aboard, found the captain, announced that he was eighteen and looking for a job. Short-handed, the captain accepted the skinny kid's obvious fib, and signed him up. And James Alec became a sailor.

For the next six years my father visited many ports around the world. One of the most frequent ports of call was Tampico, Mexico. James Alec found himself at home among the Mexican people. He was intrigued by the similarity of the culture to that of the South Louisiana Cajuns. He looked forward to his visits with the Mexican people, cultivated their friendship and dated more than one charming *señorita*.

But one day in 1917 the idyllic visits came to an end. When the ship tied up to the Tampico dock, the captain announced that no one would be allowed to go ashore. General Pershing had invaded Mexico in search of Pancho Villa, and now the Mexicans hated Americans. To go ashore would invite a fight, and very likely, arrest by the authorities.

James took the captain's prohibition as a challenge. Late that night he and a buddy slid down the lines attaching the ship to the dock and headed downtown. As they strolled down a dusty street, they suddenly found themselves in front of a military post.

"*Alto!*" a soldier ordered, blocking their path with his rifle. My dad and his buddy took off running. After a couple of blocks, my father dove through the window of a tiny hovel and hid under a bed. Hours later, he hurried back to his ship and climbed aboard, thanking God for his escape.

It broke James Alec's heart that the happy, friendly people he had come to care for were now his enemies. A dream was born in his heart: Some day he was going to return to Mexico. As a friend. And maybe even live there for a while.

*The Bible does not provide us with a background for its enigmatic introduction of Caleb in Numbers 13:6. Here and in following chapters I imagine what this background must have been, based on the Biblical text. Kenaz, the founder of the Kenizzite tribe, is mentioned in Genesis 36:42, and I Chronicles 1:53. Fifteen times, in four different books of the Old Testament, Jephunneh the Kenizzite, father of Caleb, is mentioned (See Joshua 14:14 *et al.*).

Chapter Two
Following the Dream
1919-1929

Jephunneh grew up, married and had a son. He named him Omar, and from his earliest age Jephunneh taught him the truths he had learned from his grandfather Kenaz about the God Yahveh. And he prayed to Yahveh with his son every night. He told his son about his cousins who lived in Egypt, and about his dream of one day visiting them. He also planted in his son's heart the dream of returning to Hebron in the hill country, the land of his ancestors.

In time, Jephunneh's father died. Since Jephunneh was the eldest, he received the major portion of his father's herds. When he was old enough, Omar began accompanying his father each day in his search for grazing land. This was an arduous, often discouraging task because Edom was an arid territory, and there were often long periods of drought.

One day Jephunneh came home very excited. "Today," he told his family, "I was at the city gate conversing with the elders, when a man appeared, driving his cattle before him. He showed us a document with the seal of Pharoah, giving him permission to graze his cattle in Goshen, in Egypt. Talking with him, I learned that such documents are not hard to come by. For the Egyptians, herding cattle is an abomination, so a foreigner with cattle is no threat to their way of life. And besides, Goshen is inhabited by ... " (a dramatic pause) ... "the Israelite slaves."

After six years at sea, my father returned home and married his pretty redheaded French sweetheart, Marie. This was a big change for her. The youngest of eight children, Marie's mother died giving birth to her. She became the favorite of her father who presided over a family that was part of the Louisiana rural aristocracy. Until his fifties, Marie's grandfather taught violin in a studio on the *Champs-Èlysèes* in Paris. Then he sold his studio and purchased a large plantation in south Louisiana. Marie's father saw to it that his children spoke Parisian French, not the Cajun French of their neighbors. And he insisted she not share the household labor with her four sisters. She had a beautiful pony she loved to ride, and every time her father traveled to New Orleans he brought her new riding clothes. She was eighteen when her father died and immediately lost her favored status. Without a doting father to defend her, her brothers and sisters saw to it that she learned how to wash dishes and hoe cotton.

When Alec Carter appeared and announced he was ready to settle down, she didn't waste time deciding. She needed to get away, and besides, she had lost her heart long ago to that Irish boy with the carefree grin and big black motorcycle. A judge married them, and he took her to Port Arthur, Texas, where he went to work in the Texaco Refinery. After three years, a son was born. Then, four years later, I came along. By this time, my dad had set himself on an obsessive path that he was confident would make him a wealthy man. He had left the refinery and opened a dry cleaner. Then a second. Then a barbershop. Then another. Besides, he was dabbling in real estate. He installed his family in an imposing two-story home in a privileged section of Port Arthur. I was unaware that, like my mother, I was the spoiled youngest child. I have on my chest of drawers a well-preserved eight by ten full color portrait of a handsome little boy with long blond curls and a confident smile. And there is a small black and white snapshot of me raiding the cash register at my dad's barbershop.

My family was also prospering spiritually. Years before, a famous cowboy evangelist had put up a tent downtown and converted hard-hearted, hard-drinking men by the dozens. My dad was one of them. After hearing one of Preacher Crimm's hellfire sermons he drove home, poured his bootleg whiskey down the drain and vowed never to drink again. He joined Procter Street Baptist Church.

As for my mother, she had no interest in Daddy's new faith. Her father had taught her as a girl that all Protestants were "either niggers or poor white trash." When she married a Baptist, she lost her right to her church's sacraments. She gave up mass, but never gave up her prejudices against Protestants.

I was still a baby when, one rainy Sunday afternoon, my Uncle Frank and Aunt Bessie called. "Marie, our car broke down, and it's raining. We hate to ask you because we know Alec's out of town, but we have to go to our church because we sing in the choir. Would you mind taking us?"

My mother agreed. When they arrived at the church, Aunt Bessie said, "Marie, it's an awful night, and I hate to think of you driving back home alone. Why don't you just come inside with us?"

My mother wrinkled her nose. She'd never in her life set foot in a Protestant church. Not a chance!

My Aunt Bessie must have been persuasive, because at last my mother consented with the understanding she would sit on the very last pew.

Mama told me many times that she remembered only two things about the pastor's sermon: first, it made her shudder because it was something about snakes. Second, from the moment the pastor opened his Bible, tears began to flow, and she couldn't stop them.

The next Sunday morning my mother returned. When the invitation was given, she placed Baby Pat in Bessie's arms and walked down the aisle.

My mother was truly converted, but she was determined not to become a fanatic.

At her insistence, we spent many of our summer weekends on Galveston's beaches. The rest of the year she often found other things to do on Sunday. But as the years passed God worked in Daddy's life. He was named a deacon and became faithful in church.

He prayed with me and my brother every night. And he told me about his trips to Mexico as a sailor, and of his dream of one day returning to share the Gospel with the people he had come to love.

Omar had just celebrated his tenth birthday when his father Jephunneh came home waving a document. "It arrived! The elders at the gate just delivered me this permit from the Pharoah for us to settle in Egypt!"

The following weeks were filled with activity, finding a buyer for their home, paying off their debts, and most difficult, saying their farewells. Everyone had the same question. They could understand why Jephunneh might want to graze his cattle in Egypt, others had done the same thing. But why were they going to make that fearful empire their home? And, even worse, why did they want to live among their hated cousins, descendents of Edom's brother?

Jephunneh had the same answer for all of them: "Yahveh has given me a dream, and I must follow it."

A big crowd bid them farewell at the gates. Afterward they shook their heads and muttered, "Jephunneh is out of his mind. He'll be back by the end of the year."

The trek to Egypt took a week. It was little more than a hundred miles, but cattle move slowly, and they must be fed and watered, and besides, Omar's three younger brothers required constant care. When they arrived in Egypt they followed the Nile north until they came to the fertile region known as Goshen. Jephunneh had heard that the Israelites were grouped as tribes, and in spite of being slaves, the elders of each tribe governed their people. Jephunneh had no idea where they would settle, but he was convinced that when they came to the place God had ordained, they would know it. They moved from tribe to tribe, speaking with the elders, who received them with reserve, for these were descendents of the despised Edom, the brother who had sworn to kill their father Israel. Besides, they were so burdened by the tasks given them by their Egyptian masters they had time for little more than eating and sleeping. Certainly no time to help strangers.

When Jephunneh and his family came to the tribe of Judah, they encountered an elder searching for a lost milk cow. Jephunneh and Omar joined him in the search. After a while, they spotted a lone cow grazing in the distance. The animal, seeing Jephunneh's herd, lowed and trotted toward them. The elder was grateful and invited them to pitch their tents near his stable.

The next day, Jephunneh and Omar found good pasture for their cattle. That night Jephunneh led his family in a prayer of thanksgiving for their new home. Each day afterward they found time to help the elder with his small herd when he returned from his long day of building the Pharoah's palaces.

One day, Omar returned upset from the school he now attended. "Do you know the nickname the other kids have given me? Caleb!"*

His father shook his head. I'm sorry, son, but I warned you to be prepared for prejudice."

"It's not fair! I don't like them calling me a dog."

"Get used to it, my son, life is not fair. I'll tell you how to overcome their prejudice: accept the name they gave you, and live in such a way that Caleb becomes a name of honor."

As his twelfth year approached, Caleb said to his father Jephunneh one night after prayers: "Father, when I was very small you shared with me your dream of coming to live with our Israelite cousins. Your dream became my dream, and Yahveh made our dream come true. Now He has placed in my heart the desire to take the next step."

"And what is that, my son?"

"I ask your permission to become an Israelite."

Jephunneh stared at his son, startled. "But, Omar -- "

"Please do not deny me, Father. The fulfillment of our dream will not be complete until we occupy once again the hill country of Hebron. The prophets of the Israelites are telling their people that soon God will free them from slavery and take them back to their homeland. If I hope to be a part of that return, I must become one of them."

The next night Jephunneh took his son for an interview with the elder who had been their host from the beginning. The elder, very pleased, explained to father and son what the requirements were for Caleb to become a proselyte: he would have to be thoroughly instructed in the verbal tradition. Like all other male Israelites, he would be circumcised. Third, he would have to be adopted by one of the families of the tribe of Judah. No, that would not mean he'd have to leave the family of his father, Jephunneh, but his adoption would make it possible that his genealogical line become a legitimate part of the Israelite nation. His adoptive father would be his guide in his preparations and would, at the appropriate time, recommend he be inducted into the tribe.

So Omar became a part of the family of Hezron. After six months of intensive preparation, in a solemn ritual, the elders of Judah laid hands upon him. He was entered into official records as "Caleb, the son of Hezron." ** *Thus the nickname given to him years earlier by jeering little boys became a name of honor.*

One Monday morning Daddy told my mother he believed God was calling him into the ministry. My mother blinked. "What does that mean? That you're going to sell your businesses and become pastor of a church?"

"It could mean that!"

"Me a pastor's wife? I'd rather be dead!"

As the months passed, the debate continued. One Saturday Daddy talked Mama into a weekend trip to New Orleans. He wanted to visit the Baptist Bible Institute. Just a visit, my mother need not worry.

Again and again, on the way to New Orleans, Mama repeated that she would never consent to being a pastor's wife. Sitting in the back seat with my brother, my blood ran cold. Did this mean my parents were going to divorce?

Saturday night my father slept little, complaining of a sharp pain in his side. Sunday morning, as we began our return trip, he was running a fever. By the time we reached home he was groaning in agony. My mother called our family doctor. Dr. Young poked my father's side, took his temperature and blood pressure, and called for an ambulance.

The next day they told Mama to call in the family. Daddy had a ruptured appendix, and there was nothing they could do for him.

Mama hurried downstairs to St. Mary's Hospital's chapel. Later, she would give her testimony: "I fell on my knees and told God I knew why Alec was dying: God had called him to be a preacher and I had rebelled. I told God, 'Oh Lord, please heal Alec. If you do, I promise I'll never rebel against you again, as long as I live!' And God spoke to me. He told me I was forgiven, and that Alec was going to get well."

Mama took the elevator back to the seventh floor. As soon as the doors opened she could hear my father's groans. When she walked into the room Daddy's five brothers and two sisters were gathered around his bed, tears running down their cheeks.

They stared at my mother in surprise, because her face was shining. "A wonderful thing just happened, God told me Alec is going to get well!"

They looked at one another, shaking their heads. "Poor Marie," one of them said.

"She's beside herself. Someone take her home so she can get some rest."

I remember the ride home in our big black Pontiac that evening. I was in the back seat. I stared straight ahead at the long silver-colored hand grip that stretched across the back of the front seat. What was going to happen? Had God really spoken to Mama? Or, when we returned to the hospital next morning would my father be gone? I had no idea, I only knew that, whatever happened, our lives would never be the same.

The next morning Daddy was still alive, but barely. On his evening round, the doctor told us he was doubtful my father would last the night.

My mother went down into the chapel again. Desperate, she cried out to God: "Lord, I was so sure you spoke to me. Was I wrong?"

Then she heard in her heart the words of a familiar hymn: "He has never broken any promise spoken, He will keep His promise to me." Within a week my father was home, fully recovered.

So it happened, that very early in my life, a divine truth was branded upon my soul:

God does not tolerate disobedience.

God is patient with our growth pains and he gives us a lot of slack as we learn how to know and follow His will. But outright disobedience brings His judgment.

During the next months, my father dedicated himself to preparations for the big change that had come into our lives. He sold his barbershops and his dry cleaners and closed his real estate office. In August we sold our home. My mother wept when we delivered the keys to the new owners, but she did not complain. God had given us a dream and we must follow it. The dream for now was to leave Texas and move to the prairies of South Louisiana, where Daddy would enroll in Acadia Baptist Academy, "the school of a second chance."

*The Hebrew root of Caleb is *kelebh,* "dog," or *chaleb,* "raging with canine madness.".

**In Numbers 13:6; 14:6,30 and Joshua 14:6 Caleb is called "the son of Jephunneh the Kenezzite." But in 1 Chronicles 2:18, the official register of Israel, he is called "Caleb, the son of Hezron."

Chapter Three
Growing Under God's Discipline
1929-1935

For the next twenty-six years Caleb placed himself alongside the people he had adopted as his own. As he moved into young manhood, although he was not a slave as the others in his tribe, he took his brothers' burdens as his own. Each day after fulfilling his duties to his own family he would go out to where the Israelites labored and lend a helping hand. Quite often he persuaded the guards to let him take the place of someone too weak or too ill to bear the heavy loads. On more than one occasion Caleb presented the complaints of his people to their Egyptian masters, and was able to win his case.

A year after his adoption into the tribe of Judah, one of the elders awoke him at midnight, and signaling that he was not to speak, led him to a house in the center of the encampment of the tribe of Judah. Larger than the humble dwellings occupied by the Israelite slaves, this house was built of stone. His host knocked at the bronze door, and when it was cracked open mumbled a password. The door opened, and facing them was a young man dressed in a linen robe, holding a spear. The elder led him inside. Half a dozen sputtering lamps illumined a bronze casket resting on a bench covered by a rich purple tapestry. Stamped upon the casket was the royal Egyptian seal.

"Caleb," his host told him, "behold the resting place of the bones of our father Joseph. We have told you his story, how he became second only to the Pharoah, and later brought his father and brothers from Canaan. On his

deathbed he told his brothers, 'I am dying; but God will surely visit you, and bring you out of this land to the land of which he swore to Abraham, to Isaac, and to Jacob.' Then he took an oath from the children of Israel, saying, 'God will surely visit you, and you shall carry up my bones from here.' Many of us believe that day is near."

As time passed, Caleb and his contemporaries married and took upon themselves the responsibilities of family. Often, when a conflict arose among the people, he was called upon to preside at a tribal conclave, because the people had learned he would judge fairly. His friends forgot that he was ever named "Omar," and pronounced his name Caleb with respect.

Arriving at the Acadia Baptist Academy, we were assigned a small white clap-board house without screens or electric lights, and a two-hole toilet in the back yard.

Within a year the Great Depression descended upon America. The Federal Government froze the banks, and we lost the money my father had received from the sale of his properties. But the option of leaving school was never considered. God had brought us to ABA and He'd see us through. Mama and Daddy struggled to stretch the few dollars we received each month. Daddy preached somewhere most Sundays and would bring home bags of potatoes, tomatoes and eggs. In the Spring we canned blackberries and figs, and in the fall, peas and okra from our garden. I can still see in my mind's eye the walls of our kitchen lined with shelves Daddy had built from floor to ceiling, filled with quart jars of fruits and vegetables. We always had a cow for milk, clabber and butter. Daddy somehow managed to employ someone to help Mama with the washing and ironing. We were never without an automobile, though I had to sit with my brother in the rumble seat, and the tires were usually worn smooth.

I now know that I had entered God's school of discipline, in preparation for living the poem He had written for me. I learned from my parents a lesson that I was to remember time and again in the years ahead:

"Seek first the Kingdom of God and His righteousness, and all these things will be added unto you (Matthew 6:33).

We had it tough but lived better than most of the other families in our neighborhood. One cold Saturday morning Mama told me: "Pat, I put our tithe money in an envelope behind the stove, planning to place it in the offering plate Sunday, but God just told me to take it over to Mrs. Ibsen." The Ibsens lived next-door. They and their seven children had arrived a few months before from California.

Mama stuck the envelope in her apron pocket and hurried out the back door. When she returned, tears were shining in her eyes. Mrs. Ibsen had told her they'd had nothing to eat in the house, and she'd been asking herself -- and God -- what she was going to put on the table at noon.

A funny thing about those tough days: I can't remember ever feeling sorry for myself or blaming my parents. I do remember quite vividly what happened on Monday nights. Without fail, half a dozen student families got together at the Bourgeois house, and Mrs. Bourgeois baked corn bread in a huge, hinged pot. We stuffed ourselves with cornbread and milk and laughed till we cried at the stories the preachers told about their weekend adventures. After more than seventy years one story told by Mike, a red-headed Irish neighbor, is still fresh in my mind:

"Saturday I didn't have fifty cents to buy a bus ticket to my church, so I decided to thumb a ride. A holiness preacher picked me up in his Model T Ford. All along the way it was one 'glory hallelujah!' after another. After a while I found myself wondering why the seat seemed to be getting hotter by the minute. The hotter it got, the more excited that Pentecostal preacher seemed to become. He kept bouncing up and down, shouting, 'Glory to God, I got Holy Ghost fire in my soul!' After a while I could stand it no longer. I yelled, 'Preacher, stop this thing and let me out. The only fire I got is in the seat of my pants!' Glaring at me like I was the devil himself, he pulled over to the side of the road. As I got out, I saw where the heat was coming from: the car seat was soaking wet with gasoline!

"The preacher hopped down and pulled up the seat cushion. No wonder, the gas tank cap had fallen off! Right away he stopped shoutin' hallelujah and started raisin' Cain with God for letting it happen."

By this time Mike was rolling on the floor, and we were all laughing with him.

The Bourgeois had five girls. Rosalie was the oldest and I hated her. My friends and I were always hatching up schemes to do something awful to her, but nothing ever worked out. I don't know why I hated her, she must have been a good girl because every Saturday night, without complaining, she bathed all her little sisters in a tin washtub, starting with the oldest and working her way down. By the time she got to the baby, it must not have done much good, because Mama told me she used the same water from start to finish.

I was seven when Daddy got his diploma and we loaded our beat-up furniture into an open truck and moved to B.B.I., the Baptist Bible Institute in New Orleans. The first year we lived in a tiny apartment. By the second year we couldn't afford the thirteen dollars a month rent. We had a choice: give up on Daddy's studies or take drastic measures. For Mama and Daddy it wasn't hard to decide, they'd take the drastic measures. The Institute lent Daddy a small vacant lot. He built a wooden floor, and staked out a tent on it. That's where we lived for the last year of Daddy's studies. There must have been moments when I compared our tent with the two-story house Daddy built for us in Port Arthur, but if I did, I don't remember.

Daddy was now traveling every other weekend to preach in the little French town of Chicot, about a hundred miles to the north. When he had money to buy gasoline we went with him in a rickety Model A Ford. The weekends Daddy took the train Mama, my brother Junior and I attended tiny Clay Mission, located in New Orleans' historic Garden District. I still remember those Sunday mornings walking to church under the spreading live oak trees, the white colonial houses that lined the streets, and the clanging street cars. I most remember one Sunday morning when the pastor stood before the pulpit while we sang "Just As I Am." I felt a strange warmth in my chest, and found myself walking down the aisle to take the pastor's hand. I'm sure nobody there was especially impressed by the little seven-year-old kid standing up front, but to this day I still remember it as my first experience of God speaking to me so clearly there was no doubt what I should do. And I continue to enjoy the warm, exciting personal relationship with the Son of God that began that day

The weekends we traveled to Chicot with Daddy were always an adventure.

I never saw, except at weddings and funerals, a tie or a fancy dress in the small, wooden house of worship painted a bright blue and set among shade trees. But those country people's hearts overflowed with love and they expressed their love in hearty singing, accompanied by a tiny foot-pumped organ, and in smiles and hugs, and fried chicken. The only unpleasant memories I have of those days are the yucky green tomato pies Mama insisted I eat, and having to use a second-hand fork when there was "dinner on the ground."

A part of the weekend adventure was the ride home on Sunday nights after the services. At a speed of twenty miles per hour on the rough gravel roads, the trips seemed interminable. Daddy was always worried about something happening to the car before we got home -- a failed carburetor, a dead battery -- and most of all, a blowout.

One Sunday night we were nursing a slick back tire. I was dozing in the back seat when Daddy yelled back at me, above the quiet roar of the old motor, "Pat, stick your head out the window and tell me how the tire looks." I obeyed. It was too dark to see anything, but I pulled my head back in and shouted to Daddy, "Looks fine to me."

In that very instant, BANG! and the car began bouncing on the gravel road like a ship on a stormy sea. Daddy slammed on the brakes, dropped his head onto the steering wheel ... and laughed and laughed and laughed. Soon I was laughing with him. But not my mother or Junior. Mama was too tired to laugh, and as for my older brother, he always seemed to be mad.

Rejoice in the Lord, and again I say, rejoice!

That was my parents' motto. Not that they were always laughing. But looking back, I'm impressed how, in circumstances that nowadays would seem an insult to human dignity: hard wooden floors, constantly slapping at mosquitoes or waving flies away because of screenless windows, baths once a week in a tin tub, maybe a dollar a day to support the family, "slop jars" at night instead of a bathroom, no 911 to dial for medical emergencies, my parents habitually were cheerful and optimistic.

One Monday noon Daddy arrived excited from his trip to Chicot. "Marie," he told Ma, "you know we've been praying about where the

Lord wants us to go after I finish up this Spring at B.B.I. I think I've found the place!" And he told us what had happened when the train stopped that morning at the little river town of Krotz Springs. On the platform a big man was lying prostrate on a stretcher, waiting to be loaded onto the train, his upper body swathed in bandages soaked in bright red blood.

"What happened to that guy?" he asked one of the crowd of men gathered around the stretcher.

"Oh, he got cut up last night at Moran's Bar. Dr. Young says he's done all he can for him, and they need to take him to Charity Hospital in New Orleans."

"What a tough-looking crowd!" Daddy concluded, " Looked like any one of them would've cut your throat and thought nothing of it. Reminded me of my years in the merchant marine."

Mama turned pale. "Now Alec ... "

"Don't get up tight, Hon, probably nothing'll come of it."

"Nothing will come of it? What on earth are you talking about?"

"Well, I asked one of the men standing around if they had a Baptist church in Krotz Springs. He said they did, but right now they don't have a pastor. So -- "

Mama heaved a big sigh. So you're going to ... "

"Well, I thought I'd stop off next weekend and check it out."

The following Monday Daddy arrived looking like the proverbial cat that swallowed the mouse. It was true, the church had been without a pastor for a year, and they'd invited him to preach Sunday night. After the service they'd convoked a business meeting and extended Daddy a unanimous call.

Chapter Four
Lessons From Daddy's Pastorates
1935-1938

"Atchafalaya River, straight ahead!" Daddy called, pushing back his straw skimmer. I jumped up in the back seat, where my brother and I had been dozing in the June heat, and leaned forward to peer through the darkness. It had been a long, boring trip from New Orleans, our old Model A Ford bouncing along on the rough gravel road, following the battered open-stake truck that carried our furniture.

"Hold on!" Daddy eased the car onto the railroad bridge. It was 1935, and the highway bridge promised by Huey Long was still years away. So the only way to get to the other side of the Atchafalaya River was to ease carefully along between the rails on thick cypress planks nailed to the crossties.

Halfway across Daddy braked. "Come on, let's take a look at the river."

"I don't know, Alec," Mama said, her voice tense, "what if a train comes along?"

"Oh come on, Marie, there's nothing to worry about!" He threw her a grin and opened his door.

I'd been sulking all day, not wanting to believe what was happening to us. Reluctantly I pushed open my door and stepped out. As soon as my feet touched the bridge I felt a faint vibration that moved from the soles of my feet up my spine to my brain, making me dizzy. The river!

Daddy was leaning over the rail. "Look at it, they say there's no other river like it in all the world!"

Mama shrunk back, and I imagined she must be feeling what I was feeling. The faint glow of a half moon lit up the muddy Atchafalaya surging forty feet below, rising, falling, menacing. The way the bridge shivered filled me with a premonition that at any moment the current would sweep it away, and us with it.

"Please, Alec," Mama pleaded, "I'm scared. Let's go!"

"Okay, Lady, whatever you say. Let's see who's waiting for us at the house."

How could Daddy be so cheerful? My fists clenched, I tumbled back into the car beside Junior, who'd stayed inside, sulking, not saying a word. Junior seemed to always be angry at somebody, I never was sure exactly whom.

The truck was waiting for us at the end of the bridge. Daddy pulled ahead of it and signalled the driver to follow us. We jolted down the embankment and turned into a rutted street. I breathed in the warm, humid air, perfumed by cypress trees and tarred railroad ties.

"Here's the house!" We left the street, plowed through a luxuriant growth of bitterweeds and stopped. The house loomed above us, a ragged dark shadow outlined by the light of the moon.

"Where are the church people, Alec? You said they'd be here to meet us."

"I guess they'll get here later. Come on, let's start unloading."

I slapped at a mosquito, jumped down from the car and waded through the sickly-sweet bitterweeds toward the house. On the creaky wooden porch, we waited while Daddy, in the dim light of the moon shining through a broad crack in the roof, lit the Aladdin's lamp. He'd bought the lamp yesterday as a peace offering to Mama, who'd cried when he told her they didn't have electricity in Krotz Springs.

We pushed open the unlocked door and entered the dirty, unpainted living room.

Suddenly, a scurrying sound. Daddy lifted the lamp: cockroaches, hundreds of them scattering in all directions. Mama screamed and ran from the house....

The scene remains vivid in my mind, a preview of how our life would be the next two years in that little Cajun town in South Louisiana. And of the lesson God was teaching us, a lesson that I've had to relearn dozens of times since:

Being in God's will doesn't mean things will be easy.

Krotz Springs turned out to be another of life's surprises. It would seem logical to think, after all we'd given up so that Daddy could follow God's will, that the Lord might reward us by making Daddy's first full-time pastorate a corner of heaven. But it didn't turn out that way. In fact, Krotz Springs had some of the characteristics of a corner of that other place.

Without our garden and frequent fishing trips to the bayous that abounded around Krotz Springs we might have starved to death. Daddy's salary was set at thirty dollars a month, but most months he received less than half that amount. In January the church gave him a total of $7.40. He and Mama decided it was time for action.

The first Sunday morning of February Daddy preached what we filed in our family history as the "Pork and Beans Sermon." He stood at the pulpit with a can of pork and beans in one hand and a chinaberry tree twig in another. He told the handful people seated on rough benches in the cold, unsealed wooden church about the night we arrived in Krotz Springs. Nobody was there to meet us. We were hungry, and had nothing to eat. Junior went to the store and bought a can of pork and beans. Since we lacked eating utensils, we cut twigs from the chinaberry tree in the back yard.

Then he told them how, as usual, our family had arrived at church early this Sunday morning in order to pick up the garbage in the muddy yard and sweep the cigarettes off the front steps. He asked how many families present had gotten through the month of January on less than ten dollars. Nobody raised a hand.

Then he called up Gordy, the president of the Board of Deacons, handed him a letter of resignation and told him to read it to the congregation.

Halfway through the letter, Gordy, a short, sandy-haired Irishman with big, bruised hands from his sawmill, started sniffing. He stopped, handed the letter back to Daddy and told the congregation he was ashamed of how they'd treated Brother Carter and his family. He and his family were barely surviving the Depression, but starting next month, on the first Sunday he was going to bring a tithe of whatever groceries they bought at the store on Saturday. Maybe, he said, if the rest of them felt like he felt, Brother Carter might reconsider his resignation. Everybody present stood to their feet.

Krotz Springs was unique, half Cajun French and half Scotch-Irish. A large percentage of the non-Cajuns had floated down the Atchafalaya from out-of-state, and rather than drift all the way to the Gulf of Mexico, had dropped anchor in that little fishing town. The Scotch-Irish, though many of them had chosen the river highway to escape a sheriff, looked upon the Cajuns as undisciplined, exaggeratedly emotional, living only for today. The Cajuns considered the Scotch-Irish a people without principles or culture. They put up with each other most of the time, hardly every intermarried and agreed on one thing: black people were good for only the lowest form of labor and had no place in their town. There was a law in Krotz Springs, unwritten but strictly enforced: any black man daring to remain within the city limits after sundown was an open target.

Looking back, it's hard to believe we were there only two years, because to this day my soul bears the muddy imprint of Krotz Springs' rutted streets and still mutters musical whispers of the Cajun dialect. I also still hear my Mama's soft, firm voice telling me all the things I shouldn't do, like play cards, go to the movies, or swim in the river when girls were around. Smoking, drinking and dancing were so obviously wicked it wasn't necessary that she even mention them.

Any protest, on my part brought her favorite comeback, "But Pat, what would people say?"

Mama had a special way of motivating me. She told people what a good boy I was, that I never wanted to do bad things. And I don't guess I did. Doing anything that might displease my mother would be the same as blaspheming God.

I can't remember Mama apart from her Bible. The Psalmist described Mama when he said, "I rejoice in your Word as one who has found great treasure." Until her conversion Mama had never opened a Bible. Her church had taught her that the Bible was to be read only by people who'd been to a seminary, that interpretation of God's Word by an untrained person could lead to dangerous heresies. After her encounter with God during Daddy's dreadful hospitalization, mother fell in love with the Bible. She devoured it. She memorized large portions of it and quoted it constantly. This was the key to her unique strategy for sharing her faith with others. When Mama heard that someone in the community was ill she baked them a cake, and along with the cake, shared the Good News. It would have been impossible to enter their home with a Bible in her hand, but who could forbid her entering their home with the Bible in her heart? So almost any topic of conversation was freely sprinkled with, "… like the Bible says …."

In seminary I learned that Mama may have been guilty of "bibliolatry." But as the decades have passed, more and more I've thanked God for a mother who taught me by word and example that the Bible is indeed the very Word of God. Every day, deep in my subconscious, Mama whispers to me:

Make the Bible your life's manual, believe it implicitly and devote your life to living its promises.

Daddy, like Mama, was at that time in the first bloom of a life set apart by a commision from God. He took his ministry seriously, and mostly painted in blacks and whites, not many grays. So when he found out that one of the church members kept his grocery store open on Sundays Daddy had no doubt what he should do. Mr. Robichaux's grocery, in what before had been the family's living room, was a one-man enterprise. I still remember him as a thin little person with a sad face, waiting on his customers in a sweat-stained undershirt. Seven days a week, fifteen hours a day barely provided a survival economy for him and his big family.

But he was breaking the Sabbath, and giving a bad testimony to the community.

He must close on Sundays!

Daddy and two deacons went to see him, and when he refused to take Sunday off, recommended to the church that he be expelled. There was an hour-long debate, and the expulsion was approved by only a couple of votes.

The next Sunday night when Daddy stood to preach, I heard the front screen door slam open, then the clomp! clomp! clomp! of leather boots. I turned and my heart flipped when I saw Sylvester, Mr. Robichaux's twenty-year-old son stomping down the aisle toward Daddy. Sylvester was half a head taller than Daddy and outweighed him by at least fifty pounds. I turned back to look at Daddy and again my heart did a flip-flop.

He had stepped down from the pulpit and was waiting for Sylvester, fists clenched.

The guy was going to kill Daddy! But before Sylvester could get to him, Gordy and two muscular men from his saw mill collared him, drug him down the aisle and pushed him out the front door. Daddy turned, went back to the pulpit, and without comment, read his Biblical text and preached his sermon.

I came to understand better what I owe to my father and my mother in a personality seminar. I discovered that I am a Pattern Eight, defined as a theoretical thinker and an independent risker. This personality is described by eighteen adjectives: dynamic, spirited, convincing, dramatic, optimistic, impulsive, imaginative, colorful, eloquent, enthusiastic, inspirational, charismatic, persuasive, exciting, innovative, volatile, impelling, exuberant. (My complementary pattern, Pattern Six, is less dramatic!) I concluded that my personality is a combination of the passion of my mother that made her an ardent disciple of her Savior, and the independence of my father that made him his own man.

Daddy was a small man, five-seven and maybe a hundred and forty pounds dripping wet. But he wasn't afraid of anybody when convinced he was right. I saw that trait in him again in the little town of Lottie.

Lottie, a village fifteen miles south of Krotz Springs, was a world apart. Most of the families in the small town had been there for generations. There was not a single Cajun. The congregation met in a tiny white church with a pretty steeple.

I don't remember why Daddy and Mama decided to go there after only a couple of years in Krotz Springs, maybe it was simply a matter of seeking survival in the depths of the Great Depression. I do remember our time there as the most pleasant two years of my childhood. People were gentle and kind. Every Sunday someone invited us home for dinner. Most people seemed to do their best to live a consistent Christian life.

Except for John R. Jones. I never saw John R. without his Stetson and cowboy boots. Some pastor in the past had gotten him named deacon, probably because he was the richest man in town. I can't think of any other reason, because he was seldom in church Sunday mornings and cussed "his niggers," who according to him no more had a soul than the Brahma cattle on his ranch.

About six months after we arrived in Lottie Mr. Jones and State Senator Cranston, who occupied in a big house next door to the church, had a heated argument about a highway project during a session of the Legislature in Baton Rouge. Everybody in town was talking about it, because John R. Jones had made it known he was carrying a Colt 45 on his hip and that the next time he crossed paths with the Senator he was going to put a bullet in him.

Sunday morning after church we were headed for a fried chicken dinner with the Country Smiths. Daddy stopped to check our mailbox. He had barely entered the Post Office when a pickup skidded to a halt beside our Model A. "Oh, oh!" Mama said, "It's Mr. Jones, looks like somebody's already told him about your Daddy's announcement this morning!"

When Daddy reappeared, John R. stepped down from his pickup and blocked his path. "Preacher, what's this about you kicking me out of the church?"

"Well, John, that's up to you. Come to church tonight and apologize to the Senator and there's no problem."

John R. Jones exploded. Yelling at Daddy from his lofty six-foot-four, he warned him of dire consequences. Daddy waited until he'd finished, then said quietly, "John, the Senator's going to be there tonight. He's ready to make peace with you. The rest is up to you." Turning, he got into the car and drove off.

Daddy said nothing about it at the dinner table while he gobbled down two drumsticks and accepted a second piece of Mrs. Country Smith's huge coconut cake.

That night the little church was filled. Senator Cranston and his wife were seated in the first pew. As we sang the second hymn, there was a stir in the congregation. John R. Jones had entered, and was standing at the back. I tried to make out if there was a bulge on his right hip, but couldn't be sure. When the hymn ended, Daddy passed to the front and stood before the pulpit. Without a word from Daddy, the Senator walked over and stood beside him. I'd never seen him, but with his white hair and portly figure he looked to me more like somebody's grandfather than one of the State's leading Democrats. He whispered in Daddy's ear and Daddy nodded.

"Brothers and sisters, I would like to make two apologies. First, for being a poor neighbor. Since Reverend Carter arrived I haven't come over to welcome him to our town. It's no excuse that I'm away most of the time on State business and that when I'm here on Sundays, I attend my own church. So, Reverend Carter, welcome to our community." He turned and gave Daddy a handshake.

"Second, I want to apologize for not asking the pastor's intervention in a misunderstanding I had with one of your distinguished members. Democrats and Republicans are not supposed to get along, I know, but that's no excuse for what happened between us in Baton Rouge."

Daddy put a hand on the Senator's shoulder. "Well, Senator, Baptists and Presbyterians aren't supposed to get along either. But I'm sure our Baptist deacon is not going to let a Presbyterian elder have the last word on forgiveness." The congregation turned their heads and looked at John R.

Later I remembered that Deacon Jones's wife and the Senators' wife played bridge at their club Tuesday mornings. Maybe that explains what happened next. Or maybe it was because John R. Jones could see in the faces of the people that, unless he changed his mind, he was going to be disgraced in the church where both his father and grandfather had been deacons. I don't know what he said to the Senator when he strode down the aisle and took his hand. But it must have been enough, because afterward Daddy invited everybody to stand for a prayer of thanksgiving. It didn't seem to matter John R. marched back down the aisle and out the door while the congregation sang "Blest Be the Tie That Binds."

By that time my Daddy had taught me quite well that:

God's giants are not measured by feet and inches, but by their integrity.

Maybe that's what played out in my conscience when I had to face up to "Dago".

I should explain that all the kids in my school had nicknames, and they were seldom complimentary. For obvious reasons, and to my great displeasure, I was called "Preacher." Dago got his nickname because his family was Italian. For some reason, from the day I set foot on the schoolyard, Dago took a dislike to me. His favorite way of showing his dislike was to bump into me, sometimes shoving me to the ground, and then to step away and grin at me, daring me to do something about it. I didn't know that to do. It wasn't that I was a sissy. Our house was next to the schoolyard, and at least a couple of days a weeks my mother fussed at me for coming home with my shirt torn. "Pat," she'd say, "when I hear the kids shouting 'Run, Preacher, run' I know I'll have some sewing to do when you get home, because they've given you the football and you're headed for the goal line." No, I wasn't a sissy, but I had sense enough not to take on something I wouldn't be able to finish. Dago was a year older than me, and at least six inches taller.

One day, after an especially brutal shove, I got up from the ground, and before I could stop myself, stood toe to toe with Dago, my fists clenched. He grinned and said, "Look, Preacher, we'll get in trouble if we fight on the school grounds, but I'll see you in the street after school." I lived the rest of the day in dread. Dago was going to beat me up, but good! On the other hand, I felt a morbid satisfaction knowing that at last I was going to get behind me what I'd known was inevitable.

When the bell rang, I was one of the first kids out of the building. I wasn't going to run, but maybe if I walked fast --

"Come on guys, me and the Preacher's gonna fight!"

I looked behind me and here came Dago, followed by a wake of a dozen kids.

I walked straight to the street, laid my books on the ground, and turned to face my tormentor. He sidled up just a step away and stood leering at me. Without willing it, I closed my eyes and let go a desperate roundhouse right. To my surprise, I felt an impact. When I opened my eyes, I saw that I had connected with Dago's prominent nose, and that a jet of blood was spewing out. I stared at him, unable to imagine what awaited me. To my amazement, his hands flew to his nose, he let out a yell of dismay, turned on his heel and stumbled away, bawling.

The crowd of kids followed him, and more than one looked back at me, their eyes big. From that day forward neither Dago nor anyone else dared to challenge the Preacher's potent fists!

Chapter Five
Small Town Living
1938-1943

More than once I've asked myself what difference it would have made in my life if I had spent my high school years in the city of Port Arthur, rather than in a small town in Louisiana. How much would the sophistication of city life have influenced my development into adolescence and young adulthood?

I was twelve when Daddy was called to pastor a large country church in Big Cane, close to where he'd lived his boyhood. Big Cane Baptist was a classic country church, on a gravel road four miles from the paved highway. Morrow, a village beside the highway, was three miles from the church. That's where we lived until I graduated from high school. So I spent the most formative years of my young life in a little town where I had limited opportunity for social or intellectual growth, and where my family was sometimes a victim of the pettiness of people who'd known each other all their lives, attended the same church and took for granted that the standard for the pastor and his family was absolute perfection.

I have pleasant memories of the first couple of years at the church: drowsy Sunday morning services seated beside my mother, smiling church members patting me on the head, anniversaries and huge "dinners on the ground," with long rows of tables covered with white cloths, loaded with fried chicken, potato salad, coconut cake, and iced tea.

But all that changed as a result of the cemetery controversy. The church was surrounded on three sides by a century-old graveyard. The ancestors of most of the church members were buried there, including Daddy's mother. The upkeep of the cemetery had never been the responsibility of the church. Each family had its own plot, enclosed by a wire fence. Most of these little plots were neglected, filled with weeds, each with its own colony of rats. One business meeting Sunday night Daddy proposed what seemed to him a logical solution: the church would assume the care of the cemetery. The first step would be to pull down the fences, plow up the ground and plant grass.

The reaction could not have been more violent if the pastor had proposed forbidding the use of the Bible in Sunday School. A very vocal minority declared that over their dead body would they allow a plow to pass over the dead bodies of their grandpas and grandmas. After a couple of hours the measure narrowly passed, but the fuse of a time bomb had been ignited. The proposed desecration of the cemetery was the topic of endless gossip during the week, and on Sundays provoked scowls and angry whispers.

It became intolerable for my Daddy. I remember being awakened one night hours before dawn by an agonized conversation between Daddy and Mamma. Daddy growled, "I don't have to put up with this! We were doing fine before I got into this business of trying to pastor people who are more interested in protecting their own prejudices than pleasing the Lord." Mama's answer ended the conversation. "I'm miserable too, and I'd be willing to pack up and leave tomorrow if it was up to us. But it isn't, Alec. Remember the promise we made to the Lord at the hospital in Port Arthur?

The following business meeting Daddy presented the budget for the cemetery renovation. There were endless questions about how the cleanup would be done, the danger of destoying the monuments on the graves, and accusations against the cold-hearted pastor who was willing to run a plow over his own mother's grave.

The controversy began to affect everything at church. The song leader resigned, the singing became listless, and people talked among themselves as Daddy tried to preach. The sheriff even got into the controversy, attending a deacons' meeting to remind them the graveyard was really a part of the community, since many non-members made use of it to bury their loved ones.

Daddy refused to back down, in spite of an incipient fire-the- pastor movement. Finally, at a business meeting on a hot June Sunday night, the chairman of the deacons, who until then had been a supporter of the renovation, stood to his feet and moved that, in the light of the controversy caused by the project, it be abandoned. A heated argument raged for two hours. Finally the question was called for, and the deacon's motion was approved by a majority of two votes. Daddy got up from where he was seated on the front pew, walked to the pulpit and presented the letter of resignation he had prepared that afternoon after a visit by the chairman of the deacons.

That night he and Mama talked about how we were going to get along without a salary. Mama didn't blame Daddy, but she cried a lot. The church crisis had been hard on her. She'd been having trouble sleeping and every night she rubbed liniment on her swollen knees. Thursday morning Daddy got up early and took off in the car, telling us he was going for a job interview at Camp Polk in Leesville. When he got back at sundown he was smiling. They'd given him the job! He'd shared with them his experience with his dry cleaning business in Port Arthur, and they'd decided he was just the man they needed as supervisor for the night shift at the laundry. And the salary was almost double what he'd been receiving at Big Cane Baptist Church!

After Mama, crying with relief had given him a hug, we sat down at the kitchen table, and while we ate cornbread and milk, he answered our questions.

God had called him to be a preacher, Mama reminded him. Was he abandoning his call? Absolutely not, he was sure the Lord had something in mind for him.

I felt at home at the high school in Morrow, I told him. Did this mean we were going to have to move? No, Milt Long and his wife worked at Camp Polk. Milt had told him about the opening at the army base, and he'd added that if he got the job he could ride with them. It wouldn't be easy, he'd have to work seven days a week and he'd leave every day at one P.M and get back home twelve hours later. But this was obviously the Lord's provision.

Mama's concern was answered the following week. On Monday a group of people from the Big Cane church paid them a visit. The day before, they told Daddy and Mama, they'd informed the church they were leaving to start a new church in Morrow. Would Daddy be interested in being their pastor? Within days they had signed a contract with the Free Masons to rent their hall on Sundays. Soon, a couple of dozen more ex-members of Big Cane Baptist Church joined us. It worked out perfectly with Daddy's swing shift. He had time to preach the Sunday morning sermon, then have a quick lunch before heading out for Leesville.

As I'd told my parents, I was happy at school. I made the best grades in my class and had a great time playing football at recess. Our school was too small to compete interscholastically, but that didn't matter to me since I'd have been too small to be on a team. Yes, I was happy with my grades, but unhappy with my body. I questioned God on His management of my genes. Why did I inherit the body of my father, when the Lord could have just as easily punched in a genetic code that would have given me the me the six- foot- four genes of my uncles? That way I could have stood up to John and Richard, two classmates that towered over me and did every thing they could to make my life miserable. Why they hated me, I didn't know. Maybe because I had better luck with girls than they. I'd managed to win the affection of Annette, the pretty daughter of Mr. Foster, the owner of Morrow's only grocery store and of the cotton gin in Big Cane.

Of course, falling in love had its downside, because girls could be fickle.

Annette, for example. When Ronald transferred to our school from Opelousas, the Parish Seat, he set out to beat my time. Ronald was a senior, and had an aura of *savoir-faire* about him. His vocabulary was Big Town, he wore a sharp-looking gray felt hat, and he smoked Camels. Within six months he was taking Annette to the movies in Opelousas on Saturday nights and she no longer had time for the preacher's kid.

So I went after June, her younger sister. June was a chic, attractive brunette, but not as outgoing as her sister. Still, she seemed pleased to receive me at her front door Saturday nights to sit with her on the living room sofa for a couple of hours. And she taught me how to kiss! June was shy, but not as shy as her boyfriend. I was by nature a very passionate young man, but living in Mama's shadow had kept my passions well in check, and besides, made me so aware of my sinful nature that I was painfully inhibited. As the first Valentine's Day of my courtship with June drew near I determined to buy her a big red heart-shaped box of candy. But the nearest drug store was in Bunkie, ten miles up the highway. I could have purchased June's gift on one of the family's weekly shopping trips to Bunkie, but that would have entailed putting up with my brother's jeers. So early Saturday morning I hopped on my bike and pedaled to Bunkie. All the way back I fantasized about what I'd say to June when I gave her the candy, and imagined the hug and kiss I'd receive in return. But suddenly I remembered it was Saturday, and her family would be in the house. That could be quite embarrassing! When I knocked on her door, her mother answered, smiled at me and invited me in.

"N-no thank you, Mrs. Foster, Mama's got dinner ready. Give this to June, will you?" I turned on my heel, ran to my bicycle and pedaled away as fast as I could.

But June was a sweet girl. That night when I arrived for the usual Saturday visit, she gave me a kiss on the cheek, invited me in, and offered me a piece of her candy, without a word about my mid-day *faux pas*.

About this time I preached the funeral of my best friend. He'd been my buddy since I was about seven. A small dog with a questionable mixture of genes, he showed up at our doorstep in Krotz Springs one morning. I fed him twice daily while we waited for his owner to claim him. After a week we had become inseparable, and my mother gave her o.k. to his being my pet, as long as he slept outside and behaved himself. In tribute to his pug nose, I christened him "Bull". We went everywhere together except school and church, and he paid for his food by standing watch at our front door every night and keeping the raccoons away from the chicken house. Then, a year into our friendship a tragedy occurred. Bull was caught stealing eggs. After giving him several whippings with an inner tube, Daddy announced that Bull would have to go. Accompanied by my wails of anguish, Daddy loaded him into the back seat of our Model A and took him to a farm family downriver. After a few days I stopped crying, but my heart was left with a permanent sore spot. Six months passed, and one day Daddy mentioned at dinner that he'd visited with the family where Bull lived now, and that he looked awful. Turned out that the only food available for dogs was the corn left over from the hog trough. Daddy ignored my tears, but when Mama told him he ought to give Bull a chance to prove he'd learned his lesson, Daddy didn't argue with her, just asked me to pass the biscuits.

The next Saturday morning I heard the car horn and ran to the front door just in time to see Bull shoot from the car. He bounded up to me, hugged me and licked my face, then ran into the house barking excitedly, grinning, jumping into the living room chairs one by one, ending up in front of the ice box, whining, pawing at the door.

As the weeks passed, it was evident that Bull had indeed learned his lesson. Each time he passed the chicken house his pace quickened, and not once did Daddy have to use the inner tube again.

He accompanied us when we moved to Lottie, and there I began to learn how he loved doing crazy stuff. Across the road in front of our house was a small lake with a little boat tied up at the dock. Every afternoon Bull accompanied me while I tempted cat fish with big fat earth worms. One day the boat paddle fell into the water, and while I sat there wondering how to retrieve it, Bull jumped from the boat, took the paddle in his mouth, and swam back to me, a wide grin on his ugly little face. As the weeks passed, Bull added to his bag of tricks. One day on an impulse, I stood on the shore of the lake and threw a brick as far as I could. Barking excitedly, Bull swam to where the brick had landed, disappeared into the water, came up with the brick in his mouth, and laid it at my feet.

Years later, in the little town of Morrow, we moved to a huge old house with a tin roof. One day as I was climbing a ladder to the roof, I heard panting behind me and discovered that Bull was following me. Thereafter he and I spent hours together in a little cul-de-sac on the roof, plotting our next adventure.

Not that Bull was my only friend. I had a school buddy name Emmit. We rode our bikes together, he always took my side when Richard or John picked on me, and Saturday afternoons we amused ourselves writing spy messages in a code we'd invented.

But Emmit knew my heart belonged to Bull.

One afternoon word came that Bull's body was lying beside the state highway. I searched on my bike till I found him, laid his lacerated corpse on a board, and drug him behind me to my back yard. There I dug a hole, deposited the body of my dearest friend, sang "When We All Get to Heaven," and said a prayer. I never found room in my heart for another dog.

Then there was my brother. His name was James, Mama and Daddy called him Junior and I called him Bud. This undefined name was a mirror of my brother's puzzling character. Four years my senior, Bud was not a bad person. He did well enough at school. His sweetheart was the prettiest girl in their class. He didn't drink or cuss, and didn't start smoking until he was in the army. He spent most of his spare time with Mark, June's brother, pursuing their hobby of making tiny experimental radios. He attended Sunday School and church with us. Yet at home he radiated an unspoken rebellion. I felt he saw me as a spoiled brat and that, aside from having to sleep with me on a double bed, he preferred keeping me at a distance. Sometimes he scared me. Like that Sunday afternoon I went to pick him up at the home of Georgiana, his girl friend. He'd spent the afternoon with her and now it was time for him to come home and eat supper before Sunday night church. I knocked on the door, called to him and he came out.

"Give me the car keys."

"No, Daddy said for me to drive."

"Don't be silly, I can drive better than you." He tried to grab the keys from my hand, but I put them behind my back. Finally he gave up and got into the car, slamming the door. Just before we reached a curve on the narrow gravel road, he suddenly stamped his foot on the accelerator, pushing the speedometer to 50 ... 60. The car was careening from one side of the road to the other. What would happen when we hit the curve ahead? Terrified, I screamed, "Bud, stop!"

He grinned at me and pushed harder on the accelerator.

We were going to die!

At the last instant he withdrew his foot, and somehow I managed to gain control of the car just before we reached the curve. Thank goodness no cars were coming from the other direction!

Too terrified to speak, I drove very slowly the rest of the way, breathing hard.

When the car stopped in the driveway he warned me, "Tell Mama and Daddy about what happened and I'll smash your face!"

I don't know why we never became friends. Maybe in part because of the age difference. Four years impose a barrier difficult to breach. My brother had graduated from high school and signed up with the army before I entered high school. Worse, I'm sure Bud felt my parents gave me preference over him. Did they? It's a matter of that ancient question of "what comes first, the egg or the hen?" It's a lot easier for parents to get along with a kid who is obedient and respectful than with one who seems to be looking for a fight. I'll always remember the distance between my brother and me with a guilty conscience.

I was awakened in the wee hours by mother's wailing cries. We had been dealing with her depression for some time now. The church split had been very hard on her. She had lost some of her dearest friends, and for a long time afterward, an unexpected crossing of paths with someone from "the other church" could provoke a hostile stare, and sometimes unpleasant words. Daddy's harsh work schedule was tough on her. Besides, the problem of who sat beside him every day on the trips to and from work became a sore issue. Milt and his wife sat in the front seat, and Daddy sat in the back with Myrna, an attractive young widow who also worked at Camp Polk. Mama began questioning Daddy about what went on in the back seat between eleven P.M. and one A.M. As the months passed it became an obsession with her. Daddy insisted that nothing was going on, that he and Myrna slept through the trips. But Mama became more and more upset, and once or twice a week Daddy lost hours of sleep trying to calm her.

Still engraved on my mind is a hot Saturday morning when I was in the car with my parents on the way to a funeral. Just ahead of us on the dusty gravel road was a car driven by Myrna. Mama kept telling Daddy, "The dust is awful, Alec, pass her." Daddy refused, and Mama berated him for not wanting to upset the woman he was secretly in love with.

Was Daddy attracted to Myrna? I never knew. But given the circumstances, I see no way in which they could have engaged in hanky-panky. More important, Daddy loved his wife, and was committed to his God. I'm quite sure he never entertained the possibility of being unfaithful. Finally, Daddy persuaded Mama to let him take her to the doctor in Opelousas, and he prescribed a little green pill. In a few weeks she became again the smiling, self-confident Mama I remembered from years ago. By this time the church had grown and they were building a pretty building with a nice steeple a couple of blocks from where we lived. After the new church was dedicated, they offered Daddy a substantial raise in salary if he'd quit his job in Leesville. It wasn't hard for him to decide.

After church on Sunday, December 7, 1941, I was seated in the car on the street in front of our house, waiting for Mamma and Daddy to come out. A church family had invited us for dinner. Suddenly a voice broke into the music: "The Japanese bombed Pearl Harbor this morning!" Life would never be the same. The next week in our math class Mr. Roberts the principal told us, "All you kids are running around with little stickers on your shirts saying stuff like "Slap a Jap". You think it's funny, but you'd better take this war serious. Everyone of you guys is going to end up in the army before it's over." We didn't believe him, everybody was saying the war in tne Pacific would be over in a few months.

The next year a Naval officer came to our school and talked with the boys in the senior class. As soon as we graduated, he reminded us, we'd be drafted into the army. But there was an alternative: the Naval Air Force had inaugurated the "V-12" initiative for the enlistment of pilots. The next week he'd return to apply an exam for those who were interested, and anyone who passed it would enter into a college level training program. A couple of weeks later I was advised that I had qualified.

I was ecstatic, and took a bus to New Orleans for the physical. There I was hit with the biggest disappointment in my young life: they informed me that I didn't have the 20/20 vision required to be a pilot. Except for a few points on the eye chart, my life would have taken a drastic turn. Within a year, massive air raids began against Germany, and the survival rate of the air crews was less than 50%. If I had passed that exam, would I be around today?

As we moved toward the end of our senior year the tension between Gloria Talley and me kept growing. For years we'd been in competition for the best grades in class. Now they were within a few months of deciding who would be the valedictorian. I was confident I was smarter than Gloria, but she was more disciplined than I, so we were neck and neck. I didn't like the way, when the teachers handed back our assignments, Gloria always craned her neck to see what my grade was.

A couple of Mondays before the end of school Mr. Roberts told us he would announce the name of the valedictorian on Friday afternoon. Friday came, and it looked like the hands of the clock on the wall would never get around to 3:00 P.M. Finally the bell rang for the last class, and Mr. Roberts took the seniors into the auditorium. He seated us in a circle, and sat thumbing through some papers. At last he cleared his throat, and said, "I have here the grade averages for this year, if anyone wants to check them afterward. But at the moment it appears that Pat will be the valedictorian, and Gloria the salutatorian."

No applause. I hadn't expected it. But I could feel my heart thumping and my head felt like it might lift off and bump the ceiling. Then Gloria spoke: "Mr. Roberts, if Pat dies before graduation will I be the valedictorian?" Mr. Roberts grunted shook his head and declared, "Class dismissed. Pat come with me to my office and we'll talk about your speech." I barely heard him, I was too busy thinking of all the bad things that could happen to me before next Friday night.

Two days later I was with Daddy in his shop. Woodworking was his hobby, and he made beautiful things of the cypress knees that abounded in the bayou behind our house. "Pat I got a letter this morning from your Uncle Charles. He works in the shipyards in Orange, and got you a job as an asbestos helper. You'll earn enough money this summer to pay for your first year of college."

A couple of weeks later I found myself signing the register at a boarding house across from a shipyard that churned out "liberty ships," ugly little freighters that transported tanks, bombs and food to our partner in the war, Great Britain. At that time German submarines were sending dozens of them to the bottom every month. My job was to keep my uncle supplied with the asbestos wrapping he applied to pipes running throughout the ship.

Away from home for the first time in my life, I began to learn about the reality of living in the world. The first night at supper I was pleasantly surprised when the man at the head of the boarding house table asked us all to bow our heads for the blessing. But my surprise dissolved into dismay when I raised my head and dicovered that all the steaks piled high at the middle of the table had disappeared. Soon I learned the art of keeping my fork poised and striking just before the "amen". It took a couple of more weeks for me to discover that I had picked up body lice from the common bathtub and a couple of months before I was able to get rid of them.

My biggest worry during those three months was how to win back June. The last weeks of the school year we'd had a fuss and John had swept in and made her his girlfriend. I still loved her desperately and went to sleep every night with her on my mind. It turned out to be not as complicated as I had feared. The first day back home at the end of summer, I kept watch on the street behind my house. June lived just a couple of blocks away, and I'd learned long ago to take advantage of her custom of walking to her father's store every afternoon for an ice cream cone.

There she was! I jumped up and hurried out to intercept her. She gave me a tentative smile and allowed me to accompany her to the store. I paid for her ice cream cone, and as we stood there chatting nervously I rehearsed in my mind the words I'd prepared to convince her she should come back to me. It was unnecessary. Taking a lick of her ice cream, she asked, "Will you be coming over to my house next Saturday night?"

I had just two Saturdays to sew up our commitment before leaving for college, but that was enough. The last time we were together I took off my graduation ring and placed it on her finger.

I'm in my room packing my suitcase, excited by the adventure that lies ahead; I've been accepted for the pre-med course in Louisiana College. I know my plans are a disappointment for Mamma and Daddy. Since I was four it has been taken for granted that I was going to be a pastor. But witnessing my parents' constant stress in the pastorate has convinced me I don't want to spend the rest of my life like that. Besides, I'm weary of the smirks of John and Richard when they call me "preacher."

My mother comes into my room and sits on the bed. "So, Pat, you've decided to be a doctor."

"Yes, Ma'am."

"Well, Son, there's nothing wrong with being a doctor." Then, fixing her bright green eyes on my face: "But the Lord spoke to me a long time ago and told me His plans for you."

I was eighty years old before I became aware of an unpleasant inheritance from the three months I spent in the shipyard in Orange. Jogging every day on the greenbelt in Kingwood, Texas I began to notice a shortness of breath. When I mentioned it to my physician during an annual checkup he recommended I consult a pulmonary specialist. The specialist sent me to the lab for a series of tests. A week later when I returned for the followup he told me, "Mr. Carter, you have 76% of the normal lung capacity for your age. Have you ever worked with asbestos?" My first impulse was no say "No". Then I remembered: "Surely three months handling asbestos more than sixty years ago wouldn't be affecting me now!"

"Unfortunately yes, Mr. Carter. Breathing in asbestos dust leaves permanent sword-like deposits on the lungs that are unique, and recognizable immediately."

Sounds like a parable of the life-long consequences of youthful errors!

Chapter Six
On My Own
1943-1946

Caleb married two times (1Chron. 2: 18-19). Both of his wives were from the tribe of Judah. Azubah was the wife of his youth, and bore him three children. Her name means "desolation". Was it given to her by her parents as a protest against Egyptian slavery? Or was it perhaps a posthumous name that commemorated some terrible event that occasioned her death? We have no way of knowing when Caleb married his second wife, Ephrath ("fruitfulness"), but it must have been while he was still in Egypt, because she was the mother of Hur, who played a prominent role in Israel's sojourn in the desert. Hur assisted Aaron in helping to hold up Moses' hand in a battle against the Amalekites (Exodus 17: 8-13). Later he assisted Aaron as judicial head of the people during Moses' forty days on Mount Sinai (Exodus 24:13-14).

My freshman year at Louisiana College went fast. Always hovering over me like a dark shadow was the dreadful war going on in Europe and the Pacific. May 16th, 1944 I'd be eighteen, and on that day they'd draft me into the army!

One day around the middle of April I was reading in the college library. I raised my head and found myself staring at a pretty girl thumbing through the file catalog. She had long wavy hair the color of a honeycomb, and the classic profile of a southern belle. Finally, I forced myself to turn my eyes back to my book. "Careful, Pat!" I told myself, "Remember that a few days before you left for college, you slipped your graduation ring on June's finger." Anyway, I wouldn't have had the courage to walk up to that Southern Belle and introduce myself.

The following Saturday my parents were visiting me in my dormitory room. By now Dad had resigned his church in Morrow, and they lived in an apartment in Pineville, awaiting a word from God on their next assignment.

A horn sounded out front. A few minutes later the horn sounded again.

"What's that?" Mama asked.

"Oh, it 's the school bus, a group of students visits the jail on Saturday afternoon."

"I'll bet you go, don't you Pat? And anyway, it's time for us to head for home."

My parents rose to their feet, and I was too ashamed to admit I'd never gone on a Saturday afternoon jail mission. After they left I stepped over to the window. Yes, the bus was still there, parked in front of the girls' dormitory. Well, why not? I had nothing else to do, and besides, maybe I should pay penance for what amounted to lying to Mama!

I threw on a jacket and hurried outside to get aboard, just as the bus was pulling away. As we passed through the college gates I saw my parents' car just ahead. Daddy was going slowly, and by the time we approached the boulevard fronting the college, we were quite close. Too close! Someone asked the driver a question, he turned his head, and bang! He bumped into Daddy 's car.

A dozen of us guys scrambled out to survey the damage. Luckily it was nothing more serious than locked bumpers. We juggled the bumpers until we got them separated. Of course, afterward I had to say something to my parents, so I was the last one to get back on the bus.

Someone had taken my place. Looking for an empty seat, my throat caught. There was that cute girl I'd seen in the library a few days before. And a miracle -- the seat next to her was empty!

I stumbled back and dropped down beside her. By the time we said good night at her dormitory door a couple of hours later, she'd accepted my invitation to a movie the next week.

It took me a long time to go to sleep that night. Here I was just three weeks from being drafted, and I'd met a girl who had my heart thumping. And all those coincidences: Mama motivating me to go to the jail service, our bus following on the heels of my parents' car, the collision, and then the empty seat beside that Southern Belle named Evelyn. I've asked myself what my life would have been like, except for those coincidences. Three weeks later school would have ended, I'd have left for the wars, and Evelyn and I would never have met. God's surprises!

A miracle is an event so unusual that it can only be explained as a divine intervention. That's why I call miracles "God's surprises." In my life I've experienced quite a number of God's surprises. In the Bible God did a miracle when it was necssary to bring about His purpose. Looking back on my life I can see that for the same reason God brought surprises into my life.

The day before my eighteenth birthday I volunteered for the Navy, anything better than letting them draft me into the infantry! After boot camp, because of my year of pre-med studies, they put me in the Hospital Corps. I went through a couple of months of training in San Diego, then they sent me to a naval hospital in New Orleans. Three months later I found myself in San Francisco, aboard the General W.H. Hase, a combination troop transport and hospital ship.

My first voyage was to the Leyte Gulf in the Philippine Islands. We off-boarded five thousand soldiers and took on hundreds of men wounded in General Douglas MacArthur's invasion two weeks before. For the next three weeks I had my baptism of fire nursing severely wounded soldiers and marines. After a few days in San Francisco, we headed across the Pacific again. A brief stopover at Perth, Australia, and we lifted anchor for Calcutta, India. There we received a thousand Air Force men who had spent four years in the jungles of Burma, yellow from Atabrine, the anti-malaria drug. They placed in our care one hundred seventy-five men we called "psychos." I had a number of interesting experiences with the violent cases that we locked up in tiny cells. One day I found *myself* one of those "cases!" The hold of our ship was torrid in the Pacific heat, so fans blew fresh air into those cells through vents in the ceilings, making them the coolest part of our hospital ward. One hot afternoon I pulled the mattress from my bunk into an unoccupied cell and closed my eyes for a nap. Suddenly I was awakened by the slamming of the door and a voice shouting, "Somebody left a cell door open and a psycho was about to escape!" It took an hour of pleading to convince my laughing buddies to set me free.

Instead of returning eastward to San Francisco, we headed west, passing through the Red Sea, the Mediterranean and then across the Atlantic to Norfolk, Virginia. There, an eye exam at the naval hospital changed the course of my naval career. They informed me that an infection had provoked elevated pressure in my eyes. I was admitted to the hospital, and underwent weeks of tests, aimed at identifying the unknown infection. After pulling a couple of molars, they decided to do a tonsillectomy, Navy style. Seated in a dental chair, I received a local anesthetic, and the surgeon proceeded to employ two different procedures, meanwhile explaining the techniques to the young intern at his side. When it was over, he slapped me on the back and said, "O.K. sailor, back to your ward." Not even a wheel chair? Of course not, this was the Navy!

A few days later another intern precipitated the worst six weeks of my years in the Navy. They assigned him the task of doing a spinal tap. As he began, he confessed that this would be only his second spinal tap, then apologized again and again as he pushed the big needle into the spinal cavity, trying to locate the elusive fluid, then, shaking his head, withdrew it for another attempt. By the time he'd finished I felt like someone had used a hatchet on my back.

They told me a couple of weeks later that they were through with me. Had they discovered the source of my infection? I never knew. I suspect they didn't get around to a final diagnosis. The hospital was so busy with the war wounded they didn't have time to waste on a kid who just needed a change of glasses. They sent me home for a two-week leave.

An exciting visit with Evelyn, plenty of Cajun food and it was time to return to the Navy. I saw no logical reason for going back. The war had ended, and college and romance were much more appealing. The morning of my return I swung my feet off the bed, placed them on the floor, pushed myself up and suddenly I was flat on my face, feeling like someone had zapped me with an electric cable. My back!

In constant pain, I rode the bus to New Orleans, checked in at the emergency room of the Naval Hospital, and they taped up my back and told me to hurry or I'd miss the train. This is the Navy, Sailor!

By the time I arrived at the hospital in Norfolk the next day, I was almost delirious with pain. At least now I'd have some sympathy, and they'd ask my forgiveness for the intern who had repeatedly jammed that needle into my spine and damaged my spinal cord.

I was wrong. The doctor who interviewed me didn't bother to check my back. He'd already arrived at a diagnosis: here was a homesick sailor, anxious for discharge, and dumb enough to think he could fool the Navy with the most common pretext, a bad back!

They returned me to the eye ward, and the nurses were informed of my deceit. The next three weeks were agony. The nurses rolled their eyes at my groans and offered no help, even though every time I moved on the bed or touched my feet to the floor I felt stabbing electric shocks. I began to doubt my own sanity, maybe it *was* all in my mind!

Finally it occurred to someone to call an orthopedist. He ordered a blood test, and hours later was back. "Sailor, I'm bringing you up to my ward. Your white blood count is way up, you've got a bad infection."

I cried with relief.

The treatment wasn't fun. Once a week they injected into my hip a malaria virus that drove my temperature up to 104 degrees. Several times a week they enclosed me in an oven from feet to chin, and baked me like roast beef. After three weeks they discharged me to a small Naval Air base nearby.

I spent the next six months sweating it out, waiting to accumulate enough points to be discharged. Recently a newspaper reported that a survey of the troops in Iraq revealed that most of them were unhappy and anxious to go home. Is that supposed to be news? I was in the Navy for twenty-five months, in a war that everyone agreed had to be fought, and I can't remember a day when I wasn't surrounded by men complaining about the boredom, the food, our superior officers, the foul-ups in strategy, and a dozen other problems. As for me, more and more my unhappiness had to do with my impatience to hold my beloved Evelyn in my arms. And worrying about the bad news from Louisiana College. Evelyn, a junior now, was impressed by the cool young veterans who were enrolling in college. Especially by Tom, an ex- fighter pilot. Though she didn't say so, it was more and more obvious that she was contemplating whether she really wanted to hold out until the return of her Hospital Corpsman Second class. I had been reminding myself recently that our relationship was quite fragile. We had met three weeks before my enlistment, and our only communication after that, except for several short leaves, had been by letter. Of course both of us wrote every day, but letters were hardly a substitute for talking eye-to-eye, holding hands, hugging, and kissing.

I had found a good buddy at my base, a devoted Christian from Brooklyn. Seeing my distress, he invited me to a weekend in New York City and arranged me a blind date with his sister. She was lots of fun, and I enjoyed a fantastic weekend. I still remember standing beside her at midnight atop the Empire State Building, her red hair blowing in my face.

I returned to our base with my heart feeling not quite so desperate. I still loved my pretty little Louisiana blonde, but if she decided to throw me over for that dashing pilot, there was now a redheaded Yankee who might be interested in exploring future possibilities with me.

The following Saturday I went to the USO in Norfolk to call Evelyn. She was at home for the weekend, and we were just a month away from Christmas. I considered it prudent to check on whether she was interested in seeing me on my Christmas leave.

"Hello, Evelyn?"

"Yes, hello, Pat. It's good to hear from you."

"How's everything going?"

"Fine, real fine."

"And Tom?"

A pause. "He took me out for dinner last Saturday night. Hope you don't mind."

"No problem. I was in New York City. Had a date with a pretty red-head."

A longer pause. "A red-head?"

"Yes, she's my buddy Raymond's younger sister. Real sweet." (Might as well pour it on, a little white lie wouldn't hurt.) "She insisted I come back next weekend."

"And ... and ... are you going?"

"Why sure, wouldn't miss it. Since you and Tom are hitting it off so well, I figured I have an open playing field."

A long pause. "Now just a minute, I ... "

(Is it possible? Is she crying?)

She *was* crying! It blew me away. Hearing her, my heart exploded. I wanted to take her in my arms and kiss away the tears. Oh Lord, how I loved her!

We talked a long time. She agreed never to see Tom again, and I agreed to cancel my fictitious date for next weekend. We also agreed that my Christmas gift would be an engagement ring.

I hung up, my head still spinning, and stepped over to the telephone operator to pay for the call.

"That'll be $14.65, Sailor."

I pulled out my bill fold. Oh no! "I ... I'm sorry. I don't have that much."

"Then I'll call your party and reverse the charges."

The next day Evelyn wrote and informed me of the consequences of my momentary bankruptcy. Her father had come into the living room when he heard her crying. He was still standing there, indignant, when the operator called with the reversed charges. He grunted that he wasn't about to pay for a call that had caused his beloved daughter so much pain. A night in the brig would do me good! Only more tears convinced him to change his mind.

Two days before Christmas I caught a train for New Orleans. In Georgia the train hit a car at a crossing. After two hours of waiting, with still no prospects of pulling out of the siding any time soon, I grabbed my duffel bag, hopped off the train, walked to the highway and stuck up a thumb. By dawn the next morning I was on the southern edge of New Orleans, hoping for a ride for the ninety miles that remained. A year before, Daddy had accepted an invitation to return to Krotz Springs, to the church that had been his first pastorate. An eighteen-wheeler took mercy on me, and three hours later dropped me off at that little river town with so many memories. Mama had made coffee, but I refused to take even a sip, the object of my dreams, my longing, my love was asleep just a few steps away in the spare bedroom. I had the ecstasy of awaking her with a kiss and placing a ½ carat diamond on her finger.

Immediately she jumped out of bed: "I'm going to show your mother!"

I was still sitting on the bed a few minutes later when she returned, looking downcast. "Well, did you show Mama?"

"Yes. And you'll never guess what she said."

"What?"

"She said, 'Well, you never can tell what might happen'"

By the time I was discharged, I knew I'd not be returning to my pre-med studies.

Sitting on the fantail of my ship those long ocean voyages, I'd had plenty of time to talk to God. And for God to talk to me. God had said to my heart, quietly, over and over, that of course, I had the right to continue my medical studies, but I'd just be wasting my time. He was patient, and he'd wait until I had done with making my life miserable. Once I was ready to get on with His plan for my life, He was ready also. At last I decided it would be dumb to go on being miserable. Through that experience I learned a lesson that has been repeated over and over in my life:

God, because He loves me, allows me to wander outside His perfect will, so I'll realize that the only happiness in life is obeying Him.

Chapter Seven
Marriage and Fatherhood
1946-1951

Profile
Pat Harold Carter
September, 1946

Age: 20
Height: 5'7"
Weight: 145 pounds
Education: High School, one year of college
I.Q. 145
Work Experience: Worked one summer in a shipyard, and spent two years in the U.S. Navy
Life goals: Complete his education and become a pastor
Spiritual profile: Became a Christian at seven. Grew up in a pastor's home.
Strengths: Committed to God's will
                Has maintained a positive Christian testimony
Weaknesses: Most of his convictions are inherited from his parents. Though he traveled around the world in the Navy, his outlook is quite insular. He has never considered leaving the boundaries of the state he grew up in. Outside of his conversion experience, has never made a radical decision based on an encounter with God. His principle temptations: obsessiveness, a bothersome

libido, self-esteem damaged by his small frame and feeling "different" in a hostile world.

Three months after my discharge from the Navy I decided it was time to marry the girl I loved. We had told each other we'd wait a year, until Evelyn graduated from college, so we'd have time to get to know each other better. That made sense, of course. But when you're hopelessly in love, logic tends to be unimportant. So I convinced her and we married September 5th, a couple of weeks before Evelyn began her senior year and I my sophomore year at Louisiana College in Pineville, Louisiana.

The wedding was celebrated in the First Baptist Church of the lovely North Louisiana county seat town of Minden, where Evelyn had attended high school, and her father had the International Harvester franchise. The next day we caught a plane to New Orleans. Halfway there, I was suddenly blasted by the worst headache I'd experienced in all my life. It continued after we landed and waited for our luggage.

But was I also having hearing problems? No, they really were calling our names on the public address system! "Mr. and Mrs. Pat Carter please report to the information desk." Perplexed, we hurried to the counter, where a handsome young man in a gray uniform introduced himself: "Good morning, I'm Mayor Chip Morrison's chauffeur, and I will take you to your hotel."

As we walked to the Mayor's limousine Evelyn whispered, "Uncle Lloyd did this, I'm sure." Of course. Her uncle was a state senator, and the Mayor must have been pleased to do a favor for one of the men who voted on tax breaks for his city.

I'm sorry to say what I most remember about our honeymoon isn't the luxurious room in the Monteleon Hotel, or the dozen roses the first morning from the Mayor and his wife, but that incredible headache. We finally called the hotel physician, and he prescribed a narcotic that helped me sleep through most of the five days of our honeymoon.

In the college town of Pineville, we moved into a duplex next to a couple who'd been married for twenty-five years. They were an object lesson that success in marriage doesn't depend on looks. Doug and Mabel were the homeliest couple I'd ever met, but I treasure an enduring mental portrait of them seated very close together, grinning happily, obviously convinced that they were the luckiest husband and wife in the world.

Our parents had asked us about our plans for supporting ourselves. We assured them things would work out. They did, but the first year we bought no new clothes and walked most places. We ate sparingly, but never went hungry. Every month we received ninety dollars as part of our "Veterans' Bill of Rights." Evenings I worked in the storeroom at Woolworth`s.

Besides, wonder of wonders, a country church invited me to be their half-time pastor! I'd known of that possibility before we married. Bill, who had been my freshman roommate, asked me to "fill his pulpit" one Sunday while he preached at another church in view of a call. I don't remember anything about my sermon, but I'm sure it wasn't much, because it was my very first.

A couple of weeks later Bill informed me that, indeed, he would begin a new pastorate in October, and invited me to preach again at the little church in Latanier, a country community twenty miles from Pineville. The congregation was surprised to see the "little preacher" had a new wife. And delighted when she offered to accompany our singing on the old upright piano.

After my morning sermon, Clarence, a young farmer, stood up and said, "Folks, we've been praying for a piano player for years, and here Brother Pat comes bringing us the answer to our prayers. I move we call him to be our pastor."

The vote was unanimous.

Tragedy struck three months later. Evelyn's father died suddenly of a heart attack. From that moment her family's life changed drastically. Her mother had the sole responsibility of caring for Evelyn's 17-year-old brother, 14-year-old sister and a baby boy born just six months before. She never fully recovered from her loss. For years afterward, Evelyn grieved for her father. She had been the apple of his eye, and she idolized him. I'm sure it affected our adjustment as newlyweds.

Indeed, we didn't have an easy time becoming "one flesh". Having married so soon after my return from military service, much of the getting-acquainted process that should have been a part of years of courtship had to be experienced after marriage. The fact that we were both only twenty complicated the process. Both of us had the pressure of classes. On top of this came the death of her father, an emotional trauma that probably should have been addressed by a therapist. Besides, the longer we lived together the more we realized we're personality opposites. I love travel and adventure, she prefers an easy chair and a good book. She prefers her bacon a bit soft and greasy, I like mine fried to a crisp. I like background music, but background music drives her up the wall. She seldom laughs at what I find hilarious. If I tell her a joke she exasperates me by asking questions about the details. But on one thing we've been in agreement from the beginning: God and His will is our first priority. I can't remember a moment in our lives when that commitment was ever in doubt.

The next three years I discovered a love for the pastorate that has endured all my life. We bought a beat-up little 1940 Chevy coupe that made it possible for us to get up every Sunday morning, drive to Latanier, teach Sunday School, preach, go to someone's house for fried chicken and mashed potatoes, spend the afternoon visiting, preach again that night, and arrive back in Pineville by 10:00 P.M. Those country people loved their young preacher and his wife, and we loved them! Our salary was fifty dollars a month and lots of fresh vegetables.

Evelyn has said a hundred times, with a smile, that I deceived her. She committed herself to a pre-med Freshman because marrying a doctor had always been her dream. Her grandfather was a physician, and he and his family lived in a nice home, drove a new car and took long vacations. That's what she wanted for herself. By the time I'd decided God was calling me to be a preacher, she was hooked and there was no way out! But I suspect she surprised herself when she took to being a pastor's wife like the proverbial duck to water. She taught a Sunday School class, played the piano, visited with me, and always had a smile for everybody in our congregation.

Most of our members were poor farmers. Tilford and Eula Mae were typical. They had twenty acres and a mule. Lived in a little 3-room house. At least once a month we had Sunday dinner with them, and it was always a blessed time of smiles and good will. Of course, a part of our pastoring was listening to their typical farmers' complaints. When rains were delayed, they were sure the corn was going to burn up. If it rained too much, the cotton was going to rot in the field.

Every time Mr. Crook, Tilford's father, invited us to Sunday dinner he cracked the same joke: "Eat with us today, Preacher, we're gonna have pork and grits and wine: poke your feet under the table, grit your teeth and whine."

After three years we'd both graduated from college, and it was time for Seminary. Back then it was taken for granted that any young minister who wanted to amount to anything must take three years of post-graduate studies. Strangely, those three years didn't yield a Master's degree. Three years of post-college Greek, Hebrew, and Bible exegesis earned you another Bachelor's degree. Later, the seminaries corrected that anomaly.

As a matter of course, we went to New Orleans Baptist Theological Seminary. It never entered my mind to consider a seminary outside of Louisiana, as if it were pre-ordained that I do my studies in Louisiana, then spend my life pastoring churches in Louisiana. Maybe it was because I had little guidance on mapping my future. I am struck by the fact that I remember no one ever acting as my mentor. As far as I can recall, no elderly Christian or minister ever gave me advice about projecting a plan to assure I received the best benefits possible from my education. My father was my model. I respected and admired him. But Daddy wasn't one to sit his son down and philosophize with him. In retrospect I understand why. His cultural background was limited, and I doubt that he himself ever received advice from anyone but his wife.

I entered Seminary the first week of September and three weeks later our first child, David, was born. We had thought it best that Evelyn give birth in her home town, where she could be cared for by her mother and her family doctor. After church in Latanier, before driving 120 miles south to New Orleans, I called Evelyn. She was feeling fine. Three hours later, when I walked into our apartment, the phone was ringing. It was Evelyn's mother. Evelyn was in the hospital and the birth was expected momentarily. I climbed back into our little Chevy and spent the rest of the night driving the 300 miles to Minden.

When I arrived at the hospital I was greeted with scary news: after long hours of unproductive labor, the doctor had opted for a risky Caesarean delivery. But now both Mom and David were fine.

Eighteen months later Linda was born.

Looking back, I'm surprised by the lack of memories of financial crises. Somehow we managed school and two babies without too many problems. Our second year in seminary we moved to a pastorate in the tiny village of Fordoche, some fifty miles closer to the seminary. It was a tough year for the young wife and mother. She and our two little ones lived in the small parsonage I led the church to build, and I commuted to classes Monday afternoon and returned Friday night. Evelyn also taught fourth and fifth grade. In retrospect, I'm amazed that I demanded so much of her! I've wondered what would have happened if Evelyn's father had still been alive. Would he have demanded I take better care of his beloved daughter?

Reflecting on Evelyn's dedication through those early years of marriage, I realize they were only the beginning of a long period of my taking for granted extraordinary sacrifices from my wife. And I am convinced that

God's greatest gift on this earth, after salvation, is a faithful wife.

The lovely young woman I claimed for my wife was practically unknown to me when we married. I had no basis for predicting how she would react to the demands of my ministry. I thank God for giving her the grace to respond to those demands.

Chapter Eight
The Adventure Begins
1951

Caleb lived in Egypt for some thirty years before the return of Moses.
Beginning with *his first years in Egypt he'd heard stories about Moses, and
how this adopted son of Pharoah's daughter, after a failed attempt to better
the conditions of his people, had disappeared into the vast deserts of Midian.
As the years passed and no word came from him, most people gave up all
hope of his return. But now and again, a prophet would share a word
he'd received from God: Moses had been chosen to deliver God's people
from slavery and lead them into the land promised to Abraham. In God's
time he would return. From the first moment Caleb heard about Moses he
was sure he himself would play a special role in this great adventure.*

*In his twenties Caleb met Joshua, from the tribe of Benjamin. The
attraction was mutual. They were of the same age, they both were committed
to Jehovah, and they shared the dream of one day entering the hill country
of Caanan, God's Promised Land. They began to meet together for prayer.
Soon, others joined them.*

*Caleb treated each day as a classroom to prepare him for the destiny that
awaited. Not being a slave, he enjoyed a freedom of movement denied to
his fellow Israelites. Periodically he traveled south to practice the discipline
of desert survival. He befriended an Egyptian soldier, who schooled him in
the use of the sword and the spear.*

Evelyn and I had our first experience of adventuring with God in 1951, in the last weeks of my studies in New Orleans Baptist Theological Seminary. I had learned a lot from my parents about what it means to obey God, but most of what I did now was the product of logic and instinct, rather than a consciousness of God's hand on my shoulder. For instance, I had opted for the ministry, not in response to a theophany, but because I deducted this was God's will for my life.

Then, in the Spring of 1951, I began an adventure that has continued until this day. A door opened to a new world, a world in which I began to hear God's voice in a personal way, often overruling logic, leading me into His plan for my life. I'm still a student of that world, still learning how to navigate in it, aware that I yet have much to learn. But that Spring morning I learned a lesson that I've nourished, a lesson I've lived again and again through the years:

God has a dream that He has fashioned especially for me.

I had been a disciplined student, so when I decided I wanted to pursue a doctorate in theology, the approval of the Faculty was a foregone conclusion. Why did I want to earn a doctorate? It seemed the logical thing to do. In college I'd discovered that I ranked high in the scale of academic ability. Besides, I was sure that one day I'd be a candidate to pastor one of the larger churches in Louisiana, and a Th.D. would be important for the pastor search committee. Again, logic led me to specialize in Hebrew Old Testament. Dr. J. Wash Watts, the Chairman of that department, inspired my admiration. He was a recognized scholar, the author of our textbook. His stories of experiences as a missionary in Israel gave life to his teachings.

So my future was set in concrete. Until one morning a few weeks before graduation, when a white-haired little man spoke in the seminary chapel describing his work as a missionary in California. I wasn't impressed, and struggled to keep my attention from wavering. At the close of his sermon he paused, stepped to the side of the pulpit and said, "Young men, I suppose most of you plan to carry out your ministry close to home. But let me challenge you: here in Louisiana you'll be in competition with a lot of other preachers who want the same job you're pursuing. It's different in California. Right now dozens of congregations are pleading with God to send them a pastor. How is God going to answer? Through you, young man! Lift up your eyes unto the fields. In California the harvest is plenty, but the workers are few!"

In that instant, God spoke to me! Directly, unmistakably, he whispered to my heart: "Pat, I want you in California!" Immediately, I recognized God's voice, even though I'd not had an experience like that since a Sunday morning long ago, when a little seven-year-old felt the hand of God pushing him out into the aisle to receive His Son's sacrifice on the cross.

That day was the first entry in a manual of instructions for service that God began writing in my soul:

Knowing God's will for my life is not something I deduce according to circumstantial logic. It is a revelation that comes in God's time. When God gives that revelation, his voice is as clear as the voice of someone seated across the table from me.

But what about Evelyn? What would she say? Common sense told me she'd think I'd lost my reason.

By the time I arrived in Fordoche the next night, I had worked out a plan: the Southern Baptist Convention would meet in San Francisco the following June. We'd attend the Convention and look around to see if God opened a door for us.

When I arrived at the little parsonage I found my wife stressed out by a week of trying to control thirty fourth graders for six hours day, then coming home to two hungry babies. After we got our kids to bed, I sat across from her at the table and told her what had happened to me the day before. I studied her eyes, fearful of her response. She reached out, picked up her cup of coffee, took a sip, set down the cup, and said calmly, "So we need to make a trip to California. All right, let's go." I was stunned. No questions about the validity of my theophany, no questions about how we'd pay for a trip across the country, simply a quiet acceptance!

That day I became aware as never before of how fortunate I was to have married a woman who was ready to go with her husband wherever God's plan took us.

Then, as the weeks passed, my vision slowly faded, and logic prevailed. What was I thinking? Scrap all the plans we had so carefully laid? Abandon the opportunity to spend three marvelous years with one of Christendom's greatest Bible teachers as my mentor? It didn't make sense!

I moved my family to one of the new apartments that the seminary had constructed on a beautiful new campus near Lake Pontchartrain. We had decided it was time to resign the church in Fordoche and look for a pastorate closer to the Seminary, a church that could pay me a salary sufficient for the support of my family.

It should have been a joyful summer. We were the first occupants of a beautiful apartment. I had been recognized by the staff of the seminary as one of a few graduates in whom they were willing to invest three more years of their time. Most Sundays I had a place to preach, and I was involved in enough revival meetings to keep me busy. But it turned into the worst summer I can remember. The heat was oppressive. (In the early 1950's nobody had air conditioning.) There was a plague of mosquitoes so overwhelming that we had to keep the kids indoors most of the time. And Evelyn and I argued constantly. We seemed to disagree on everything. Days would pass when we hardly spoke to each other.

In July I received a letter that set my heart to thumping. The pastor of the Proctor Avenue Baptist Church in Port Arthur, Texas invited me to preach in a youth revival the last week of August. A dream come true! Proctor Avenue was where Daddy had been a deacon and felt the call to the ministry. There Mama had found Jesus and been baptized. What an opportunity!

I spent many long hours preparing what I was sure would be the best sermons I'd ever preached.

The revival meeting turned out to be a disaster. At least that's what it seemed to me. As I preached each night I had the sensation I was a hound howling at the moon. I was sure nobody was listening, that every young person present was bored and every adult was saying in his heart that I was a hypocrite, that I didn't believe a word of what I was preaching. Night after night when the invitation was given, no one came forward.

Saturday afternoon in the pastor's guestroom I asked myself if I could survive through Sunday night. What about packing my suitcase and slipping away when nobody was looking? About 2:00 o'clock I fell to my knees and cried out to God: "Father, what's wrong? Why have you abandoned me? I'm going to remain here on my knees until you answer!"

Forty-five minutes passed, and then, as if pushed by a hand on my chest, I found myself on my back staring at the ceiling. God spoke clearly to my heart: "Pat, do you expect me to bless a Jonah? I told you to go to California and you disobeyed me. Nothing's going to go right for you until you repent!"

I sat up, disoriented for a few minutes. Then I hurried to the phone in the hall and called my wife. "Honey," I said, "we've got to make a trip to California."

"But how? We have no money. And besides, your seminars begin week after next."

"I know, but I can't begin my studies until I straighten out this business of God's will for my life."

When I arrived home Monday afternoon Evelyn handed me a copy of the Times Picayune, New Orleans' morning newspaper folded to the want ad section. She had underlined an announcement in red:

> *Free trip to California! Horsetrader Ed has purchased*
> *automobiles for his lot in San Francisco. Buy the gas and drive a*
> *late-model car to California.*

By sunup Friday morning we had deposited our children with my aunt Donie in Port Arthur and were headed west in a 1948 Olds. We were in agreement on our travel plans: on Sunday morning we'd take advantage of this trip to attend Charles Fuller's Old Fashioned Revival Hour in Los Angeles. Both our families, like millions of other believers, had listened to Fuller's radio program faithfully as long as we could remember. Afterward, we'd head for San Francisco, where we had reservations at a downtown hotel.

Halfway across Arizona the next day, a red light flashed beside the speedometer. I was about to learn another lesson:

When God prepares a place in his calendar for us, he has a way of securing our cooperation.

In the next town, I pulled into a shop.

"Your generator's dead," the mechanic informed me, "you're going to have to replace it." When he told me the price, my heart skipped a beat. That was before credit cards, and I knew immediately we couldn't pay for the repairs and still have money for our expenses in San Francisco.

I explained my plight. The mechanic replied, "Well, you've got a problem. By tonight you won't have any juice left in your battery."

"Isn't there any way I can get this car to San Francisco without replacing the generator?"

The mechanic scratched his head. "I'll tell you what you can try. It may work and it may not. Tonight park your car on a hill. Next morning give it a push, shift into first and see if the engine kicks off."

We continued on to Los Angeles, eyeing the red light and praying all the way. We did find a motel on the crest of a hill. The next morning we loaded our suitcases into the trunk. Getting in, I pushed the starter button. Nothing!

"Well, the mechanic warned us," Evelyn said.

"And now we'll have to try what he said."

"Yes, but first let's pray." Evelyn reached over and took my hand.

"Lord," I prayed, "you brought us this far. I don't know why you let that generator fail, but you know why. If you want us to get to San Francisco tonight, you're going to have to make this car start."

I got out, Evelyn got behind the wheel, and I pushed and strained, praying all the while. The car started moving slowly, then picked up speed. "Now," I yelled, "engage the clutch and shift into first!"

The car bucked a couple of times, coughed, then, praise God! the motor roared into life.

By late afternoon we'd checked into our hotel, having left the wounded Oldsmobile at Horsetrader Ed's and picked up a rental car. Well, here we were! What next? We'd already planned to make a visit the next day to Golden Gate Baptist Theological Seminary. If I abandoned my doctoral studies in New Orleans, it seemed logical to continue them in another seminary.

"What about church tonight?" Evelyn asked, as we lay on the bed recovering from our trip.

"Well, I guess we could check out the yellow pages."

She reached over, picked up the telephone directory and thumbed through it.

"A lot different from New Orleans," she said after a moment, "just half a dozen churches listed under 'Baptist'. The first one on the list is 'Bayview Baptist'. Shall we call?"

"Why not? Go ahead and dial the number and see if they have services on Sunday night."

"No, you make the call." She handed me the telephone.

I dialed the number, and a male voice answered. I asked if Bayview Baptist Church had Sunday night services.

"We certainly do. I'm Bob Mefford, the pastor, and we'd love to have you visit us. May I ask who's calling?"

I gave him my name and explained that we had just arrived from New Orleans.

"Tell him you're a preacher," Evelyn whispered.

"I graduated from the seminary in May and we're here just checking out the area."

There was a brief pause, then Mefford said, "Preach for us tonight."

I was dumbfounded. Placing a hand over the receiver, I whispered, "This guy's nuts, he's inviting me to preach at his church tonight."

"Tell him yes."

"Don't tell me what to do, woman!"

"Hello ... hello. Are you there?" asked the voice on the telephone.

"Oh yes, I'm sorry, I was just surprised that you asked me to preach without even knowing me."

"But I do know your seminary, and if you're a graduate, that's a good enough recommendation for me."

I chuckled. "Well, Pastor, how can I refuse? If you've got enough faith to invite me sight unseen, I suppose I ought to have faith enough to accept."

Following Pastor Mefford's directions, we found the church without much trouble. True to its name, it was located on a peninsula jutting out into San Francisco Bay. The congregation met on the main floor of what had been a rather large three story private residence. There were some sixty people present, and when I stood to preach my heart was warmed by their smiles.

After the sermon a young woman approached me. "Rev. Carter, she said, "allow me to introduce myself. I'm Ruth Faver. Did Pastor Mefford tell you he resigned last Sunday?"

I did a double take. "No, he didn't."

"Well, I'm the president of the Pastor Search Committee. Would you be interested in the possibility of becoming our pastor?"

Shocked, I could only stare at her. After I'd caught my breath, I answered, "I might be."

I explained my commitment to the seminary in New Orleans, and the reason for our visit. We agreed that if we returned to San Francisco I'd call her and she'd arrange "a sermon in view of a call".

The pastor and his gracious wife invited us to their home for coffee. They lived on one of San Francisco's fabled hills a few blocks from the church. Evelyn and I sat with them in their living room sipping coffee, awed by the way the picture window framed the lights of San Francisco and the East Bay, and by the unending stream of headlights flowing across Golden Gate Bridge and Bay bridge. Pastor Mefford explained that he and his wife were moving to another pastorate in Southern California, and that Bayview church had agreed to buy their house and place it at the disposition of the next pastor.

Back at our hotel we sat up until after midnight reliving our experience, half afraid we might awaken at any moment from a dream. How strange the way everything had worked together! Except for the problem with the car we would have delayed our arrival at San Francisco until late Sunday night, too late to attend a church service. And choosing to call the first church in the yellow section! And the pastor's absurd invitation to me to preach, sight unseen! It was hard to believe all this could have been coincidence.

The next morning I drove across Bay Bridge to Golden Gate Seminary in Berkeley. In comparison to the fabulous new seminary campus in New Orleans, the old brownstone converted office building was rather depressing. I was almost relieved when the academic dean, instead of being impressed by a visit from a man approved by another seminary as a Th.D. candidate, spoke rather doubtfully of the possibility of my being accepted by his seminary.

"You'll need to talk to Dr. Deere, chairman of the Old Testament Department. Mondays we don't have classes, so our teachers are at home. On the off-chance he may have dropped by his office, let me dial his extension." A moment later, eyebrows raised, he said, "Well, Frank, I didn't expect to catch you in today … oh, I see. Do you have a moment for a visitor who's interested in your department? …Good, I'll send him down to you."

Hanging up, he commented. "Quite a coincidence! Dr. Deere dropped by to pick up some papers to grade. When I called, he was walking out the door."

Frank Deere, a big man with a friendly smile, welcomed me in, listened intently as I explained my visit, and when I'd finished, reached for his desk calendar. "Pat, you're the kind of man I pray daily God will send to work with us here in California. Give me the name and address of your seminary's registrar, and before I leave my office I'll dictate a letter requesting your records. As soon as I have them I'll present your case to the Graduate Committee. We should have an answer for you within ten days."

Back at the hotel I described the visit to my wife. When I'd finished, she said, "Know what? We'd talked about spending a week here, but I think we already have all the raw material we need to make a decision, don't you?"

I went downstairs, drove to the Greyhound station and purchased our tickets.

At 7:00 the next morning we boarded the bus for the long trip home.

Almost as soon as the bus left the station we began evaluating our situation.

First, we reviewed everything in favor of our remaining in New Orleans. The faculty knew me, three years under Dr. Watts would incredibly enrich my ministry, we were near our families, and we had just occupied a beautiful new apartment. And speaking of answered prayer, what about that nice church just an hour's drive from the Seminary?

They had extended me a call, agreeing that we'd be at the seminary during the four days of classes, and occupy their pastorium weekends. Wouldn't it be foolish to leave behind all those certainties to pursue a dream that was, at best a "maybe" situation?

Off and on during the day we talked about what a move to San Francisco would require. We'd have to sell our furniture, no way we could pay movers to haul our stuff halfway across the continent! And how would we support ourselves? Even if Bayview Church called us, the salary would probably be inadequate for a four- member family.

"I guess I'd have to go to work," Evelyn said.

"I'm afraid so, Dear, at least in the beginning."

At midnight the bus paused for a half-hour rest stop in Flagstaff, Arizona. As we sleepily sipped our cokes, Evelyn remarked, "You know, I'm tired of kicking this thing around. Let's make a decision."

"I think I already have."

"I guess I have too." Evelyn checked her watch. "I saw a telegraph office in the waiting room. Why don't you send a telegram to the church that's awaiting our response to their call? That would be a good way to burn our bridges, don't you think?"

I picked up her hand and kissed it. "I'm so glad I married you!"

The next two weeks were hectic. What I had dreaded most didn't turn out so bad, after all. When I advised Dr. Watts of our change of plans, instead of scolding me for backing down on a commitment, he congratulated me for having the faith to obey God's call. Our garage sale went quite well. My parents were surprised, but pleased that their son was following the pattern they had set of placing God's will as the first priority. Evelyn's mother, who was still battling depression over the loss of her husband, asked only that we allow her and her five-year-old to visit us after we were settled.

I really should have asked the advice of my father about the trailer I bought to transport what was left of our earthly goods. Looking back, I wonder why no one warned me of the folly of trying to pull a wooden trailer over the Rocky Mountains behind a little Chevrolet coupe. Anyway, U-Haul didn't exist then, so maybe I had no other alternative. I can only suppose the good Lord must have said to His angel, "Look Michael, there they go. Without our help they'll end up at the bottom of some Rocky Mountain canyon. Assign one of your people to watch over them."

Halfway across Texas the nails on the trailer's wooden siding pulled loose and were scraping the tires. My solution was to get a hammer and a screwdriver and chip away the offending part of the trailer, a process I must have repeated half a dozen times before we reached our destination. When, on the fourth day we arrived at the dingy veteran's apartments in Oakland, the bolt holding the trailer hitch to the bumper was so worn it fell to the pavement when I unhitched the trailer. I can't explain why no one had told me I needed a safety chain!

Chapter Nine
God's Boot Camp
1951-1955

Right away we learned a lesson:

Just because you're in God's will doesn't mean you won't have problems!

The day after our arrival in California I called Ruth Faver, the president of the Pastor Search Committee at Bayview Baptist Church, expecting an invitation to preach. After a hearty welcome, she gave me a disturbing update: the church already had commitments for the next two Sundays! Next Sunday a man in his 40's with considerable pastoral experience would preach. The following Sunday, if they didn't call him, they would hear a young man who had been recommended to them. When she mentioned his name, my heart sank. Yesterday at the seminary, someone had introduced me to Paul. He was a popular evangelist who had decided to take a recess from his itinerant ministry while he was in the seminary. I didn't have a chance!

The next day, another blow. I had been driving Evelyn around Oakland in pursuit of one of the secretarial jobs listed in the classified ads. We stopped at a telephone booth for her to make a call. Afterward, I drove her to an interview. When she got back into the car, she opened her purse, then said in a low voice, "Oh no, where's my billfold?"

She must have left it in the phone booth! By the time we got back to the phone booth the billfold, with most of our money, was gone.

I don't remember much of the next days. I'm sure we must have been depressed. Isn't it fascinating to look back, and say to yourself, "If only I had known what would happen later, I wouldn't have worried for a moment." I was at the beginning of learning a lesson that I would have to relearn a dozen times:

The discouraging circumstances of the moment usually tell you nothing about what God is really doing in your life.

If we're going to govern our lives by God's promises, it's important to rest in them, whatever happens. If not, we'll live in constant stress. Evelyn and I have had to make, again and again, life-changing decisions based on what we believed was God's will. Not once did God let us down. Every time I doubted God's faithfulness, I felt abandoned, desperate. Sometimes I replay, like a C.D., the drama of those days of pointless discouragement, and tell myself, "If only you had believed, you could have lived those uncertain days in peace and triumph!" Little by little I'm learning to live that awesome promise in 1 John 5:24: "Whatever we ask according to His will He hears us. And if He hears us, we know that we (*already*) have what we ask of Him."

Several weeks after losing her billfold, Evelyn received a letter from New Orleans. The billfold had been turned in to the Oakland police, and they had written the police in New Orleans. An ex-neighbor at the Seminary had given the New Orleans police our new address. We went to the station and reclaimed the billfold. Not a single dollar was missing! In the meantime, Evelyn had found a temporary clerical job.

On a Friday, some two weeks after I'd called Ruth Faver, she telephoned with an urgent request. Could I preach Sunday? The church had voted not to call the first preacher. The second had just informed Mrs. Faver that he had accepted the pastorate of another church.

I did preach, of course. Evelyn and I knew that it really wasn't a "trial sermon", that God had been leading, both in our lives and in the life of the church, shepherding us into His plan.

(In the year 1998 we received a letter from Ruth Faver, who had returned to her native Georgia. She had secured our address from the International Mission Board. She told us she was convinced that her role in our coming to the pastorate of the Bayview Baptist Church was the most important moment of her life. That the moment I stood in the pulpit that first Sunday night, the Lord told her He had chosen me to be pastor of the church.)

A week later we moved our pitiful little inventory of furniture into the beautiful two-story parsonage, at 131 Bridgeview Drive. What an appropriate street name! Most nights, until we became accustomed to our fabulous view, Evelyn and I would sit in our darkened living room and contemplate the glittering panorama spread before us: Golden Gate Bridge and Bay Bridge, immersed in a million lights on San Francisco's hills, the East Bay and Contra Costa County.

The four years in San Francisco, 1951 to 1955, were filled with learning experiences for the young minister and his wife from Louisiana. Most of the church members were military and work-related transfers from Texas and Oklahoma. They were part of only a small minority of the Christian transplants who had an interest in joining a church. One fellow pastor swore to me that the white stuff atop the Rocky Mountains was not snow, but church letters people threw out their car window as they crossed the California state line!

I began a diary in November 1952. Reading the daily entries, I find that most of what's written there I've forgotten, that I carry in my memory only the encouraging victories and the numbing defeats. I've tended to forget those long, harsh days in the trenches, sometimes scary, often boring, when I struggled just to survive, buffeted by fluctuating church attendance, marriage crises, alcohol addictions, sicknesses of the kids, disappointments with people, angry church members, undependable church members, stingy church members -- and church members whom I came to love as God's special people. There always seemed to be economic problems. Several months after our arrival Evelyn went to work at the San Francisco Naval Shipyard. She left the job after two years to give birth to Carol. Afterward, when things got tight, she'd called "The "Kelly Girls," an agency for temporary employment.

Within a few weeks my own pattern of life was set. Three or four days of the week were dedicated to visitation and the preparation of sermons. The church, with an attendance of 125-150, required constant work just to maintain its membership because people were constantly leaving for military duty elsewhere, or to look for a job in another city. The remaining days I drove across Bay Bridge to Golden Gate Seminary and spent long hours in a tiny cell assigned to me for a daunting project: an exegesis of the Eighth Century Prophets. This exposition, plus a number of seminars in minor fields, would constitute my resident requirements for the acquisition of a doctorate in Old Testament. The long, lonely hours conjugating Hebrew words and studying commentaries often provoked headaches and indigestion.

In the midst of the constant struggle, there were adventures that showed unmistakably God's hand in our lives. One of these was my unexpected role in the future location of Golden Gate Seminary. In the early 1950's radio was still the most common source of information and entertainment. Everybody in the Bay Area tuned in to KCBS. The daily early morning feature by Jim Brady, "This Is San Francisco," was one of its most popular programs. Friday morning, December 12, 1952, as usual, Evelyn and I had our radio tuned to Mr. Brady, as I shaved and she dressed for work. I wasn't paying much attention, until Evelyn cried, "Pat, he just mentioned your name!" I listened, astonished, as the speaker described a letter I had written to the architectural firm of J. Carl Warnecke.

The Warnecke firm was the most prestigious in the Bay Area. They had received a lot of publicity for the construction of cutting edge schools in northern California, and recently of government buildings in Washington, D.C. The company was making a feasibility study for a seminary campus the Southern Baptist Convention had projected for the Bay Area. More than a year before, Warnecke's public relations representative had called me. I was impressed by the clipped British accent of the gentleman asking me for information on Southern Baptists. I gave him a summary of the number of churches, total membership and annual budget of the Southern Baptist Convention.

After the radio program, the man who had called me, Mr. Leslie, invited me to lunch. He explained that his earlier call was motivated by a letter from the Southern Baptist Convention asking if Warnecke would be interested in exploring the possibility of his firm doing the construction of a seminary. They had never heard of the Convention. The word "Southern" suggested to them a small group of black churches in the deep south. Impressed by my description of Southern Baptists, they had pursued the matter, and recently the Southern Baptist Convention had appropriated $50,000 for a feasibility study.

And now I was being featured on Jim Brady's program! And I was remembering a copy the seminary had sent me of a letter from John Carl Warnecke to Dr. Harold Graves, President of Golden Gate Seminary. The letter requested that staff members and graduate students "contribute their ideas in writing for our inspiration and direction in the master plan studies ... what is the ideal type of student you aim to produce? What conditions, then, will be most essential to this development?"

About a week before, Dr. Graves had informed me that the Warnecke firm had chosen my letter from among some forty submitted, as best fulfilling what they wanted.

But I had no idea it would be aired over CBS! Mr. Brady later sent me a copy of the script. It said, in part:

> *"Last night in Berkeley, the thirty-member board of the Golden Gate Baptist Seminary heard Harold Graves, the president, reveal plans for a multi-million dollar seminary which will arise in the East Bay Area. For suggestions on how this was to be done, the Warnecke office turned to the people themselves -- the students and ministers who will be studying and teaching there. And I'm proud to say that Pat Carter, of 131 Bridgeview Drive, here in San Francisco, was one of those whose ideas will find expression in the new buildings. I wish I could read you everything he has written, because I think this young minister has captured more completely than anyone I know, the spirit which has made California and the East Bay so attractive to people all over the country.*
>
> *He speaks of California's long tradition of independence and freedom, the wide sweep of the Pacific stretching 700 miles along our coast. This freedom, he feels, is expressed in California*

architecture, where hills, sunshine, glass and redwood combine.
Since the Baptists have been historically a freedom-loving people,
this should be expressed in the seminary.

Finally, he comments on the spirit of simplicity inherent in
California living. The ornate, pretentious, have little place in our
modern spirit. Because, as he says, the Baptist faith appeals by
its simplicity, that too should be in the buildings.

So I'm looking forward to the day when I can go again to the
East Bay and see a vision of the future being made into a reality.
And I'm proud to know that a San Francisco minister, and a San
Francisco architectural firm will help bring the spirit of the west
alive again.

In the months that followed I was invited to John Carl Warnecke's firm several times for chats with Mr. Warnecke and his staff. I was excited when the Seminary acquired a large property on Strawberry Point, a wooded peninsula jutting out into the Bay just north of the Golden Gate Bridge. The seminary campus that was constructed in the years that followed evokes the ideals expressed in my letter. Unlike Southwestern Seminary in Fort Worth, whose lofty golden dome dominates the prairie for miles around, Golden Gate seminary folds into the wooded hills, and seems a part of them. Its unpretentious buildings, quietly beautiful, express not only the topography of its surroundings, but also the spirit of openness and simplicity I emphasized in my letter.

The most concrete accomplishment of our four years in San Francisco was the construction of a church building on a hill overlooking San Francisco's busiest thoroughfare, Bayshore Freeway. A year after his story about the seminary, Jim Brady featured our church in his program, "This is San Francisco":

This morning I want to tell you about a church. It is a symbol of what
people can do for themselves when they have the spirit and the will to work.
I'm speaking of the Bayview Southern Baptist Church ... overlooking
Bayshore Freeway and Alemany Boulevard. Any night, and Saturdays,

too, you can go out and watch the members of the congregation working
under the direction of the pastor, Rev. Pat Carter.

Sounds romantic, building your own church! But this was a
strategy born out of necessity and carried out in desperation. It became
apparent a year after I assumed the pastorate that our church was
outgrowing its facilities. We began looking for property, and at last
located a lot on a hilltop overlooking the major freeway feeding traffic
into town from the south. Our problem was money. We hadn't any!
Finally, we issued $40,000 in bonds backed by the Broadway Plan, a
Christian organization. The bonds paid 5% and were guaranteed by
the church property. This occasioned two daunting tasks: first we had
to sell the bonds to church members and friends who had faith in us.
Second, because this amount of money wasn't sufficient to entrust the
construction to a contractor, we would have to do most of the labor
ourselves.

Two years of my diary are filled with the perils I endured as general
contractor. We engaged an engineer named Robert Fenway to do the
foundation and other basic construction. My inexperience led me to
accept his offer of working on the basis of cost plus ten percent. It
didn't take long for me to realize the catch 22 situation into which
we had fallen. The more our construction cost, the more profit for
Mr. Fenway! This gentleman gave me more digestive upsets and
headaches than anyone before or after. And the poor congregation!
Every Sunday their young pastor harangued them about the need to
sell more bonds, and for more people to show up each night and on
Saturdays to consecutively dig the foundation, pour the concrete floor,
stucco the outside walls, apply sheetrock to the inside walls. Of course
that young pastor was there in his blue jeans any time anyone else was
present. Added to the stress of the construction itself were the stressful
meetings with protesting labor unions and companies we owed money,
besides petitions from the neighbors concerned about parking. As
a consequence, I lost twenty pounds, my seminary studies suffered,
my conscience constantly plagued me for neglected pastoral duties,
I was impatient with my children and short-tempered with the wife
who worked forty-hour weeks to help the family pay its bills. How
our marriage survived such a stressful period is a testimony to God's

grace! Evelyn later confessed to me that if her father had been alive, she probably would have taken a vacation from her obsessive husband.

Finally we moved into our building on April 1, 1954. It was far from completed, but we had sold our other property to a civic club, and they were unwilling to wait any longer for occupancy. Two weeks later we celebrated the appearance of our younger daughter, Carol.

The following months were difficult, as we were surprised by a downward spiral in attendance and finances. I entered a period of deep depression, because the church owed money to a building supply company, and we had no way of paying. In June the California Baptist Convention lent us $4,000, taking bonds as collateral. Our struggle continued month by month, until finally, on December 5th, we had our official dedication ceremony, with the attendance of many people from neighboring churches and dignitaries from the State Convention. The building was beautiful, with white stucco walls and a tall redwood tower visible to the thousands traveling below.

By that time I was physically and spiritually exhausted. And I was discouraged about my seminary studies. The national accrediting agency had notified the seminary months before that until they acquired a larger library, they could no longer offer doctorate degrees. My professors had assured me that I would be allowed to complete my graduate studies, but warned me my Th.D. would not be recognized by other seminaries.

We made a Christmas visit to our parents in Louisiana. On our return we stopped off at Southwestern Baptist Theological Seminary in Fort Worth, Texas. Studying their catalog, I was fascinated by the Th.D. in Philosophy chaired by Dr. John Newport. Dr. Newport offered seminars on themes that had intrigued me for a long time: the problem of evil and suffering, Marxism, which at that time seemed to be conquering the entire world country by country, and philosophical problems related to biblical interpretation. My good friend C.W. Brister, who had just completed his Th.D. studies, arranged a visit with the Dean of the graduate department, Dr. Robert Baker. Dr. Baker encouraged me to consider transferring to Southwestern.

The trip back to California was a disaster. In the plains of West Texas the next night, we suddenly realized that the trunk lid had come open. I braked, and we discovered that all the children's Christmas presents had been scattered over the highway in the last hour or so. The children were devastated when we decided it wasn't worth turning around. The following morning in New Mexico I lost control of the car downhill on an icy mountain highway and slammed into another automobile. Minutes later a car behind me repeated the same maneuver and rear-ended us.

By the time we arrived in San Francisco I felt as if I had a burning coal in the pit of my stomach. This had been happening frequently in recent months. A doctor's visit revealed that I had a severely inflamed stomach. My doctor warned me that, unless I found a way to lower the stress in my life, I'd soon have ulcers.

Maybe it was God's time for a new start. We had come to California with a lifetime commitment, but by now we'd learned that our calendar is not always God's. Was His plan for us now to make my graduate studies our priority? But that hardly seemed logical, since we were in the state with the biggest missionary challenges in the country. Not logical, but logic is secondary when you're seeking God's will. We decided the time had come once again to put out a fleece. We listed three goals that had to be met before we'd feel we had a mandate to move toward another horizon:

(1) The remaining Broadway Bonds would have to be sold.

(2) We must pay our debt to the Convention.

(3) Most important, there must be an influx of new people, experienced disciples who would be capable of moving the church forward after our departure.

These were ambitious goals, since we would have to leave before the end of June, in order to plug into Southwestern's program of studies. Only God could do it!

And God did! In the next five months we received 47 new members, more than had joined our church in all the previous year. The debt was paid off and the remaining bonds sold.

On June 6, 1955 we said a tearful goodbye to these people we had come to love so deeply, and headed east, again pulling a trailer behind us.

Why did God take us to California? That He led us, there is no room for doubt. But here we were, after only four years, headed for a new adventure. What had been accomplished?

A few months after our arrival in San Francisco, the associational missionary cornered me in the seminary: "Pat Carter, tell me why you came to California."

"Because God brought me."

He punched a finger in my chest. "Let me tell you, there's only one reason why Southern Baptists are in California, and that's because of our position on baptism and the Lord's Supper."

After that encounter, I had a difficult time feeling friendly toward him. We lived on different planets. He was a representative of a group who were convinced the Southern Baptist denomination had been chosen by God to teach some fine points of church tradition to the denominations that had preceded us in California. I had no desire to be a denominational warrior, I was sure God had not brought us with that purpose.

I had learned that neither did God take us to California for the purpose I nurtured in my young, ambitious mind. I had envisioned a huge church building on our hill, housing a congregation of 1000 people, dwarfing the two-story 50X100-foot building we had first erected with so much sacrifice. The huge church never evolved. There was, of course, substantial progress. We began the pastorate with 150 members, and when we left there were more than 300. During four years we had a total of 300 additions, 94 of these by baptism. Church receipts more than doubled and the value of church property grew from $13,500 to $105,000. This was in 1955, so to appreciate these finances in twenty-first century dollars multiply the figures by 10.

After we left the unthinkable happened. The city decided to place a highway interchange exactly where Bayview Baptist Church had recently built their beautiful sanctuary. They expropriated the property, and the reimbursement was only enough for the church to purchase a small building a few blocks away. In the ensuing years the membership dwindled. I'm not sure the congregation even exists now.

On balance, was the expenditure of so much prayer, preaching, visitation, back -breaking hard work and heartache a failure? For several years after the city's takeover of our beautiful church on a hill, that question tormented me.

Then, ten years after our departure, several of the former members of the Bayview Baptist Church promoted a reunion in South San Francisco. We were on our first furlough from Mexico, and traveled to California for the reunion. Some fifty adults were present, from about fifteen congregations in the Bay area. I listened as one by one they stood to relate what they were doing in the Lord's work: teachers, Sunday School Directors, others in evangelism and work with women. It slowly dawned on me what made our four years in San Francisco worth while: our impact upon the lives of individuals. Wasn't that similar to Christ's ministry? He left no institutions, only persons with the fire of His message burning in their hearts. Institutions are necessary, but too many times they become the projection of a leader's ego, and the people's loyalty is not so much to Christ as to the charisma of their leader. When that person leaves, the institution dwindles. On the other hand, an individual born again and committed to Christ has the powerful, quiet presence of the Holy Spirit within, guaranteeing that God's Word, and a mentor's investment, will not return void. So from that experience I learned a lesson:

People are more important than institutions.

I suspect that God's major purpose in taking us to California was to place us in a training camp for the future plans He had for us. In those four years we learned a great deal about discerning and following the Spirit's leadership, witnessing, relating to people different from us, reacting positively to disappointments, and simply surviving in a hostile climate. Those lessons would be invaluable in the ministry in another country that God was preparing us for.

Yes, It's All About People

Until San Francisco, there had been a unifying factor in the churches I'd known. The overwhelming majority of the members had grown up in the same town. Later, in large cities, I learned that people of the same cultural level tend to cluster. The Bayview Baptist Church was different. The overwhelming majority of the people were transplants from other states, and besides, there were striking cultural differences.

Take the Dumas and the Davis families, for example. Otis and Clara Dumas were from a humble rural background in south Louisiana, with only a few years of formal education. Otis worked in the city dump. Clara, his wife, was a large-bodied, big-hearted woman who dedicated an impressive amount of her time and energy to yelling at Otis, who wore a hearing aid. I remember the Sunday when we were seated in their living room after a fried chicken dinner. Clara began berating her husband for a recent failure. He sighed and closed his eyes. Suddenly she yelled, "I see you, Otis, don't you dare!" Otis' fingers were inside his shirt front, turning off his hearing aid!

In contrast, Janice and James Davis were from Nashville. James had a doctorate in nuclear science and was an executive in a government laboratory dedicated to atomic research. Janice had a Masters in education. It was stimulating to sit at their kitchen table, coffee cups in hand, and engage in a wide-ranging conversation about the dangers implicit in the cold war with Russia and her atomic capabilities, national politics, critical problems in the Biblical text … and the future of our church. James was a deacon and the Director of our Sunday School, and Janice loved her church with all her heart.

Then there was Mrs. Gilliland. I still remember the first Sunday she appeared in our church. She had struggled to locate us, and entered just as I stood to preach. I was unable to speak for a moment, threatened somehow by that tall, elegant woman in a wide straw hat. Mrs. Gilliland, an export of the Alabama Baptist aristocracy, had been recently widowed, and had come to San Francisco to live near her only son. She became a very special friend to her young pastor and his family. She was a dedicated intercessor, and many years later in Mexico, we received letters that said such things as: "this morning I awoke before dawn, and the Holy Spirit told me to spend an hour on my knees praying for you."

Besides, I was impressed at the consecration of our military men. They brought to their Christian lives the discipline earned in military service. Marine Sergeant Brent came to us from Pennsylvania, by way of Okinawa. How he loved the Lord! He had been converted in a Methodist church, and it took a while for him to become convinced that he needed to be immersed. But once convicted, he submitted to that discipline. He was one of the most faithful laborers in the construction of our new house of worship.

Quite a contrast, the discipline of Brent, to the lifestyle of the Luthers. I had the blessing of leading them to faith in Jesus Christ and baptizing them. Joe worked at a dozen different jobs during the time I knew them. When things were going well they spent money like it was going out of style. When things were going bad, I could count on him hitting me up for a loan, which of course turned out to be a gift. The same lack of discipline ruled in their church life. I found myself on Sunday mornings glancing at the door, wondering if today the Luthers would make it, or if they were sleeping off some late night adventure.

In contrast to the Luthers, who were a constant trial of patience, the Butlers were a sudden and resounding disappointment. Carl was Director of Sunday School when I became pastor. I never had doubts about whether he'd be there; he usually beat me by fifteen minutes. Each Sunday morning in the general assembly, before we split for classes, he presented a well-prepared devotional thought. But after a few months, I began to worry about what I saw on his wife's face. Always, while Carl was giving his devotional, Eula kept her eyes fixed on him. What was that expression on her face, anger, fear, maybe hatred?

Late one Saturday night Eula appeared at our door with their three small children, her face bruised, lips bleeding. Seated in our living room she told a sad story: at least one Saturday a month her husband spent the day in a bar, and returned home to yell at her and pound her with his fists. Early the next morning Carl came for his family, the picture of innocence, remonstrating with his wife for abandoning him. A couple of days later I knocked at their apartment door and there was no answer. Peering through a window I was startled to see a vacant living room. We never saw the Butlers again.

And of course there were good people who had bad children. I never met Jo Ann's ex-husband. I only knew he had left her and a four-year-old son ten years before. I admired Jo Ann. She worked long hours at a low-paying job, but always had a smile on her face. Johnny always seemed to be in trouble at school, and at church picked on the smaller kids. One Sunday morning after church Evelyn walked up and down the aisles, wringing her hands. "I know I left my purse right there in my chair while I was shaking hands with the people, and now it's gone."

"You know, others have complained of losing things," I told her. "We've got a thief in the congregation. This has gone far enough!"

"Any idea who it could be?"

"I'll bet its Johnny. He was suspended from school a couple of weeks ago for stealing a classmate's allowance." After church Jo Ann was looking for him, and suddenly he appeared with a smirk on his pimply face.

"Then he must have hidden the purse nearby."

"Under the church!"

I gave one of the kids a dime to crawl beneath the church and see if he could find Evelyn's purse. After five minutes he slithered out smiling, the purse swinging in his hand.

"Ill bet Johnny comes back this afternoon to retrieve it," Evelyn said.

"I'm going to find Mr. Johnson and see if he can come back and set a trap. He's a detective, and he'll know how to do it."

Fifteen minutes later Mr. Johnson appeared with a small box in his hand. "This is a powder we use in our work. We place it on a surface and it stains the thief with a bright indelible purple."

That night, as usual, Jo Ann drug in her son Johnny for the weekly young people's meeting. It didn't take a detective to see the bright purple stain. Mr. Johnson collared him, got an admission of guilt, and with his mother's permission took him to the police station for a stern lecture. I don't know how Johnny finally turned out, but at least we had no more complaints of thefts in our church.

Yes, it's all about people. And there were others: Mr. Banducci, an elderly, pious deacon who was never quite convinced that his young pastor was worthy of his confidence. And Jake, the alcoholic I baptized with such high hopes that, being indwelt by the Spirit, he'd never take another drink. When his wife threw him out for backsliding, I persuaded Evelyn that we offer him the downstairs guestroom. Late one night three months later, after sharing our table with him most days, getting out of bed half a dozen times to go pick him up at a bar, repeated acts of tearful repentance that lasted less than a week, I threw his belongings into his suitcase and placed it outside our front door, refusing to answer the doorbell when it rang again and again. And like the Butlers, Jake dropped out of sight.

Last of all, a tip of my hat to dear Mrs. Brown. A quiet, unobtrusive grandmother, she came to our house every day to stay with the kids those months when Evelyn was working for Kelly Girls. Never a complaint, either from her or from our children. I'm thankful for the contribution she made to the lives of kids who were the innocent victims of the often inept struggle of their dad and mom to be worthy interpreters of God's Poem. So many interesting personalities! And the most fascinating of all bore the name San Francisco. Living with her for four years was like being in love with a charming, beautiful, rather disreputable lady.

A city of hills. To get to our street you had to place the car in second and roar up a steep incline. For the last ten seconds before reaching the crest, I always prayed I wouldn't meet another car careening downward. Thankfully, my prayer went unanswered only once. Our insurance companies struggled for months trying to define whose fault it was, and never quite agreed.

A city of lights. I never tired of that perpetual Christmas tree outside our second floor picture window: in front, a million lights illumining that royal city, to the left the lights of Golden Gate bridge, to the right the lights of Bay Bridge, and in the distance, of the East Bay.

A city of fog. My favorite escape when I felt stressed out was to drive in the late afternoon to a quiet green park atop Twin Peaks. There I could watch the fog rolling in from the Pacific like a great white cumulous cloud. This fog was our air conditioner. Sometimes I reminded myself, as I pulled on my jacket, that just thirty minutes away over Bay Bridge, beyond the reach of our ghostly fog, people had their air conditioners going full blast. At times the fog became disruptive. At night I sometimes found myself easing downhill for a meeting at church, unable to make out anything three feet beyond the hood of my car, praying I would not bang into something or someone.

A port city. San Francisco had been my homeport when I was in the Navy. I can still remember the scary feeling as my ship slipped westward beneath Golden Gate Bridge and I felt the sickening roll of the Pacific, knowing that for the next two or three weeks I'd see only a gray sea by day and at night a black, star-spangled sky. That the next time we dropped anchor I'd find myself in another world. And being a port city produced a complex metropolis: fragrant China town, fisherman's wharf with its salty air and fried oysters. Golden Gate Bridge, a gold bracelet on the wrist of an elegant lady. And the Hunter's Point Naval Shipyard, just half a dozen blocks beyond our church, its scrabble of cheap apartments like carbuncles on the buttocks of an elite lady.

After three years in San Francisco, Evelyn and I were quite sure God had picked us up and dropped us into the middle of that lost, intriguing city, with the purpose of investing the rest of our lives there.

But He is the God of the unexpected! Although we didn't know it at the time, He was preparing us for something greater.

Chapter Ten
We Become Texans
1955-1958

Headed for Texas! Twenty-five years earlier, when I was four, my parents had snatched me away from Texas to become a Louisianian. But now I was headed back to my native land, accompanied by a wife and three children. We had traveled from New Orleans to San Francisco pulling all our possessions behind us in a trailer. And here we were again, pulling another trailer with everything we owned toward Fort Worth. Not much progress in four years in the accumulation of earthly goods! But we had been enriched in things much more important than clothing and furniture. Having received an abundance of proof that our Heavenly Father was guiding us, we traveled over the Rockies and across the desert with a song in our hearts.

Our family had changed: we had gone to California four years earlier with two children, and now there were three. David was seven. He had grown into a handsome, self-assured kid. From his teachers there were never any complaints about his academic discipline, but more than once notes had come from school about fights with fellow students. Linda, five, was a quiet, rather timid little girl, always ready for a hug. Carol was a year and a half old. We referred to her as our "carpet baby," because we paid for her unexpected arrival with money we had been saving to buy a carpet for the living room.

As for finances, God's promise of His presence was the only bank balance we possessed. If someone had asked me how I proposed to support a wife and three children while I did graduate studies, I'd have said I had no idea, but I was certain God did, and that was enough. Our friends from student days in Louisiana College and New Orleans Seminary, C.W. and Gloria Brister were moving to a pastorate, so they had offered us their rental home across the street from the Seminary campus. I had been warned that the great majority of student body husbands worked at secular jobs to finance their studies and put food on the table.

Logically, what we were doing was very risky. First, because I couldn't be sure I would be approved as a Th.D. candidate by Southwestern Seminary. In spite of my acceptance for doctoral studies by both New Orleans and Golden Gate Seminaries, I would not be an exception to Southwestern's policy that a candidate for their doctoral program take one week of stringent exams over the entire Master of Theology course. This rule was complicated by the fact that I had done my Master's program in another seminary, and four years had elapsed since my graduation. Besides, how much similarity was there between the Master's program in the two seminaries? And how much would I remember of what I had studied in New Orleans? I couldn't afford to ignore such odds, so I planned to invest five months of intense private study in preparation for the entrance exams.

We arrived in Fort Worth on June 17, 1955. The Bristers wouldn't be vacating their house until July first, so we would store our furniture in their garage and, in the interim, visit our families in Louisiana. While we were unloading the trailer, C.W. told me: "I'll be back in a few minutes. I want to run over to Mr. McKiver's office and advise him of your arrival. He helps locate work for students. There's no possibility of employment by a church anytime soon because they've got a long waiting list. Your only real hope is a job with a local business."

Twenty minutes later C.W. returned, his face bright with excitement. "Pat," he said, "I can't believe what just happened. When I told Mr. McKiver about you he sat there looking at me for, maybe thirty seconds. Then he said, 'Fifteen minutes ago I received a call from the First Baptist Church of Burkburnett. Their pastor has resigned and they need a supply preacher. He held up sheet of paper: "This is a list of more than 150 students who're looking for a place to preach. I really should send one of them, but you know what? As you were telling me about your friend Pat Carter the Lord whispered to me that I should send him."

We took a break for a glass of lemonade. My hand was shaking so much I could hardly hold my glass. "C.W.," I said, "I'm flabbergasted at the goodness of God! Would you lead us in a prayer of thanksgiving?"

So the next weekend Evelyn and I drove from my parents' home in Louisiana to Burburnett, a county seat town about a hundred miles north of Fort Worth. First Baptist Church averaged 500 in Sunday School. They invited me to return the following Sunday. And the next. In mid-July the Deacons informed me they had voted to recommend to the church I be called as pastor. But there was one requirement: I'd have to give up my plan for studies at Southwestern Seminary.

The offer was attractive. A church this size would be a stepping-stone to larger pastorates. And what a relief it would be not to have to worry about finances ... nor about that entrance exam in the fall, whose outcome was far from certain. But Evelyn and I didn't have to talk a long time to agree on our answer. God had brought us to Fort Worth to study at the seminary. No other alternative, however tempting, could be considered.

When I informed the deacons of our decision they asked me to continue serving as supply preacher until they found a pastor.

We were now in our rental house across the street from the Seminary campus. I had begun my regimen of 8-10 hours a day of study in the library, in preparation for the entrance exams in November. And I had secured a swing shift job at Arrow Freight Line, loading trucks. But then, an unexpected setback: one Sunday morning I awoke with severe abdominal pain, and struggled to make it through two sermons and the drive back to Fort Worth. That night I was admitted to the hospital, and the next morning they removed my appendix.

I'd be two weeks in recovery. How would we stay afloat financially? We did'nt lose sleep worrying. God would provide!

And He did. A friend in my dad's church sent us a small check every week. Daddy loaned me a couple of hundred dollars to pay our most pressing obligations. But what would we do when the Burkburnett church called a pastor and no longer needed my services? I wrote in my diary on August 11, "Something is going to have to break very soon, or we'll definitely be in bad shape."

Again, another divine intervention! I had yet to meet Dr. Cal Guy, the Missions professor at the Seminary. But in mid-August Mr. McKiver called and informed me that Dr. Guy had arranged for me to preach the following Sunday at Southside Baptist Church in Palestine. They were looking for a supply pastor. With the permission of Burkburnett First we went to Palestine the following weekend.

From the very first Sunday, we fell in love with Palestine and the people at Southside. Some 120 miles south of Fort Worth, Palestine, a city of 15,000, nestles in rolling pine hills. The church, true to its name, was on the south side, located in a curve of Highway 287. For the past eight years the congregation had been worshipping on the first floor of a two-story educational building set back on a four-acre lot, waiting for someone to lead them into sufficient growth to build a sanctuary. And the people! On the way home from the first weekend we agreed that Palestine seemed like a little corner of heaven. After four years in the tough, sophisticated metropolis of San Francisco, where, if you knocked on a front door an unfriendly eye stared at you through a peephole, the openness of the people in Palestine, their smiles, their hugs, overwhelmed us. Why, even strangers on the streets nodded and smiled at you!

It wasn't hard to say "Yes!" to their invitation to be their supply pastor. The next Sunday we made our last visit to Burkburnett, and were blessed with a nice love offering.

And the last Sunday of August, 1955 we began our ministry at Palestine. Less than a month later we accepted their invitation to be fulltime pastor, with generous provisions: I could spend four days a week at the seminary, the salary would be twice what we had received at Burkburnett, and they would begin construction soon on a parsonage.

God's loving care had been so obvious these past four months! Far beyond what we could have imagined, our every need had been supplied, and except for one Sunday in recuperation from the appendectomy, I hadn't missed a Sunday in the pulpit! We could attest to Paul's affirmation: "My God shall supply all your needs, according to His riches in glory in Christ Jesus."

We didn't know it at that time, but God was preparing us for future plans He had in mind. And He was in the process of writing on our hearts a very important lesson:

Once you are sure of God's will, move ahead, unafraid, resisting any detour.

In the two months that followed we lived joyfully and expectantly in the pattern the Lord had set for us. Five days a week I was in the library, poring over notes supplied by helpful fellow doctoral candidates who had done the Master's program at Southwestern. Among these were men who would distinguish themselves in Baptist work in the decades ahead: Kenneth Chafin became Director of Evangelism for the Southern Baptist Convention, Russell Dilday became President of Southwestern Seminary, Jerold McBride pastored large churches in Texas and Oklahoma and was named Director of Evangelism for the Oklahoma Baptist Convention. Half a dozen other new friends became Seminary professors, Presidents of universities, etc. My horizon was expanding!

October 11th, Foreign Missions Day at the Seminary, I had an experience both unexpected and troubling. It was the custom on Foreign Missions Day for a missions personality to speak in chapel and appeal to students to consider serving overseas.

I didn't plan to attend; I must not allow myself to be detoured from my rigorous study discipline. And besides, the question of foreign missions had been settled for me a long time ago. I had attended dozens of "foreign missions days" in six years of seminary in Louisiana and California, and had never felt an inclination to respond to the invitation at the close. I believed I knew the reason why: my gift was the pastorate, no doubt about it, because I loved teaching and preaching and the care of the flock.

The bell sounded for chapel, and the study carrels around me emptied. A twinge of conscience changed my mind and sent me to the balcony of Southwestern's huge chapel. A missionary appointee to the Philippines was the invited speaker. I found myself looking frequently at my watch. I was wasting time! Those Greek notes I was studying had me scared, I really needed to apply myself. I sighed with relief when the invitation hymn began. On the second verse, as I wrote later that day in my diary, "something got hold of me. I made it through another verse, but I couldn't stop weeping. Finally, I could take it no longer, so I stumbled down the balcony stairs and went to the front, along with about twenty-five others."

I told Dr. Guy, the missions professor, that I'd come down simply "to show I'm not a coward." I walked away wondering what had brought this on, since I had resolved the question of foreign missions a long time ago.

I decided to share my experience with Evelyn and check out her reaction. When I entered the house, she was in the kitchen washing the dishes. Her back to me, she said, "What are you doing home? It's a long time till lunch."

I answered, "Well, I just wanted you to know there was a missions emphasis in chapel today and when the invitation was given I went down to the front."

She turned, drying her hands on her apron and said, quite calmly, "Pat, four years ago we uprooted our family and moved to California. Five months ago we uprooted the family again and came to Fort Worth. I'm tired of this running around. Tell you what, if you think God is calling you to missions, you go ahead. I'm staying here with the kids."

That settled it. I knew the Foreign Mission Board didn't appoint divorcees!

I spent the first week of November struggling through the entrance exams. They were tough: four days of objective questions and the final day writing thematic papers. The weeks following were stressful. What would I do if I failed the exams? Would that mean we had misinterpreted God's will about moving to Fort Worth?

In December they advised me I had been approved. I learned that, of the fifteen who took the week of tests, several had been rejected. Among these were two who, like me, traveled from California. I wrote in my diary: "It's good to have all the uncertainty and strain of the past months behind us. But you know -- it was fun!"

In January I enrolled in the Philosophy Department. The doctorate in Philosophy offered by Dr. John Newport fascinated me. In my two years of residence I would have the opportunity for concentrated research in vital areas of the human struggle: evil and suffering, the nature of the universe, the Marxist world challenge, the meaning of Biblical inspiration. Evelyn also enrolled in three courses.

We settled into our new routine. Five days a week we were at the Seminary, and weekends we spent in Palestine. The children were happy. David and Linda had adjusted well to their new school, and Carol was a joy to have at home. We were grateful for the way our children were reacting to a rather stressful existence. David was bright and feisty. Linda seemed to be surviving reasonably well as the ham in the sandwich, squeezed between a hyperactive older brother and a demanding younger sister.

In early summer we moved into a handsome new home in Palestine, a block from the church on a quiet wooded street, and appreciated four months of freedom from the weekly trips to the seminary. But I had trouble enjoying leisure time. In late June I wrote in my diary: "I'm too tense and nervous. I suppose it's just my nature, I certainly wish I could get over it, I do want to be an enjoyable person to be around!"

By November, 1956 we were initiating plans for the construction of a sanctuary. In January a local bank granted us a loan. Month by month the church progressed in attendance and finances. In March we had the excitement of a groundbreaking service. I was thankful that this construction was going to be different from the struggle we endured in San Francisco. We had sufficient financing. There would be no worry about bruised hands and a sore back, because all the work would be done by contractors! More than once I remembered that less than two years ago I was engaged in a stressful battle to finish construction, pay off a crushing debt and arrive at a decision about a monumental change in the life of my family. The months since then, though stressful, had been marked by continual blessings from the Lord.

These blessings continued. In June, 1952, I was appointed a teaching fellow in the evangelism department of the seminary. I would be teaching several classes and grading papers. I was thrilled because I would be working closely with Dr. C.E. Autrey, renowned preacher and teacher. Dr. Autrey had recently come to the Seminary from the post of Director of Evangelism for the Southern Baptist Convention.

.

The last Sunday in June we moved into our beautiful new colonial style worship center. There were 278 in Sunday School and more than 300 in the service. By the end of August, when we celebrated two years in the pastorate at Palestine, we had much to celebrate. We had doubled our Sunday School attendance. Most Sundays, our beautiful sanctuary, with a capacity of 350, was comfortably filled. As I moved toward the completion of my residence at the Seminary prospects were bright. I had learned that the students who graduated with a Th.D. in Philosophy were known as "Dr. John Newport's boys", because their mentor, a man of enormous influence, took them under his wing, recommending them to pastorates of leading Texas churches. Besides, another possibility surfaced: Dr. Autry informed me that he had recommended that I be invited to teach Evangelism as a resident member of the Faculty.

But there were also negative currents. The Supreme Court decision ending racial discrimination was impacting, not only the schools, restaurants, and public transportation, but also the churches. Many were expecting an invasion of blacks demanding membership in white churches. One Friday I returned to Palestine from the Seminary just in time to learn of an unscheduled meeting of the men of the church to treat this matter. Strong feelings were expressed. One of our most influential deacons, a rancher, insisted we take whatever measures necessary to assure that no black person would ever be allowed to attend Southside. He proposed that the ushers be instructed that should a black appear at the door, they be informed they were not welcome. I rose to inform the men that should the church approve such a measure, they would have my resignation. Finally, after heated arguments, the group agreed to turn the matter over to the deacons. The deacons put the issue on the back burner. But from that day my relationship with the rancher cooled. It was heartbreaking for Evelyn and me, because he and his wife had been among our dearest friends. I wrote in my diary, "The race issue is terribly explosive. God alone can save us now from some terrible outcome."

This intense pressure affected my state of mind and added to a haunting feeling in my heart that, in spite of the church's prosperity, something was wrong in my life. I noted in my diary that I was not praying enough, I was a failure as a personal soul-winner, and I was a hypocrite. The pressure continued to build. I remember one Thursday afternoon as I was driving home from the Seminary I almost lost control of the car on a sharp curve, and a voice whispered, "Let it go, you'd be better off dead, anyway!" For several days afterward I felt shaken, depressed. These problems caused me to seek to draw closer to the Lord. I instituted a discipline of going aside three times a day for prayer.

In April, 1957 I submitted my thesis subject, a study of the Biblical teaching on physical healing. This was the product of a research paper on the subject that I had presented in a seminar titled, "Faith and Healing." I found myself going deeper into the Word than ever before, and beginning to recognize doubtful traditional Biblical interpretations that I had accepted as a matter of fact all my life. I became more and more conscious of a liberating force within me, freeing me from prejudices that were the product of my upbringing. I began to have repeated intuitions that ahead lay a special revelation from God. Late at night on April 10th I was praying, and afterward wrote in my diary, "Such a horrible fear came upon me that I seemed to sense the physical presence of Satan. I rushed to my desk to get my Bible, and when I picked it up it dropped to the floor. I saw that it had fallen open to 2 Samuel 5:24, 'And let it be that when thou hearest the sound of a going in the tops of the mulberry trees, that then thou shalt bestir thyself, for then shall the Lord go out before thee.... ' I am certain --absolutely certain - - that this was God's word for me. Now, I shall wait for the sign he promised."

In June I wrote, "God is so real to me. What a wonderful adventure, learning to live with Him. Day by day I continue to feel his love grow deeper and deeper in my heart. I feel at peace with God and in touch with him daily. A real revolution is taking place in my life!" In July I did something I had never done before. I spent the entire night in prayer in my church office. As the months passed I became ever more aware that I was on the verge of something special. November 13, I noted, "As I prayed tonight I felt very strongly that God was trying to impress something upon my mind. I couldn't understand what it was. I felt the Holy Spirit very close, but somehow I couldn't understand." A week later I wrote, "I feel strongly that God is moving in my life for a very special purpose. This moment I saw a verse, Matthew 22:14, in a new way. God seemed to be saying, 'I have chosen *you* for a very special purpose.' Oh Lord, here I am, send me!"

Just two weeks later, on December 4, 1957 God's answer exploded into my life. There was another Foreign Missions Day in chapel. And again, just as two years before, I decided at the last moment to attend. When the soloist sang "Jesus Is the Sweetest Name I Know," a supernatural peace invaded my heart, and as missionary appointees gave their testimonies God began to impress quietly upon my soul, "Pat, this is it, I am confirming what I said to you two years ago. I want you in foreign missions." An explosion, yes, but this time a quiet explosion, no tears, not even the need to go to the front. Just an absolute certainty.

The rest of the afternoon I had a quiet confidence that this time God would do in Evelyn's heart what He had done in mine. We hadn't mentioned the question of missions once in the past two years, but I was sure that God's time had come and He would complete what He had begun in me.

Each Thursday I drove back to Palestine, where Evelyn lived with the children, for the the mid-week prayer meeting. That night after the service we put the kids into their beds then sat together on the living room sofa. Taking her hand, I quietly related what had happened. She sat for a long time without speaking. Then I saw a tear coursing down her cheek. Turning to me, she said, "This morning, at the same time you were in chapel, I was sitting here preparing my Sunday School lesson. Suddenly the living room became very bright, and I found myself sobbing in surprise. I don't know how long it continued, but when it was over I asked myself out loud, 'What was that about? What was God saying to me?' I guess I know now, but let me sleep on it."

The next morning when she awoke she said to me, "Honey, I'm ready to go!"

For six weeks we told no one, because we wanted to be absolutely sure about our decision. I wrote in my diary December 14, "I'm battling the trepidation and doubts that had to come. Such thoughts as 'It's going to be so hard to tell my parents ... I'll never have the freedom of preaching in a foreign language the way I do in English ... Did God really speak to me, or was it my imagination?' Oh Lord, help me to ride out this storm. I'm trusting in you. Help me and sustain me, I pray."

January 24, 1958, I wrote: "Again, the sun is shining in my heart concerning our missionary call, just as I felt it would. I feel more than ever that this is God's will for our lives."

So the appointment process began. On February 15 we met with Miss Dawkins of the Foreign Mission Board and she told us that they felt we could best serve at the Seminary in Torreon, Mexico, and that they were looking toward appointment in December. In May we attended the orientation conference at Baylor. To our surprise we encountered half a dozen friends from college and seminary days there. In late June we informed the church of our decision. They were sad, but few were surprised.

Now my residence at the Seminary had been completed, and in July I had my long-awaited oral exam before the Graduate Committee, something I had looked forward to with apprehension for two years. I talked without stopping for two hours. At the end Dr. Newport and the Committee told me that if it were allowed, they would add "with honor" to my passing grade.

In August Evelyn and I passed our psychiatric exams. Two weeks later we had our physicals. An unpleasant surprise! The doctor told me my history of arthritis might present a problem for the Board. In early September Dr. Elmer West called from Richmond and informed me that the doctor's prognosis of my arthritic condition made it impossible for him to recommend my appointment. I protested indignantly: the arthritis was only an occasional problem, usually occasioned by stress. If the Board refused to appoint me, I was certain I had ahead of me half a lifetime of active, fruitful service. Were they going to deny my carrying out the ministry to which we were sure God was calling us? He recommended I consult with a specialist.

A week later I visited a specialist in Dallas. I was relieved when he agreed there was not sufficient medical evidence to impede my appointment. A few days later a call came from Richmond: Evelyn and I had been approved for foreign mission service! I wrote in my diary on September 22, 1958: "The pattern for the next thirty-five years is set. What does God have in store? I feel that we have come to the end of a very long road, and to the beginning of another."

We drove to Richmond for the appointment service October 14, 1958. We were surprised to discover that Billy Graham was a member of the Foreign Mission Board, and would preach the sermon. Evelyn even had her picture taken with him! Then we spent a week in New York City fulfilling dreams we had nurtured for decades.

Back home we went through the painful ritual of saying goodbye. The Associational Women's Missionary Union celebrated their annual meeting in our church and designated this meeting "Carter Day", giving us a nice love offering.

The last Sunday was bittersweet, so many expressions of love and many tears.

I noted in my diary the next day as we were packing to leave, "They act as if we had died. I hope and pray they will snap back and go on in the fine way they have." (They did! Southside Church grew later to be the largest Baptist church in Palestine.)

We spent the next six months at Southwestern Seminary. Since I was going to teach in the Mexican Baptist Theological Seminary, the Board wanted me to complete my thesis before we left, thus fulfilling all the requirements for the Th.D.

Chapter Eleven
Acquiring the Tools
1959-1960

Becoming a missionary means beginning a new life, in a sense dying and being born again into a new world. In order to be effective in this new world one must acquire the tools. The most important of these is the language. So we spent the first year of our missionary life in a language school in San Jose, Costa Rica, beginning in April 1959. A more ideal place could not have been chosen. In 1959 Costa Rica, with a million inhabitants, was the only true democracy in Latin America. San Jose, the capital, was a beautiful, mile-high city with a pleasant climate.

Everything was supplied to make it possible for both husband and wife to dedicate full time to language study. We were provided an attractive home and a bilingual Jamaican maid, Berenice. I still remember the first morning we awoke in our new world. The maid was in the yard speaking to someone in Spanish. Of course we had no idea what she was saying. Evelyn mumbled sleepily, "You know, she could be plotting our murder, and we'd have no idea!"

Within a week we were busy with schoolwork. Each of us was placed in a group of only four people. I faced a challenge, because the other three members of my class had studied Spanish before. I set up a rigorous schedule for myself. After a morning of intensive activity in class, I applied myself to another six hours daily of private study.

As the months passed, we were surprised at how quickly we were acquiring the language. But not as quickly as our children. David, eleven, was having to repeat the fifth grade, not only because of the language problem, but also because of a school system different from the United States. Linda had a private teacher. Carol, five, was in a day school. They seemed to soak up words and expressions, and were soon asking us questions about the language that we were unable to answer.

We had an unanticipated blessing, the opportunity of becoming friends with people of other denominations who, we discovered, loved the Lord as much as we did, and were highly motivated.

There were sixteen Baptist couples enrolled. After a couple of months I recorded in my diary a sobering phenomenon: "I enjoy the friendship of the Southern Baptist students here. However, I can't help but feel there's something lacking in our fellowship. Our get-togethers are usually hilarious, but the spiritual dimension is missing." Added to this was the lack of spiritual input at church. We attended the *Iglesia Bautista* in *Barrio Guadalupe* Sunday mornings. It was a frustrating experience to sit though a service and for the first several months have no idea of what the preacher was saying! After a while I found food for my soul by meeting each Monday night with a small group of Navigators. These missionaries, whose controlling motivation was Bible study and spiritual growth, made a lasting impact upon my life.

By September I was able to understand a lot of what was going on at the church.

Not that what I heard was especially helpful. I discovered that Pastor Muñoz was not much of a preacher, and there were rumors of a movement to fire him. The leader of the movement was confronted in a Sunday-afternoon business meeting, and after hours of heated discussion, expelled from the church.

In November I taught my first Sunday School class. I noted in my diary, "I can now speak fairly well without any preparation, if I take my time." Opportunities began to come my way. I was invited to speak in chapel two days on my doctoral thesis about divine healing in the Bible. Later they asked me to speak on the same subject at a pastor's retreat. In December I was named President of the student body.

In April, 1960 we completed our language studies and returned to Fort Worth, to await the documents we would need for entry into

Mexico. Time went slowly, and we lived through discouraging months when it seemed that the applications would be denied, and we'd never get to Mexico. I used the time to begin preparations for my classes in the Seminary in Torreon, Coahuila, Mexico, a desert city some 350 miles southwest of Laredo, Texas.

Chapter Twelve
A New Life in the Desert
1960-1961

"Moses and Aaron brought together all the elders of the Israelites, and Aaron told them everything the Lord had said to Moses. He also performed the signs before the people, and they believed. And when they heard that the Lord was concerned about them and had seen their misery, they bowed down and worshipped." (Exodus 4:29-31)

The return of Moses after forty years of silence was a surprise to most of the Israelites. But not to Caleb. He had nourished through all his years in Egypt the dream that Yahveh had given him. And had visited regularly God's prophets whose hearts burned with the assurance that deliverance was near. Throughout the weeks of the plagues, when time and again the elders were ready to throw in the towel, Caleb and his dear friend Joshua exhorted the people to have faith. More and more Moses and Aaron sought out Caleb and Joshua, seeking their counsel. When at last Moses stood before the Red Sea and raised his rod, Caleb was close by. When the sea parted, his shout of joy was an explosion of the hopes and prayers he had nourished for nearly forty years.

"Then Moses led Israel from the Red Sea and they went into the Desert of Shur."

(Exodus 15:22).

Is there any other place on this planet where two such disparate worlds are separated by only a narrow, shallow river? After more than forty years working in Mexico, I continue to be impressed by the differences between the United States and its southern neighbor. Language is the most obvious, but not the most important. The differences are the product of the roots of the two cultures. The United States (Mexicans are offended when someone refers to the United States as "America." "We are Americans also," they insist. Then how about "North America"? Mexico is also part of North America! So it's safer to speak of "The United States", though technically the same problem exists, since the official name of Mexico is "The United States of Mexico.")

The United States had its roots in immigrants from northern Europe who brought with them Biblical values and a work ethic. In contrast, Mexico had its roots in Spain and the Roman Catholic value system. The Thirteen Colonies were formed principally by families seeking refuge from both religious and economic problems. In contrast, Mexico was occupied by Spanish *conquistadores*, soldiers and fortune hunters whose principal goal was the acquisition of riches. Besides, the civilizing influence of mothers and children was absent, so the infamous *machismo* became an integral part of the Mexican culture. The people who settled the Thirteen Colonies had a passion for liberty. Because of the religious persecution they had suffered in England, they were determined to establish freedom of worship as a basic principle. In contrast, the *conquistadores* brought along Roman Catholic missionaries with a passion to impose the absolute rule of their church. The North American continent had its native inhabitants, but they were relatively few and primitive in their culture. These Indians were exterminated, or expelled from their homelands, and had very little influence in the formation of our nation's lifestyle. In contrast, the native population of Mexico descended from a sophisticated cultural history. Instead of expelling these natives, the Spanish absorbed them, using them as slave labor and intermarrying with them. So until the present time the "Indian" strain is dominant. Only about ten percent of the population is genetically European, twenty-five per cent are genetically pre-Columbian and the remainder are *mestizos*, a mixture of European and indigenous.

Another impact upon the soul of Mexico, seldom mentioned, but the theme of my novel, *Charming the Serpent*, is a history of thousands of years of dominance by demonic gods. This influence continues in a prevalent superstition, demonic oppression and the presence of witches everywhere.

After the Conquest, The Roman Catholic Church, failing in its attempt to persuade the native population to abandon their gods and embrace Christianity, resorted to a subtle syncretism of Christian doctrine and pagan tradition. Many of the Mexican saints are baptized pagan gods. The most striking example of this syncretism is the Virgin of Guadalupe, a Christian version of Tonantzin, the ancient goddess of nature, whose shrine dominated the same hill where the Basilica of Guadalupe in Mexico City has reigned since the fifteenth century.

Neither Evelyn nor I had ever set foot in Mexico before our entrance with documents giving us the right to reside in our adopted country. But from the time we occupied our hotel room in Laredo, to await the approval of the passage of our household goods, we began to experience the trauma of impinging upon a world radically different from the one we had grown up in. Instead of the immediate rubber stamp by immigration authorities that we had taken for granted, we suffered through nearly a week of rejection and threats. We became very discouraged, began to feel like criminals, and almost gave up hope. Finally, our customs agent made the necessary "arrangements," and we found ourselves being waved into the country by smiling officials who had accepted from the beginning that we would be approved, once we met their conditions.

My parents had driven to Laredo to take us to our destination. The trek to Torreon across 350 miles of desert is still as fresh as yesterday in my mind. That was before the blessing of automobile air conditioning, so a journey through the desert, with six of us jammed into Daddy's sporty Pontiac, was far from pleasurable. Ninety per cent of travelers into Mexico pass through Monterrey, and then fifty miles to the west, in Saltillo, turn south toward Mexico City. But we took the less-traveled western route to Torreon, located squarely in the middle of the great northern desert. By mid-afternoon of the second day, when we arrived at that city of a quarter of a million inhabitants, we were tired, grumpy, scared, and very hungry.

I wrote in my diary August 18, 1960, "We like Torreon very much. We are impressed by the wide, clean streets and the beautiful eucalyptus trees." Torreon's economy centered upon agriculture. Irrigation was brought in from a dam 125 miles to the west, and the rich desert soil produced an abundance of wheat and grapes.

We were impressed by the seminary campus. The Mexican Baptist Theological Seminary had been founded here nearly sixty years before, and had later moved to Saltillo, where it suffered through the Revolution of 1911-1917. Later, seeking freedom from persecution by the recently installed Marxists, the Seminary spent some ten years in El Paso. In 1946 the Foreign Mission Board purchased almost an entire city block in Torreon and began the construction of the seminary plant. This construction continued through the years.

The first Monday in September we enrolled our children in the American School. I wrote:

> Carol Anne is starting the first grade. She is big for her age, cute as can be, and very bright. Linda has begun the fifth grade. She is a very sweet little girl and gets cuter as the years go by. David, because he lost a year in Costa Rica, is entering the sixth grade. He's a handsome young fellow, and somewhat small for his age."

Just a week later we celebrated David's twelfth birthday. I wrote,

> Think I'll paint a word picture of him. He is very blond, sharp as a cricket, and never meets a stranger. Our biggest problem is to keep him from talking too much. He seems to be a sincere Christian. He still is not too serious about his studies, and I do not know yet what his capacities are. At times he gets pretty cantankerous around the house and as a whole is the hardest to get along with. But outside the house he is all personality and makes a good impression.

Reading my diary account of our first years in Mexico, I'm reminded of a man thrown into a wide river with a fierce current, trying, at the same time to survive, to fish, to dive for pearls, meanwhile swimming around frantically, eager to discover what else he might do. I was continually under stress, trying to adjust to complex relationships with the federal government, the local churches, my fellow missionaries, and my own soul. As a "fisher of men" I suffered constantly from guilt, doubting that I was responding adequately to the spiritual needs of the lost people all around me. And I was constantly seeking ways to be a better teacher and a more productive servant. In the midst of so much obsessive activity I kept reminding myself of my responsibility to be a good husband and father. I suspect that many times I was not a very pleasant person to be around, and that my fellow missionaries and my wife must have asked the Lord more than once to slow me down!

My first year's assignment in the seminary was New Testament Greek and Theology. Fewer than forty students were enrolled, and I soon learned that I shouldn't expect too much of them academically because most had only completed elementary school. They were the product of a poor educational system, of very humble living conditions and of tiny churches struggling to survive.

I tried to maintain a healthy relationship with my co-workers. A few weeks after arriving I wrote, "There are many problems among the missionaries, most of them due to a clash of personalities." The faculty assigned me the supervision of the mission work of the students, but the local missionary vetoed this, complaining I would be encroaching on his territory. I soon discovered a long-existing tension between the President of the seminary and the oldest missionary couple on the staff. This couple had already given notice they were going to ask for reassignment. At the conclusion of the previous school year another veteran couple had left to work in a distant part of Mexico, and gossip was that their departure was due to unhappiness with the administration of the seminary. The librarian, a single lady, complained that the President made changes in the library without consulting her. I wrote in mid-September: "There is harmony on the surface, but just beneath, tempers seem to be on edge. A rather strange situation, God's servants working together, but no real unity of the Spirit among them. It is a wonder we accomplish as much as we do!" Then, typical of Pat, the new missionary who suspected that God might have brought him to Mexico to solve everybody's problems, I added: "My prayer is that I may be able to make a contribution to our becoming a working unity. The Lord continues to impress me with the possibility of a ministry along the lines of bringing to bear the Holy Spirit and His power more fully and perfectly in our lives."

Besides, I suffered from the intuition that I was not fully accepted by my fellow missionaries. I was the first missionary to be assigned directly to the seminary. The other faculty members had come to Mexico as evangelists and had later taken on their teaching responsibilities as a secondary assignment. I was also the first to come with a doctorate, and I realized later that some feared this might be the first step in changing the seminary from a practice-oriented institution into academic isolation.

The missionaries spoke constantly of the possibility of being expelled by the Government. We were careful never to refer to ourselves as "missionaries," and legally the seminary did not exist. In 1917, at the end of a bitter six-year civil war, a new constitution was written. The revolution in Mexico was somewhat similar to the Boshevik revolution in Russia in the same period, and some radical measures in Mexico's constitution reflected the Marxist concepts being installed in Russia. All the church buildings were expropriated, and churches were forbidden to acquire property. Priests and evangelical ministers could no longer vote, own property or wear religious garb in public. Religious schools were forbidden. Foreigners were denied the right to be church leaders. That, of course, placed missionaries in a vulnerable position.

I slowly learned that the federal government had the practice of winking at violations of religious prohibitions. They were aware of the existence of the seminary and the presence of foreign missionaries, but they chose not to make an issue of it. However, some missionaries developed a fear of being constantly watched, under the threat of being jailed or expelled from the country. This phobia was epidemic in Torreon's missionary family. For instance, when we were looking at a house for rent, the owner asked what I did, and David piped up, "My daddy teaches in a seminary." The missionary lady accompanying us laughed nervously and said, "Pay no attention to what that little boy says, his daddy is retired." Some missionaries complained that their phones were being tapped.

An additional tension was the ever-present corruption in the culture. It was generally understood that nothing was impossible, if you were willing to pay for it. This included Border crossings, favors in the courts and traffic violations. I found out about traffic violations soon after arriving. I was driving down *Boulevard Cuauhtemoc* toward the seminary one afternoon, when a traffic cop on the corner blew his whistle and signaled me to pull over.

"What's wrong?" I inquired.

"You were speeding, *Señor*."

"Speeding? But there are no speed limits posted."

"Everybody knows the speed limit on this street is thirty kilometers per hour. You were going fifty. I can write you a ticket and it will cost you fifty pesos. But give me twenty-five pesos, and we'll forget about it."

I informed him it was against my principles to pay bribes. He began to argue with me. The discussion continued for half an hour, and meanwhile one of Torreon's frequent dust storms blew in, and I could feel my hair filling with desert sand. The policeman told me about his family's poverty, and added that his little son had polio. He needed money to pay the physicians.

"Look, officer," I said, "I'm sorry about your little boy. If you should stop me one day on the street and tell me you needed money to pay his medical bills, I'd help you, but I'm not going to pay a bribe."

Finally he shook his head, and said, "*Señor*, you just don't understand. Forget it!" and turned on his heel and walked away.

The next day I was driving down the same street, when I heard a shrill whistle. I braked, looked toward the sidewalk, and saw it was yesterday's traffic cop! When he approached the car, I protested. "Look, officer, I wasn't speeding, I remembered your warning of yesterday."

"You're right, you weren't speeding. But remember what you said yesterday? That if I stopped you on the street and told you I needed money to pay my little boy's doctor bills you'd help me?" Smiling, he held out his hand.

I reached into my pocket, pulled out a twenty-peso bill, handed it to him, and drove away, shaking my head.

Another surprise in those first years was the church services. I had brought with me my gringo stereotype of the Mexican: a smiling, guitar-playing, extrovert. But the atmosphere in the churches turned out to be something quite different. With few exceptions, the hymns were mostly uninspiring translations of songs I'd sung all my life. The sermons in the Calvario Church, which met in the seminary chapel, were too long, and tended to be more lecture than sermon. We became members of the Horeb Church, located in one of the poorest *colonias* of the city. Brother Poncho, the pastor, was a graduate of the seminary, a pleasant young man with a winning smile. Sunday morning services were poorly attended because Sunday morning was market day. More people came Sunday night. The services began about eight and often continued until after ten. In the summer, the desert heat was stifling. No fans, of course. In the winter the church was unheated, so I wore two pairs of socks, two pairs of pants and a sweater under my coat. Sometimes the preacher's face was almost hidden by my steamy breath.

I always welcomed opportunities to preach. Early on I learned to bring along a sermon when I visited a church, because quite often, when the time came for the preaching, the pastor stepped to the pulpit and announced, "We're pleased to have Brother Carter visiting with us tonight. He will bring the message." The first time this happened I outlined a sermon in my mind as I walked from where I was seated to the pulpit. After that, I always had one tucked away in my Bible.

Still in the process of learning the language, I often made mistakes, and the trip home became a classroom, as my wife and children reviewed my errors. Sometimes the mistakes were ludicrous. I remember the time I preached about Paul and Silas locked up in the Philippian jail. Halfway through I saw David elbow Linda, and they covered their mouths to stifle belly laughs. Later, on the way home, I remonstrated: "Do you kids know how embarrassing it was to have my children laughing at me in the middle of my sermon?"

"But Daddy," David answered, "do you know what you said?"

"What do you mean?"

"You said Paul and Silas spent the night in a pumpkin!" And my twelve-year-old explained to his dad that the word for dungeon in Spanish is *calabozo*. But I had used the word *calabaza,* which means "pumpkin".

My wife got a big laugh out of that mistake. But a couple of weeks later I had my revenge. She came home puzzled from a speaking engagement at a meeting of the Women's Missionary Union. "When I began my talk, the women laughed. I didn't mean to tell a joke, I can't imagine what I said wrong."

"Well, repeat your words."

"I said, '*Hermanas,* I am the *habladora for today.*'"

When I burst out laughing, her face reddened. "You too?"

Then I explained: The dictionary defines, *habladora,* as "speaker". But in Mexico *habladora* means "gossiper"!

"Go and make disciples." That was Christ's last command to his people. And that was what had brought us to Mexico. Besides, twelve years in pastorates in the States had bred in me a need to be actively involved in spreading the Word. I enjoyed teaching my classes, but that wasn't enough! Early in December I was in the Christian bookstore talking with the manager. He asked me if I had ever seen a map of the *ejidos,* the country villages surrounding Torreon. When I replied that I hadn't, he showed me a map taped to the wall. "Here's Torreon," he said, "and all these little black dots you see are the *ejidos* scattered over the desert."

I whistled in surprise. "How many are there?" "Over a thousand within a hundred kilometers. And you know what, the Gospel has been preached in less than ten per cent of them."

A bell rang in my heart. In one of those villages, God had an assignment for me.

Somebody was waiting for me to go and share the Gospel!

In the days that followed I'd take one of the blacktop roads heading off into the countryside, and as I drove, pray that the Holy Spirit would impress upon my heart the place he had chosen for me. One day I passed a tiny *ejido,* no different from hundreds of others scattered over the desert: a few dozen adobe huts set on bare dirt streets, desolate in appearance, with nothing green growing in the dry brown soil. But the moment I saw the name of the village, Albia, something clicked in my heart. A hundred yards past the sign, I made a U-turn and entered the town. I located the *juez,* the leader of the village, and asked him how many families lived in his town. Then I asked his permission to return before Christmas and leave a bag of fruit and candy in each home.

We took the kids to the market and bought oranges, tangerines and candy. Then we spent Saturday morning filling 267 brown paper bags with the fruit and candy, and in each one we placed a Gospel of Luke. Saturday afternoon David and I went to Albia. At the door of each house we called to the occupants (You can't knock at an abobe house!) When the door was opened we explained that, in the name of the Christ Child, we were presenting them a Christmas present. Then we asked permission to return the following Sunday and explain about the Jesus in the Gospel of Luke. There were a lot of smiles, but not one acceptance of our offer to come back! When we'd completed our rounds we returned to the car, tired and discouraged.

"What happened, Daddy?" my twelve-year-old asked. "I thought you said God had led you here."

I had no answer.

I started the car, and as we turned onto the highway we saw two young men with their thumbs up. (Ever since, David has insisted they were angels!) I stopped and invited them into the back seat. As we drove toward Torreon, I explained what we had done and shared our disappointment that no one seemed interested in the Bible.

"*Senor*," one of the youths told me, "there's only one person in Albia who has a Bible, *Señor* Domingo Roman. He and his family are away today. Why don't you come back and visit him?"

The next Sunday afternoon I returned. Until this moment there remains a vivid image in my mind of what happened. As I entered a wide gate in the adobe wall enclosing the Roman's house, Domingo and his wife were seated on the ground shelling corn. As soon as he saw me, *Don* Domingo rose his feet, his arms opened wide, smiling from ear to ear. "You must be Mr. Carter! They told me about you. *Bienvenido!*"

He invited me to sit in a cane chair, then disappeared into his house for a moment. When he returned, he was dusting off a small black Bible. "My cousin went to work as a *bracero* in the United States two years ago, and when he came back he gave me this Bible. I've been waiting ever since for someone to come and explain it to me!"

I stayed for more than two hours, explaining to Domingo and Mathilde God's plan of salvation. They were fascinated, and invited me to return the following Sunday. I drove home shaking my head in astonishment.

Thus came into being our first outpost in Mexico. Soon our entire family was visiting Domingo and Mathilde and their eight children once a week. I preached, Evelyn played the little portable organ, and our kids taught a children's Sunday School class. Soon Domingo and Mathilde and Alberto, their eighteen-year-old son, invited Christ into their hearts. As the weeks passed, other families joined us. Before we could baptize Domingo and Mathilde it was necessary to help her obtain a divorce from her first husband, then have the civil marriage to the man she had been living with for twenty-five years. I still remember my surprise that they had been living together unwed for so long. Later I learned that this was the custom among a large percentage of the poor people. (I attributed this to the fact that Mexico was a third-world nation. Isn't it interesting that, since then, this lamentable practice in a third-world country has become an accepted custom in the United States?)

I was pleased to see striking family and social changes developing as the result of Christ's rule in the Roman family. Before, a large portion of Domingo's meager income was devoted to drinking and gambling. Now he used that money to clothe and feed his family. Alberto had been content with just an elementary education, but now he attended night school in Torreon. And this country boy who had slept all his life on a straw *petate* on a dirt floor now made a good living selling vacuum cleaners from door to door!

The church in Albia prospers until this day. They have a comfortable concrete block house of worship that seats 100 people. For many years their pastor was *Jesus* Roman, whom I remember as a mischievous six-year-old who often slipped away in the middle of a church service. *Jesus* is now a prosperous farmer with a tractor and a small herd of cattle. Albia taught me a lesson that guided me throughout the following years of missionary work:

In every town there's someone whom the Holy Spirit has prepared to receive God's Word. All that's lacking is a person to be a bearer of that Word.

That perception stirred my heart to initiate a new project. I was concerned that, at the current rate, there was little hope that a significant portion of the hundreds of *ejidos* around Torreon would ever hear the message of salvation. So we formed "The Caravan of Evangelism." My father's church in Louisiana sponsored our purchase of a pickup truck and a movie projector. One of our mature students, Arturo Alarcon, became the director of our team of four seminarians. Each "Caravan" began with an initial presentation of the Gospel, and a week later, a follow-up. We'd enter a village and drive down the streets announcing that in fifteen minutes we would show a movie of the life of Christ. In those days before the entrance of TV into the rural areas, movies had a strong appeal. Often as we drove along the dirt streets making the announcement, the kids would form a wake, shouting "*cine! cine!* movie! movie". Finding an empty lot, we parked the truck, pulled up the screen on the bed of the pickup, and projected the movie. Hundreds of people would gather. After the movie one of us would preach a short evangelistic sermon, then issue an invitation. Usually there were dozens of professions of faith.

The first attempt in a village always involved the possibility of opposition, usually in the form of a shower of stones. This could happen in an *ejido* with a fanatic Catholic population, or with a communist cell. If stones began to rain down, we lowered the screen, cranked up the truck and got out in a hurry.

The long-term, follow-up to our missionary work was carried out by neighboring churches that we trained ahead of time. I wrote in my diary, "I envision hundreds of new missions scattered all over the desert, each one with a pastor enlisted from the congregation."

As the months passed, the list of new missions grew: La Union, Nuevo Gomez Palacio, Anna, Bilbao, Maravillas, etc. I never compiled a final list, but God did bless in a special way. Sometimes I imagine myself entering heaven and being embraced by dozens of smiling Mexican *campesinos* saying, "*Gracias, gracias.*"

One of the most difficult issues for the new missionary is the problem of identification. What can he do to appear less like a foreigner? Looking about, during my first year in Mexico, I discovered that most Mexican men wore mustaches, so I began to cultivate one. This made me the object of boisterous jokes on the part of my fellow missionaries. In response I wrote a poem and read it at the annual

Christmas missionary dinner. The reaction was uproarious laughter and a consequent suspension of abuse. In the years that followed I was invited numerous times to read my poem at welcoming parties for new missionaries. Here's a part of that monumental work:

A MUST FOR EVERY MISSIONARY IN MEXICO

Since arriving in this country I have heard the constant cry,
"My dear friend the thing important is you must identify.
Forget your Yankee customs, like a vet'ran spout your Spanish.
Teach your mind the rhumba rhythm, and your troubles quickly vanish."

So we started at our house a resounding revolution,
The Magna Carta of the Carters: a calypso constitution.
Of that land north of the *Rio* I'm as quiet as a mouse,
And with that phrase, *"mi casa es su casa,"* everybody owns my house.

When I'm sipping sweet *atole* with *hermanos* (brothers) at the church,
I always ask for seconds, though my stomach gives a lurch.
When I meet a distant brother, whatever be his name,
My *abrazo* (hug) is sufficient for a bear to blush in shame.

But my brothers, here's a problem, and forgive me if I shout:
How dare you sit *contentos* with your bare face hanging out?
Look about you, think a moment, sit in quiet contemplation,
Are you blind? Can't you see? Your upper lip lacks decoration!

Why, a thicket lushly sprouting is a sign that you're a male,
Clothe that region labiodental that lies so bare and pale.

No, all's not a bed of roses with a mustache on your face,
In the eyes of certain erstwhile friends you've fallen in disgrace.
Hear their cynical sarcasm's: "Razor dull? What happened to your lip?
Your mouth is dirty, wash it off. Your wife gone on a trip?"

But besides the advantage of identification

There are certain other strong points of strategic vegetation:
When your work is going badly and your spirits start to slip,
Why, a mustache helps you stiffen up that sagging upper lip.
And when you're tramping through the country without water on your hip
It filters out the insects when you stop to take a sip.

You're practically indecent, get some cover for that chasm.
In the morning use your razor blade with less enthusiasm.

So come along, you sinners, and join the milling throng.
Let your face become a forest as you raise this marching song:
"Let's identify completely while the whiskers multiply,
A mustache for every missionary in Mexico -- or die!"

Chapter Thirteen
Living With Crises
1960 - 1963

The first three years in Mexico brought one crisis after another.

The first affected the seminary. When I arrived I learned that the Board of Trustees had invited a Mexican couple from the Baptist Spanish Publishing House in El Paso to join the staff the following January. They were in their fifties, and highly respected, both by nationals and missionaries. Their coming would help offset the often-expressed criticism that the seminary was an institution of gringos. It was considered a notable coup that the Seminary Director had convinced the Mexico Mission, the organization of Southern Baptist missionaries in Mexico, to offer the Delgados a salary equal to that received by missionaries.

A couple of months after our arrival I was seated in the Director's living room, chatting with him. The phone rang, he picked up the receiver, and as I watched I saw his brow crease, his face slowly turning red, and heard him say, "No, it can't be. How could they do that? I can't believe it!"

Finally, he hung up and dropped his head into his hands. When at last he looked up, he told me in a quiet, hoarse voice, "The call was from the Mexico Mission Executive Committee. They are having their quarterly meeting. They decided we had offered the Delgados too much salary, and have cut it in half."

"But haven't the Delgados been advised of the salary?"

"Yes, they have." His voice broke as he said, "I don't see how I can tell them what has happened!"

In the days that followed we lived in a funereal atmosphere. The Director was crushed. I remember standing one day at the gate of the seminary, when he walked up to me, opened his mouth to speak, and broke into sobs. Within a week he wrote a letter of resignation, and left the seminary.

Eventually the Executive Committee reconsidered and rescinded their decision. But by that time the word had been leaked to the Delgado couple and they decided to remain at the Publishing House.

The illness of Alfredo Muller was a crisis that endured for most of the first year after our arrival. Professor Muller was a brilliant Hebrew scholar and a pillar of the seminary faculty. By the time we arrived his prostate cancer was so advanced that many days he was unable to leave his bed. The man fascinated me, and I spent time each week at his bedside soaking up his wisdom. I suspected it might be providential that I was engaged at that time in discussions with Broadman Press to publish an adaptation of my doctoral thesis on divine healing. Maybe God wanted to use me to help this noble man find health! I prayed for him constantly, looked for ways to make our prayers for healing more effective, and brought to his bedside persons reputed to have the gift of healing. Professor Muller was sure that God was going to heal him, and made plans for what he would do once he was whole again. One afternoon he showed me an array of camping equipment he'd bought for the new life that awaited.

I agonized as month after month his condition worsened. How could I accept that he was doomed to die, when the Bible teaches that salvation includes the whole man, spirit, mind, soul and body? It became a crisis of faith for me. One morning very early the phone rang. It was his wife.

"Pat, Alfredo passed away just a few minutes ago."

I jumped in my car and drove over. When she opened the door, Mrs. Muller held a scrap of paper in her hand. "I found this by his bed. Alfredo must have written it just before he died." I read the unforgettable words, written in Spanish in a shaky hand:

Dark river is the Jordon I cross.
Take my hand O Lord,
I see the lights of my heavenly home.

I have used that poem innumerable times at funerals. I cannot explain why God didn't heal Alfredo Muller here on earth, but I'm glad he left a written testimony to that moment when Christ's hand reached out and gave him the perfect healing for heaven.

Mr. Muller's sickness and death was one more step in my long journey to understanding and applying the teaching of the Bible concerning sickness and healing. The journey began as I wrote my thesis and experienced a gradual enlightenment, studying my Bible and researching the writings of Christian scholars. My research obligated me to abandon the traditional stance that is careful not to put God on the spot in the time of sickness. I learned that God expects us to ask for healing. And that he does heal.

I had witnessed the miraculous healing of my father. I had witnessed it again in an instantaneous healing Evelyn received in the Spring of 1958. We were in Fort Worth after our appointment to service in Mexico, and I was working to complete my dissertation on the Biblical teaching concerning sickness and health. One of the questions I faced was the validity of the gift of healing. When I read in the newspaper that a British Episcopalian woman who claimed to have the gift of healing would be ministering in St. Matthew's Cathedral in Dallas, I determined to meet her. Evelyn and I attended a service at which she spoke, and she granted my request for an interview. Afterward, as I greeted her husband, Evelyn chatted with her,.

Later, driving back Fort Worth, Evelyn suddenly remarked, "Oh no, it's gone!"

"What's gone?" I asked.

She told me what had happened: While I was interviewing the lady's husband, Evelyn walked over to her and asked a question: "Have you every prayed for someone with hay fever?"

For years, the months of April and May had been a severe trial for Evelyn. She suffered day and night, sneezing constantly, trying to control a dripping nose, her eyes red and watery.

"She didn't answer my question. Instead she reached out, placed her hand on my shoulder, and began to talk about God's love. Suddenly I felt an electric shock. I was surprised, but made no comment. Afterward, I didn't mention it to you, because it seemed so strange."

Evelyn sniffed. "But guess what? Since that moment my hay fever has disappeared!"

That was fifty years ago, and not once has Evelyn's hay fever returned!

Evelyn received a miraculous healing. But why doesn't it always happen that way? In research for my thesis I attended an Oral Roberts service at a stadium in Shreveport, Louisiana. At the time, Mr. Roberts was famous for his "healing campaigns" throughout the United States. That night hundreds went forward for him to lay hands on them and declare dramatically: "Demon of sickness, be gone!"

After the service Mr. Robert's support staff invited me for coffee and cake. I was impressed by their sincerity and openness. They confessed that no more than five per cent of the people Oral Roberts prayed for experienced a miraculous healing, but insisted that if it were necessary to pray for a hundred people in order to bring healing to five, the effort was worth it.

I have learned that physical healing will not always come to the people we pray for. But I am as convinced as I was in the first moments of my discovery of the wholeness of Biblical salvation, that I should always pray for healing.

We should always pray for healing, because we are God's children, and our Father has told us that healing is one of his gifts to us. At the same time we must remember that we live in a world whose ruling prince is Satan. Our Father is infinitely wise, and the healing he grants will be the healing that he himself wills. I have come to believe that our emphasis should not be so much on the instant healing of disease, but on preventing disease through a discipline that promotes health. Physical health is a part of the salvation that comes to us through the blood of Christ. But we must cooperate with Christ by creating an environment for health with a healthy diet, avoiding vices and regular exercise. Equally important is the cultivation of a mind free from stress, fear, anger, and bitterness. I

have learned to practice this discipline, and through the years have seen the disappearance of one sickness after another, including the arthritis that in my thirties almost prevented my appointment to mission service.

Speaking of crises, I learned to solve many of them *"a la mexicana"*. One of my first lessons came as the result of my involvement in a tragic accident. The afternoon of June 19, 1961 I was speeding down a broad boulevard headed eastward out of the city of Torreon for a preaching engagement. Suddenly, just ahead of me, a small child darted into the street. I didn't have time to apply the brakes. I felt a bump, and looking back saw a tiny form in the street, kicking convulsively. By the time I got to him he was lying in a pool of blood.

This was before cell phones, so I scooped him up and raced to the Red Cross. There they gave him emergency treatment and transferred him to a hospital. The word was that he might not live. As I waited at the hospital a policeman appeared, explained to me that in Mexico, if blood was spilled in an accident, the person responsible was placed under detention for a minimum of seventy-two hours. It was midnight. The patrolman took me to the police station and booked me. By that time my wife and several missionary colleagues had found me. Word had come that the child had cranial fractures and that an eye was severely damaged.

The next day my parents arrived for a scheduled visit. They, of course, were shocked, and their having to be a part of this difficult time increased the tension. Soon I was suffering nausea and diarrhea. I spent all day and another night at the station. Late the next day they informed me that I would be transferred to the city jail. I was taken to a gloomy, gray two-story building and led inside to a large common cell holding 20-30 drunks, drug addicts and cut-throats. I was scared!

I had learned by that time that in Mexico there is always an alternative to a seemingly impossible situation. So I inquired of the man with the keys. He informed me that, for fifty pesos (four dollars) I could rent a private cell. I handed over the fifty pesos and he conducted me upstairs to my "private room," a bare cell without a bunk or even a chair. But at the moment it looked to me like a luxury suite!

Later that night Mr. Pierson, a veteran missionary, was given permission to bring me a mattress. By midnight, utter exhaustion from two days with little sleep knocked me out until dawn. By noon the next day our lawyer had made the necessary arrangements for me to be released on bail.

The justice system in Mexico is quite different from that in the United States. I never appeared before a judge, nor had any direct contact with my own lawyer, nor with the prosecutor. About a year after the accident an article appeared in the local paper entitled, "Pat Carter *Bien Preso*," which meant that I had been sentenced to a jail term. But again, I never received any word from the courts or from my lawyer. In time, all the necessary "arrangements" were completed, and the matter faded away.

Romans 8:28 certainly applied in this case. I had a number of opportunities to witness to the father and mother of the injured child, who eventually recovered completely. They attended our church and made a public profession of faith. Also, I came to have a stronger appreciation for my colleagues whom, in so many ways, showed their love and concern. This crisis deepened in me the sense of family that is, perhaps, the greatest blessing of being on the missionary team. After this event, I was less conscious of my colleagues' "failures" and more appreciative of their sincere devotion to God's work and their love for one another. Now I was willing to give them permission to be human.

Crises, so many crises! And among those I lived in my first years of Mexico was the ongoing battle between the free world and communism. Soon after I was released from military service in 1946, a battle of nerves, dubbed the "cold war," began between the United States and Russia, and continued for decades. Then came the Korean War. I still remember my dread as I responded late one night to a notification from the U.S. Government. As a member of the Naval Reserve, I must report for active duty. Later, I was thankful when they advised me that, because of my enrolment in a seminary, my reactivation would be postponed until my graduation, so that I could serve later as a Naval chaplain. Perhaps I should have pointed out to them that by the time of my graduation my period of enlistment in the reserve would have ended!

Reading my diary, I'm reminded how much of my life I've tended to live from day to day, dreading what might happen tomorrow. In an entry in March, 1961 I mentioned my battle with depression because of "the darkness of world conditions." In April I lamented that communist Fidel Castro was now in control of Cuba. Two weeks later I commented on the success of the Russians in becoming the first to put a man in space, and that the astronaut reported God was nowhere to be seen. "All this indicates the slow advance of communism by lies, deceit, hatred, and all the other weapons, evil and immoral, that can be imagined. The U.S. meanwhile is preoccupied by race riots, the attempt of the Catholic Church to grab public funds, and the economic recession." A week later I wrote about the ill-fated invasion of Cuba. "The invasion was a miserable failure. The forces were wiped out by Russian tanks and planes. There were protests all over the world and riots throughout Mexico. U.S. prestige has hit a new low. Right now the communists are riding high. Kennedy spoke last night, and said that if it is necessary the U.S. will go it alone. Things look very bad for the future." In August I complained, "World conditions continue very somber. In Berlin there is evidence that war may break out." In September I was even more discouraged: "When I see the continued progress of communism and so many indications that the U.S. is becoming more and more corrupt, I feel that perhaps God plans to use communism as his rod to purify Christianity by fire. We are living in very turbulent times. Maybe God's plan is to allow communism to take over and destroy all vestiges of organized Christianity in the world." A year later I trembled as Russia placed missiles in Cuba, and President Kennedy threatened war.

What turbulent times I have lived, all my life! Soon after I was born the great Depression fell, then war with Germany and Japan, then with Korea and China, and then the cold war with Russia that endured for forty years. Meanwhile, Vietnam and Watergate. At the turn of the 21st century, world terrorism took the stage.

Always, dangers abound that could destroy life as we know it. Isn't it amazing that God has preserved America in spite of all its failures, and my own life, in spite of all my fears! Surely there's a lesson to be learned from these decades of daily worries about dreadful things.

Most of the bad things I've worried about never happened. And most of the bad things that did happen came as a surprise. So, as God's child and Christ's brother my theme should be the same as Paul's, as he was chained to a Roman soldier: "Rejoice in the Lord always! and again I say, Rejoice!"

Yes, I worried a great deal about world events. And also about the things happening in my own heart. Reading my diary I find laments again and again about my own spiritual failures, and my longing for spiritual growth. October 3, 1960, I expressed this longing as follows: "My constant prayer is that my spiritual hunger may increase more and more, and that the great desire of my life be the infilling of his Spirit. I don't know of anything else that would be of more service in the kingdom." In April of the following year I lament that I had been unsuccessful in persuading the Seminary staff to meet once a month to pray: "We are not a unity, we are just little islands working at the same task but without the spiritual power that would make us conquerors. Oh God, I recognize the spiritual poverty of our lives. Is there not something we can do about it? Oh God, show me the path I should tread!" The next month I complained, "How hard it is to keep optimistic and a warm relationship with God! I have tried to understand what the cause is. Is it because of simply being in a foreign country? What is the reason? I do not have the hunger for God that I should have and I do not pray as I ought. I am just lazy spiritually. Oh God, help me!" And a few months later, "For so long I have longed for my life to be a channel of God's power. Oh, how I long to see a demonstration that God is God. Somehow we are choking off his power. When will we see this power liberated?"

In September of that year I invited the Seminary students to join me every Wednesday morning at 6:00 A.M. in a "Fraternity of Prayer." Eleven signed up.

A couple of weeks later I commented with joy about the way this group prayer meeting was strengthening my own life and the life of the students. "If God will show me the way, I am willing to dedicate the rest of my life to a personal quest and to helping our people to deepen their spiritual life." By December I was discouraged, because attendance in the prayer group was lagging.

My struggle continued through most of 1962. In September I visited the doctor because of stomach pain and the loss of appetite. He gave me "tranqulizer pills" and I berated myself for my obsession with work. I ended the year with this comment: "I find myself still asking the question, what is going to be the sum total of my life? Is it really going to count? Am I going to leave a mark that makes people say, 'There walked Pat Carter?' I get desperate sometimes. How I want my life to count!"

Reading my comments after more than forty years, I can see how the desire "to make my life count" must have caused my wife stress. In January 1963 she accompanied me on an automobile trip to the state of Chiapas, about a thousand miles south of Torreon. After our return I wrote in my diary: "We spent all week on campus with the people, sleeping on the floor of a tiny potato shed outside the main house. On our return trip we spent one night in Mexico City in a downtown luxury hotel, as a reward for our potato shed experience." But then I complained, "On the return it seemed that our desire was more to divert ourselves than to live close to the Lord. We did nothing particularly wrong, I suppose, but a general spirit of worldliness left me with an empty heart. I want God to give me an absolute hatred for the things of the world and an absolute love for his work."

The year 1963 was filled with soul searching and crises. In July I philosophized,

> I see more and more that for religion to have power it must be of the heart, something that I instinctively feel with the heart. The heart must rule and the mind follow, not vice-versa. When my heart is happy and in communion with the Lord, then my head is happy. When my head begins to rule and my heart goes into eclipse I enter into a time of doubting and unhappiness. Oh God, give more of this foolish, glorious faith that keeps me moment by moment in your presence.

My last entry or 1963:

> Dreams ... dreams ... are they meant to be realized, or are they nothing more than a mystical part of life that gives it a golden

glow and makes it worthwhile to live, but are never to be realized? I have dreamed much and realized little. As I grow older I find that I am less idealistic and more realistic, that is, less optimistic. With all that one might desire, there remains a deep, unfulfilled void. Is not the gray and the ghastly of life the guarantee of heaven, that out beyond, the gray will turn to gold and the ghastly to glory?

Struggles, struggles, struggles. Those first few years in Mexico were indeed like being thrown into a deep river with a powerful current, and fighting desperately to survive. Now, I believe I understand better the meaning of my struggles. I agree with my favorite Biblical expositor, Alexander Maclaren, who declares that "the very signature of the Christian life is yearning after unaccomplished perfection."*

*Alexander Maclaren, *Expositions of Holy Scripture, Second Corinthians, Galatians, and Philippians,* p. 262.

Chapter Fourteen
In the Land of the Mayas
1963-1965

In the summer of 1962 I traveled with two other seminary teachers to Merida, the capital of Yucatan. We had been invited by Pastor Aurelio Mandujano to spend a week discipling a new church that met in his back yard. I had no idea that this trip would result in a major change in my life, and that of my family.

We boarded a bus in Torreon Friday at 8:00 P.M. When I awoke at dawn I saw fields of corn and beans, quite different from the harsh, dry desert I had become accustomed to. I saw endless fields of corn and beans. At 10:00 A.M. we arrived at Mexico City. There we transferred to another bus for the twenty-eight hour trip to Merida. The first six hours we traveled from the highlands down to the coast, passing first through grape fields, then fields of pineapple, and later banana groves. Leaving the port city of Veracruz, we traveled for most of the day along the coast of the Gulf of Mexico. At that time they were constructing the first highway from Villahermosa, in the state of Tabasco, to Merida. We boarded five different ferries: three times we crossed broad rivers and then took a ferry to Isla del Carmen in the state of Campeche and another to return to the mainland. I remember being awakened at 2:A.M. Saturday night to walk across a bridge. It was still under construction, so the bus had to cross without passengers. As we traveled, surrounded by palm trees fronting on mile after mile of virgin sandy beaches, I felt myself part of a living picture postcard. When we left the state of Campeche and entered Yucatan, the scenery changed. No longer lush forests, but rocky ground, only able to support the fiber-producing hennequen plant. Finally, Sunday afternoon, we arrived at Merida, after a total of forty-two hours on the bus. Pastor Mandujano met us and took us to his home

Late Sunday afternoon a group of members arrived at the tabernacle of palm branches in the pastor's back yard, returning from a mission in a country village. They reported that a mob had invaded the house where they were having services, tore up their Bibles and threatened them with bodily harm if they returned.

Here was truly an outpost for God in a needy land! Seven years before, Pastor Mandujano had moved to Yucatan from his native state of Chiapas, in Southwestern Mexico. He came at the invitation of a group of people who had been converted through a radio program from Cuba. Twelve miles north of Merida in the port city of Progreso, Mandujano founded a church. Since then he had organized six more, five of them in villages scattered through Campeche and Yucatan, and one in the capital city of Merida.

Merida is called *la ciudad blanca*, the white city, because of its thousands of white native stone houses. The downtown streets are paved in the red brick that served as ballast for centuries on ships arriving from France, Yucatan's principal trading partner. The Mayans are very short in stature and the men are renowned for their large, round heads. Most of the women wore the beautiful flowered native dress called *huipil*, and most of the men were dressed in white cotton shirts and pants. I was impressed by the exceptional friendliness of everyone I met.

As the week progressed, I fell under the spell of the land of the Mayans. I slept little, cried often, and by the end of the week was suffering from a bad case of diarrhea.

The harvest was so plentiful and laborers so few! All the way home I prayed, asking the Lord to make it clear to me and to Evelyn if He was calling us to work in that field.

By the time I arrived back in Torreon I felt quite sure that God wanted us in the Yucatan peninsula. Beside the pressing need there, my first year in the seminary had convinced me that I would be a much better teacher if I spent some time on the field. In July, accompanied by Evelyn, I made a return visit to Yucatan. My wife was impressed by the need, and told me she was willing to make the move.

In June of the following year the Mexico Mission approved our transfer, with the understanding that we would work in the Yucatan Peninsula until furlough, and afterward return to the Seminary. This support by our brother and sister missionaries was an enormous blessing for Evelyn and me. It was our first experience in Mexico of the way the Holy Spirit could move in giving unanimity to some one hundred people working as a family in Christ. The fact that any major decision on the part of a missionary had to be approved by so many people could be daunting. But during all our years in Mexico there was never an occasion when I doubted the desire of my brothers and sisters for the best for myself and my family. This sense of family was a unique and blessed experience. The sense of family included the children, who had the custom of calling their parents' co-workers "uncle" and "aunt".

The next month the Mexican Baptist Convention named me field missionary of the Yucatan Peninsula, including the states of Yucatan, Campeche, and Tabasco, plus the territory of Quintana Roo. In August we made the move.

Moving to Yucatan was like entering a different country. In fact, until fairly recent times Yucatan had been a sovereign nation. Separated from the rest of Mexico by jungles and swift rivers, for centuries the only communication was by boat and airplane. Most of its commerce was with France and Cuba. The native language of a large portion of the population was Mayan. Also, the historical background was distinct. For many centuries a sophisticated, religion-based civilization built pyramids, studied the stars and existed as city-states scattered throughout the jungles. The impressive cities of Uxmal and Chichen-Itza are reminders of an empire that flourished for several hundred years, then vanished. Until today no one has come up with a satisfactory explanation of how people who surpassed Europe in architecture and astronomy became the poorest, most backward region in Mexico.

Yucatan was, and still is depressingly poor. For centuries the henequen fields provided a workplace for the people. A plant similar to cactus, henequen produced, not tequila, but a tough fiber that was once sold throughout the world. But at mid twentieth-century plastics began replacing henequen, and by 1960 the factories that converted the plant into fiber could only survive with a heavy subsidy from the federal government. As a result, most of the rural people barely survived. In the capital city there were striking contrasts. Downtown was scrupulously clean, with gleaming stone palaces and beautiful French colonial homes set on broad boulevards. But the majority of the people in the suburbs lived in shacks. In the countryside the men still arose at 4:00 A.M. to go to the fields. They worked until 11:00 A.M. and then left the steaming fields to spend the rest of the day in their hammocks. Drunkenness was common. On Sunday afternoons the parks were dotted with men dressed in spotless white cotton, lying in a drunken stupor.

In spite of the grinding poverty, the Mayan people were exceptionally friendly and generous. Always, when we visited a congregation in the country, the church service was preceded by a meal of tacos and a rice drink called *horchata,* served in someone's home on spotless white tablecloths. In our mission in Albia near Torreon, we had become accustomed to people with unwashed faces and dirty clothes, because of the scarcity of water. In Yucatan, though there was no surface water, underground rivers supplied cool, clear water. Every day at 4:00 o'clock, after the mid-day siesta, everyone in the family bathed and dressed in clean white clothing. Then they walked to the central plaza for a chat with the neighbors.

A week after we arrived in Merida, Pastor Mandujano departed for the United States in the company of a group from a Hispanic church in Detroit. He had been in bad health for several months, and they persuaded him he needed to seek medical help in the States. During the six weeks he was away I found myself trying to fulfill the pastoral duties.

Within a few months we purchased a large property downtown, thanks to a gift from Southern Baptists. An abandoned stone building dating back to colonial days, it required extensive repairs. At first we had services in a large room across the street from the *Cantina Canario.* It was disconcerting to be preaching, and suddenly find myself facing a parishioner from the neighboring bar standing at the back waving his arms in imitation of my gestures. As our congregation grew, we moved to the patio in the center of our property.

Our family soon learned that the tropical heat would take a lot of getting used to. The three years we had spent in Torreon the desert heat was ameliorated by water-cooled fans on the roof. Merida was almost a thousand miles nearer the Equator, and the addition of the moisture from the Gulf, only a dozen miles away, made for an oppressive heat most of the year. At that time air conditioning was largely unknown in Yucatan, so we made out with fans and slept on hammocks at night. By noon the heat had sapped our strength. Evelyn and I struggled with depression brought on by that oppressive tropical heat.

And the insects! I remember vividly our first night in our new home, a comfortable dwelling with three bedrooms and a tall avocado tree in the front yard that produced fruit the size of footballs. We were seated in the living room, quite content, when a large insect entered from beneath the front door. Behind came another, followed by another, until there was a line of insects several yards long, marching from the front door to the kitchen.. I found myself waiting for the sound of a drum and a fife! The next day a scorpion fell on Evelyn's shoulder when she opened the kitchen door. Thankfully, the scorpion didn't sting her.

Once a month I traveled to the three missions in the jungles of Campeche. I would drive some four hours to the railroad town of Candelaria, and there board a train. After a half-hour ride I'd get off at the first mission, where I would preach and visit with the lay pastor. At night I would sleep in the home of one of the members. I always brought my hammock with me. When bedtime came, all of us would hang our hammocks on hooks in the little round one-room dwelling, and I'd try to rest amid the snores, moans and coughs of mom and dad and half a dozen children. The next day I'd ride a horse down the railroad tracks to the next mission, and the third day to the mission in *Triunfo,* perched on the banks of a wide, deep river. The train passed only twice a week, so on the last night of my pilgrimage, after the service, I'd ride a horse twelve miles back to where I'd left my car. When Pastor Mandujano accompanied me, we'd take turns on the horse.

Three hundred miles west of Merida was the city of Villahermosa, Tabasco. The name means "beautiful city," and it was well-named. Back then, before the discovery of oil, it was set in a virgin forest, traversed by a wide river with a powerful current. Year-round the area produced exquisitely sweet watermelons, bananas, cantaloupes, pineapples and mangoes. It also produced swarms of hungry mosquitoes! I remember the first Sunday night Evelyn and I attended a service in the small church. When we arrived they were singing, accompanied by a continual waving of dozens of colorful handkerchiefs. "What a beautiful way of keeping time with the music," I whispered to Evelyn. But when the hymn ended, the handkerchiefs kept waving, and we realized the handkerchiefs were keeping time with another kind of music: the humming of the clouds of mosquitoes that had come to feast on the worshippers.

The church at Villahermosa was an example of the curious contradictions of the Yucatan Peninsula Baptists. They were a very hospitable people, and went out of their way to express their concern for the visiting missionary. But among themselves, they were a big family of jealous children, often at war.

The drive to and from Villahermosa was always an adventure. Most of the way I traveled on sparkling beaches with groves of tall, majestic palm trees. I also had to endure three ferries. There was always a long line of automobiles waiting for the arrival of the ferry. Beginning some ten miles before the boarding dock, the pace of the traffic began to pick up, as the travelers jockeyed for position. A couple of miles from the destination the narrow rutted road became a race track. I'll never forget a race between two red Volkswagen bugs. They sped at more than seventy miles an hour, first one, then another taking the lead. When we got within sight of the ferry they increased their speed, bouncing along side by side. Some fifty yards from the river one floor-boarded the accelerator and turned suddenly in front of the other. I watched in awe as the little car made a couple of spins on two wheels. Finally it regained its balance and raced ahead. As soon as the cars stopped the doors popped open and the drivers, jumping from their cars ran toward each other. I expected a fist-fight. But no, they hugged, laughing hilariously and pounded each other on the back.

Then there were the "northers". Midway between Villahermosa and the city of Campeche was Isla del Carmen, an island surrounded by a bay some five miles wide that opened into the Gulf of Mexico. This meant two ferry trips, the first to reach the island, then the second at the other side, to return to the mainland. In nice weather the trip to and from the island were pleasant half-hour voyages. But quite often in winter a strong north wind whipped up such waves that the ferry was forced to anchor, and wait until calm weather returned. This meant, if one was caught on the mainland, a wait of twenty-four hours or more, without restaurants, hotels or rest rooms. One pre-Christmas trip fourteen-year-old David accompanied me. On our return we arrived at the Isla del Carmen bay on a stormy Christmas Eve, and found ourselves at the end of a half-mile line of vehicles. We spent the night in the car, trying to sleep, fighting mosquitoes and praying for the wind to calm. We arrived back home Christmas night, to the relieved hugs of Mom and David's sisters.

As the months passed I found myself spending more and more time trying to solve problems in the churches and missions. They seemed to be endless! Some had to do with the backgrounds of the people. The Presbyterians had preceded the Baptists by some fifty years, so many of our parishioners were disgruntled former members of those churches. Frequently I dealt with spiritual problems. During one period I found myself at the same time trying to heal a church split in Villahermosa, confronting the lay pastor of a mission in Luna, who was accused of sleeping with a divorced church member, and mediating an on-going fight between the pastor of Seye and Pastor Mandujano.

Pastor Mandujano was a classic charismatic personality. In Merida, standing before the congregation, playing his accordion in accompaniment to the piano, the violin and the bass viol, he infused excitement into the services. On mission trips, when we arrived at an unevangelized village, he would stand in the square and crank up his accordion, and people would come flocking. On the other hand, quite often I was called upon to mediate problems occasioned by his changeable temperament. It was a joy, during the less than three years we were in Merida, to join Pastor Mandujano in baptizing hundreds of new believers and to see an enormous growth in membership and attendance.

The Mayan people were open and childlike. Sometimes that childlikeness deteriorated into childishness. My diary is filled with references to disappointments with people. There was the case of Carlos. A former boxer, he earned his living driving a taxi. He had an impressive testimony, was a deacon and faithful member of the church.

We made him the leader of our Caravan of Evangelism in Yucatan. Then a pastor and his family from the United States came for a visit. Overwhelmed by the needs of Carlos' family, they "adopted" them, and invited them to move to Michigan and live in their home. When the Carlos and his family departed they left even their clothing behind, because the pastor had promised to take care of their every need. I'm sure that pastor never considered the damage they had done to our church and the work in Yucatan.

Then there was a bright young man named Luis. He occasionally attended our church, and considered himself an intellectual, challenging most of the basic precepts of the Bible, including Creation, the inspiration of the Bible and Christ's substitutionary death on the cross. Here, I thought, was a good opportunity to apply what I had learned in my studies for a Ph.D. in Philosophy. For months I visited him once a week, and was confident that, one by one, I was demolishing his arguments. The day came when he told me he had no other questions. I invited him to take Christ as his Savior, and to my surprise he looked at me blankly and shook his head. He never returned to church.

One of my greatest disappointment was Teodoro. The Sunday before he was baptized I wrote in my diary: "Teodoro shows signs of becoming an outstanding worker. I believe God is going to do something significant through him." But as the months passed, problems surfaced. There was gossip about his involvement with one of the young women in the church. One day he confessed to the pastor that the past week he had spent the night in the home of this girl's parents. The mother had slipped into his room, he said, and kissed him awake. We decided the time had come to buy him a one-way ticket back home to Villahermosa.

Many wonderful experiences with special people! And also disappointments! I was in the process of learning an important lesson:

I must learn how to be a servant to people without conditions. Otherwise I will become their victim.

John explains how Jesus lived this truth:

Now while he was in Jerusalem at the Passover Feast, many people saw the miraculous signs he was doing and believed in his name. But Jesus would not entrust himself to them, because he knew all men. He did not need man's testimony about man, for he knew what was in a man (John 2:23-25).

Jesus was never deceived by men. Jesus "did not entrust himself to them," yet he died on he cross for them! That's why he could say, in the shadow if the cross, "In this world you will have trouble. But take heart! I have overcome the world." (John 16:33). Then he went out to be crucified by the world. What a challenge for me! If, like Christ, I give myself to others without unreal expectations, Christ makes me an overcomer.

It became apparent our first year in Merida that the school system would not meet the needs of our children, so in the next two years we had to devise difficult solutions. Our fourteen-year-old Linda went to live with the Hartfields, a missionary family in Mexico City, so she could attend the American School. Fifteen-year-old David transferred to the Acadia Baptist Academy in Louisiana, where Dad had attended two generations before. Mom guided eight-year-old Carol in the Calvert Course, a home study.

Giving up two of our children in their mid-teens left us with a sense of guilt that contributed to periods of depression. On December 2, 1963 I wrote in my journal: "I had a great deal of trouble last week with the feeling that life is nothing but spinning my wheels and not really accomplishing anything. Even reached the point of wishing I was not in the ministry. Then, after the first good night's rest in a week, I got straightened out."

One of the ways of escaping these depressions was devoting my spare time to writing. In 1964 Evelyn and I decided we should invest our $500.00 in savings in a fiction course in titled "Famous Writer's School." As the months passed I began to submit stories about Yucatan to Christian magazines. Quite a number sold. Then I began my first attempt at a novel, and developed the discipline of arising before dawn each morning and spending a couple of hours writing.

As the months passed, I felt more and more that my future was with the seminary.

Van Gladen, the Director, mentioned in a circular letter his desire to return to field work. In a conversation with me he encouraged me to return to the seminary and suggested I was the logical person to succeed him as Director.

In December, 1965 we said goodbye to the Mayan people and headed to the United States for our first furlough. I wrote in my diary: "As I leave Mexico I go with great thankfulness for many blessings from God. These 28 months in the Yucatan that I had suspected might be a time of rest have instead been a time of much activity and some heartening successes."

Chapter Fifteen
Exploring the Land
1966-1967

Caleb and Joshua became Moses' faithful servants. They encouraged him when the people murmured about the lack of water and food. Together they praised God when water gushed from the rock and manna and quail fell from the sky. In the first testing of the Israelite army, a battle against the Amalekites, Caleb fought at the side of General Joshua. Later, he pleaded with Aaron not to give in to the impatient, complaining people while Moses and Joshua were on Mount Sinai receiving God's Law. And he stood by Moses when he returned to destroy the golden calf and set things in order.

When Moses named twelve men, one from each tribe, to explore the land of Canaan, no one was surprised that Joshua was named from the tribe of Ephraim and Caleb from the tribe of Judah (Numbers 13: 6,8). During the forty days in the land of Canaan Caleb more than once felt he must be dreaming, seeing the fulfilment of the vision he had nourished for close to forty years! As they walked through the hill country, he marveled at the riches of the land. Very late one night the twelve spies slipped into Hebron and found their way to the Cave of Machpelah, where lay the bones of Abraham and Sarah and Isaac and Jacob. The tears Caleb shed were a mixture of sadness for the seven hundred years this sacred place had been in the hands of pagans and joy at the prospect of its reconquest.

But as the journey ended he was shocked to discover that only he and Joshua were persuaded that God could give them the land. The other ten spies were panic-stricken by the walled cities and the giants they had seen.

Their report to the people provoked a disaster. When the ten declared, "We can't conquer those people, we seemed like grasshoppers in our own eyes, and we looked the same to them," the people wept. When Joshua and Caleb tore their clothes and cried out to the assembly, " The land we passed through and explored is exceedingly good ... do not rebel against the Lord, do not be afraid of the people of the land, because we will swallow them up" the people took up stones to kill Moses and Joshua and Caleb.

A Rhyme:
Caleb was forty years old when he was sent to spy out the hill country in Canaan. (Joshua 14:7). I was in my fortieth year when I was sent to spy out the hill country in Mexico City:

In January, 1967, after a year's furlough, we returned to the seminary in Torreon. And to a huge challenge: during our furlough Van Gladen had resigned the presidency, and the Board of Trustees had named me to replace him. Soon after we arrived, I wrote in my diary, "Everything is bright with promise. Of course there are problems, but I have the feeling this is the opportunity for which God has been preparing me."

At the first meeting of the Seminary Board of Trustees they instructed me to give priority to a feasibility study of the relocation of the Seminary. This was not a surprise. During my years in Yucatan I had served as a member of the Board of Trustees. One November I was returning from a meeting, accompanied by another member of the Board, Julian Bridges, who worked with university students in Mexico City. During the fourteen-hour bus trip from Torreon to Mexico City he poured out his heart about his conviction that the Seminary should be in the Capital of the nation. At midnight we arrived at the outskirts of that enormous city of fifteen million inhabitants. Our bus topped a hill, and suddenly, the city lay before us like an enormous lake of fire.

In that moment, the Holy Spirit spoke to me: Julian was right; this is where the Seminary should be!

During the twenty-eight hour ride from Mexico City to Yucatan, my soul churned with that new vision. The day after my arrival I sat down at my typewriter and wrote to Van Gladen, recommending that we consider a relocation of the seminary, and giving my reasons.

The possibility of moving the seminary was a very delicate issue. For most Baptists, the seminary "belonged" in Torreon. It had been there since its founding in 1903, with brief interludes in Saltillo and El Paso, due to political problems.

Torreon, a modern city of a quarter of a million inhabitants, was a green oasis in the middle of a vast desert, kept alive with water brought in from the *Palmitas* spillway 125 miles to the west. The seminary occupied most of a city block. On one corner of the property was Calvary Church. The classrooms were in this building, because at that time the Constitution of Mexico required that all classes on religion be conducted on church property. There were dormitories for male and female students, a library, a dining hall, half a dozen apartments for the faculty, and an office building.

After the meeting of the Board of Trustees I sat down and made a list of more than a hundred people in the United States. I wrote and asked them to pray daily for God to make his will plain to me and to others who would be involved in the decision to move or not to move. In the months that followed, I kept them informed on developments. Their frequent letters were a constant encouragement.

I appointed a committee to help me carry out a thorough investigation: missionary opportunities, the attitude of the churches, housing and the possibility of purchasing a site. We soon found that many people in Mexico City opposed our coming. Forty years before, a comity agreement with the American Baptist Convention had given them exclusive rights to missionary work in that city. Besides, the American Baptists sponsored a seminary in the borough of Tlalpan in the southern part of the city.

Discouraged by this opposition, we investigated the possibility of relocating instead to the city of Guadalajara. In April I presented to the Seminary staff an analysis of the advantages of moving to that city. The next week Howard Stevens, a Seminary professor, accompanied me to Guadalajara. We presented the project to the pastors and missionaries, and they gave their hearty support.

The following week Mr. Stevens and I traveled to Mexico City, and were surprised to encounter enthusiasm among the pastors about the possibility of our relocation. Two weeks later we took the seminary choir to Mexico City, where they presented concerts in a number of the churches. I wrote in my diary: "I was amazed at the friendly reception we received and the strong support our seminary has in that city. But a visit with the President of the Tlalpan Seminary elicited a strong negative response. He and his Dean reacted as if we were plotting to blow up the city."

On my forty-first birthday, May 16th, I wrote, "We're approaching the time when we'll have to make a decision on the location of the seminary. I still haven't been able to decide. The easiest thing would be to remain where we are. In my own heart Guadalajara is still running stronger than ever." Two weeks later I wrote, "I believe that at last I've reached a conclusion: we should move to Guadalajara."

On Sunday morning, June 11th, I had one of the most startling epiphanies of my life. I quote what I wrote in my journal that afternoon:

I am 90% certain that God spoke to me this morning in church and gave me the answer I've been waiting for. God's word is: he wants us in Mexico City! Yesterday we had a meeting of the Board of Trustees. I presented my study, which was heavily slanted toward Guadalajara. Victor Muñoz spoke at length about the great missionary opportunities in Mexico City, but I didn't feel like he said anything new. After four hours of wrangling, the Board agreed they could not recommend that we relocate to Mexico City.

This morning as I sat waiting for the beginning of the service I was searching in my Bible for a text I could use for a sermon I had been invited to preach in the annual meeting of the National Union of Baptist *señoritas*. As I thumbed through my Bible my eyes fell on the words of Paul to Agrippa in Acts 26:19: "Oh, King Agrippa, I was not disobedient to the heavenly vision." I thought, "That would be a great text for my talk to the *señoritas!*" Suddenly I found myself sobbing, and an inner voice told me that being disobedient was exactly what I was in danger of doing -- that God had spoken to me two years ago and told me the seminary should move to Mexico City -- that this was the vision he had given me and I must not turn my back on it. All during the service I wept as the Lord continued speaking to me. Even now, at 3:45 P.M., when I think on what happened, I am weeping again.

So, as I say, I am 90% certain that this is the moment I've been waiting for, when God would take all the facts and fears and reactions and unscramble them into an answer that would reveal His will. I know that all the problems that are involved here will be worked out, difficult as they may be. God isworking. Blessed be his holy name!

By Wednesday the 90% certainty had become 100%, so I sat down and wrote the members of the Board, asking them to forgive me for making a recommendation that was contrary to the will of God.

After mailing the letters, I asked myself: what happened to connect me suddenly with God's face, as surely as tuning in to a channel on T.V.? I arrived at this conclusion: it was the fruit of the prayers of the people I had asked to pray for me. From that experience I learned a lesson:

Concerted, persistent prayer releases the initiative of God. There are things that God wants to do, but he waits until we ask him to do it. Whatever important decision we have to make should be bathed in prayer, meanwhile awaiting God's confirmation in our heart. To do this we need the help of others.

Since then I have placed as a #1 priority finding persons who are dedicated to the ministry of intercession and who are willing adopt the work God assigns me as their "project." I update these persons on my needs and draw upon the prayer power they generate for my life.

I'm concerned that, as far as I can discern, many in Christian leadership have not learned to practice this powerful dynamic. They believe in prayer, but have no experience of a dynamic partnership in prayer with others. This is a tragedy, because:

God has assigned an intercessor for each of his servants. They should find that intercessor and hook up with him.

In July, at the annual meeting of the Mexico Mission, the organization of missionaries in Mexico, I presented my recommendation that we move the seminary to Mexico City. I was surprised at the near unanimity of the affirmative vote. After much debate on on the question of which city we should relocate to, we found ourselves in a deadlock. The next day we reopened the matter, with the understanding that there must be an agreement of at least three-fourths of those present. After another long debate a vote was taken on moving to Mexico City. The vote was incredibly close, one more negative vote, and the motion would have failed!

Then came the moment I had most feared: the presentation of our decision to the Baptist leadership in Mexico City. This meeting took place in August, 1967, in the downtown First Baptist Church. Some forty five people attended, including officials of the Central Baptist Association, the staff of the Tlalpan Seminary, and missionaries from the American Baptist Convention.

I wrote in my diary the following week: "The meeting in Mexico City last week was one of the worst trials I have endured in my entire life." In the large room designated as our meeting place, the President of Tlalpan Seminary arranged the chairs in a circle. In the center of the circle he placed a chair for me. This young man was the son of the physician who had founded a prestigious Christian hospital in nearby Puebla. Born and raised in that city, he spoke Spanish like the native he was. Six feet five, this handsome *caballero* had recently graduated from the University of Chicago with a Ph.D. in public relations. In recent months, after his return to Mexico, he had practiced with great success the techniques he learned in acquiring his doctorate. At the annual meeting of the Mexican Baptist Convention in Monterrey a month before, he had hosted a gala banquet with hundreds of pastors as his guests. He brought down the house when he declared that *mole poblano*, not blood, flowed in his veins. (*Mole poblano* is a Mexican meat sauce used in festive occasions.) He brought down the house again when he sang as a solo Mexican Baptists' favorite hymn, *Jesus es mi Rey soberano*. By the time he presented his ambitious plans for the seminary he would be guiding, he had the pastors in the palm of his hand.

When I learned of his conquest of the good will of Mexico's leaders, my heart sank. I'd already had battles with my conscience about our proposed "invasion" of Mexico City, and this seemed to confirm my doubts.

As I took my assigned place in the assembly room, surrounded by Mexico City's Baptist elite, I felt like Daniel being tossed into the lions' den. I read a paper prepared by our seminary board, explaining the reasons for our proposed move to Mexico City. When I had finished, the assembly exploded. A pastor protested that he was offended by my declaration that God had spoken to me. Who did I think I was, a reincarnation of the prophet Amos? The revered elderly pastor of the First Baptist Church rebuked our seminary board for not consulting with the Mexican Baptist Convention before making their decision. The Executive Secretary of the Central Baptist Association jumped to his feet, his face red with anger and made a dramatic threat: "My father was a revolutionary, and blood of the Revolution flows in my veins. I am ready to shed that blood to see that your seminary does not come to Mexico City!" I was shocked, because a couple of weeks before this man had told a small group of us who interviewed him that he saw no problem with our plans for relocation to his city.

The bitter assault continued for three hours. Not a single person came to my defense. One prominent pastor, who the week before had written a letter assuring me of his support, sat through the meeting without opening his mouth.

I left the meeting shell-shocked, and remained numb for days afterward. A week later I wrote in my diary: "I'm still living in the backwash of the Mexico City meeting. I find myself hating the thought of moving to that city and having to deal with people who said the things they said to me."

I couldn't believe my eyes when a week later I received letters from the First Baptist Churches of both Mexico City and nearby Puebla, congratulating me on our plans to move the Mexican Baptist Theological Seminary to Mexico City! I was beginning to learn how the loyalty of people can change overnight.

In any public meeting, people tend to decide how they'll vote on a controversial matter, not on principle, but on whom they perceive

to be in the position of power at that moment.

Chapter Sixteen
In the Eye of a Storm
1967-1970

With the coming of summer I occupied myself with one of the most challenging duties of the president of a seminary, working with prospective students. This is a task sometimes inspiring, sometimes discouraging. Many who applied had insufficient academic preparation. In the past most of the students had only finished elementary school, a reflection of the culture of Mexico. Now we were encouraging every prospective student to at least complete high school. Others lacked the minimum age of twenty, or had not been sufficiently active in their church. We also required that the prospective student give ample evidence of a call from God. Weighing this evidence could be a daunting task. By the beginning of our school year we had enrolled sixty students.

Then on September 3, 1967, a fabulous surprise. I wrote in my diary: "A MIRACLE HAS HAPPENED! I've been selected as a winner by Guideposts magazine and will make a trip to New York City for a Writers' Workshop. It seems like a dream, I'm still having a hard time taking it in."

Guideposts is one of the most popular Christian magazines in the U.S. Founded in 1945 by Norman Vincent Peale, author of *The Power of Positive Thinking*, it features testimonies of people whose lives have been changed by an encounter with God. That year they had initiated an annual contest that has continued ever since: they invite their readers to send in a story, and from these they choose winners who are brought to New York for a week-long workshop. The telegram I received informed me that I had been chosen as one of 24 winners from 1100 entries.

I spent the week in a retreat on Long Island, receiving training from editors of Guideposts and Readers Digest. One of our principal speakers was Katherine Marshall. Upon my return I wrote in my diary: "I think that week was equal in excitement to any week I have spent in my entire life. This is the big break I've been waiting for. I can feel destiny vibrating in every fiber of my body." I was convinced that soon I would be a "successful writer."

That was more than forty years ago. Since then I've published three books in Spanish, one novel in English (Several others are unpublished), and maybe a dozen articles in magazines. Nothing like the "success" I expected at that time, but tomorrow's another day!

As the year 1967 came to a close, the possibility of moving the seminary to Mexico City appeared almost non- existent. On December 18 I wrote:

Last week's meeting of Mexican Baptist leaders in Mexico City on the possibility of a union of seminaries was very negative. I came back telling myself we were going to remain here in Torreon after all.

All day long I felt blue about the future of the seminary. This morning I came to the office in great need of a word from the Lord. I thumbed through my Bible, asking him to speak to me through His Word. And He did: Acts 4:19 says, "Whether it be right in the sight of God to hearken unto you than to God, judge ye." And again, John 16:33: "These things I have spoken unto you that in me you might have peace. In the world you will have tribulation, but be of good cheer, I have overcome the world."

In these two passages comes again so very, very strong the reaffirmation of what God said to me on June 11. WE MUST GO TO MEXICO CITY. If all the world is against us, if it costs us the support of every church in the convention, if I lose every friend I ever had WE MUST GO TO MEXICO CITY. Why? Because this is God's will! That is sufficient. I am willing to talk, to compromise, to be patient, but now I know better than ever this one basic thing that must not change: God has said we must go to Mexico City and therefore we will go.

In January I went to Cuernavaca for the annual meeting of the Theological Schools of Northern Latin America. Afterward, I wrote, "One of the professors of the Tlalpan Seminary told me his staff is convinced that if our seminary moves to Mexico City they will be swarmed under, so they are going to 'fight to the death.'"

1968 was another year of conflicts, failures and blessings. The question of the seminary relocation was always on my mind. I wrote on January 9, "Humanly speaking, the move to Mexico City scares the wits out of me. I can see us being crucified, because the president of Tlalpan Seminary is very efficient at getting people to see things his way." A few weeks later our professor of music returned from a meeting of the National Baptist Council with the following report for me: "The President of Tlalpan Seminary has everybody in his hip pocket."

One night in February I was so worried I slept only three hours. The supervisor of the dining hall had informed me that a student from Monterrey, a part of Tlalpan Seminary's "territory" had told her that at mid-term he was going to transfer to that seminary. I lay for hours mulling over the foolishness of this competition that made us enemies. When I finally got to sleep about 3:00 A.M. I had worked out in my mind a plan for uniting Mexico's three seminaries. The next day I interviewed the student who had made the threat and he told me he'd just been kidding!

Still, I continued to push the idea of a united seminary. Within a few months that possibility was dead. Tlalpan Seminary announced that they were committed to entering the recently founded Theological Community. An international theological foundation had purchased a large plot of land next to the National Autonomous University and invited all the denominational seminaries in Mexico City to move onto that property. Each seminary would have its own classrooms, the chapel would be shared by all, and there would be an opportunity to share professors.

As the months passed and there seemed to be little progress in the planned relocation, I fought depression. What concerned me most was my frequent doubts about the validity of the encounter I'd had with the Lord a year ago, an encounter that had convinced me God wanted us in Mexico City. On May 5th I wrote in my diary:

Though I've had many mystical experiences about the seminary moving to Mexico City, the developments since then leave me with the question of my ability to interpret God's will, and a deep, inexpressible puzzlement about the way I have gone through life believing that God has spoken to me directly through such experiences. If I have been wrong this time, how many other times have I been wrong, and can it be that the entire basis of my spiritual life, and my way of interpreting God's will is wrong? That's a gnawing worry deep within me that will not go away. Of course we might still move to Mexico City, but it would take a major, major miracle. It has come to the point that the only thing that makes me think we should go to Mexico City are those intuitions I have had. And I am not yet ready to give more weight to my intuitions than all the evidence that can be stacked on the other side.

At the annual meeting of the Mexico Mission in July, I presented to my fellow missionaries the recommendation of the seminary Board of Trustees that, in the light of the opposition, the seminary relocate to Guadalajara. However, when a vote was taken, the majority were still in favor of Mexico City. Later that same day, after more debate, the vote was 26-12 in favor of Mexico City. We adjourned, agreeing to pray for God's leadership.

The next morning I moved that we have thirty minutes more of debate, then vote with the understanding that to be valid, any decision must have a 75% majority. When the vote was taken, we were dumb with shock: 34-11 in favor, a total of 74%. One percentage point short!

Bob Fricke, one of the faculty members most vehement in his opposition to moving to Mexico City, stood to his feet, tears in his eyes. He declared that he could not live with his conscience if his vote thwarted the will of the majority. His change raised the affirmative vote to 76%.

In November we started looking for property.

Meanwhile there were encouraging developments in my writing. Word Publishers expressed interest in the possibility of publishing a novel I had submitted to them, if I made certain revisions. I made the revisions and resubmitted the manuscript. Readers Digest sent me a retaining fee of $250.00 in response to a query on a possible story. In addition to these, at the end of 1968 I was awaiting word on a manuscript sent to Christianity Today, had sent a query letter to Guideposts in Spanish, had completed four sermons for *El Pastor Evangelico* and was beginning a series of six lessons for a Spanish Young People's quarterly.

Meanwhile we struggled through numerous family crises. Evelyn had an appendix operation in June and the doctor did some additional internal "rearranging". She was in bed for six weeks. My frequent trips into rural areas provoked amoeba and typhoid. Fatigue and depression followed. In her last year of high school Linda decided she was in love with her boyfriend Jorge. Before she left for college they agreed that when she graduated she'd return and marry him. But by the end of her first year, Jorge was complaining to me about her "cold letters."

The year also underscored my growing understanding that, whatever else happened, what mattered most was my progress in "being fashioned into the image of Christ." On October 31, 968 I had an unexpected encounter with the Holy Spirit. Later I described the experience in my diary:

> In my devotional that morning I was trying to pray after reading a little booklet entitled "Victory in Christ". The booklet emphasizes the need to ACCEPT, not ask, to be conscious that every moment Christ is living in us and working through us. I confess that I had become impatient with books about the "miraculous" results of the filling of the Spirit because I had sought that sort of thing off and on all my life with little result. Aware of my skeptical attitude, I had been praying that God would help me to change. Reading the book, "something got hold of me" and I had the most unusual sense of another Presence that I've had in all my life. Since then I've been more acutely aware of God's presence, and conscious of the fact that I've have moved

into a new relationship with myself and with the Lord. I don't understand yet all that has happened. I am trying to be careful in my estimation and let God move me along in this new relationship as he wants to. The essence of this relationship is to let grace work through the Christ who lives in me, to stop "trying" and accept what God is already doing. Was this a "filling", or a "baptism" of the Spirit? I believe it was. But I am not anxious to give this experience a name. I only want to respond to what he has done and what he wants to do.

A week later I wrote about a "victory over besetting sins and a consciousness of the presence of the Lord. The most constant factor is a happiness that at times simply overwhelms me."

At the end of 1968 I wrote that I was trying every day to place myself completely under the direction of the Spirit, that I was experiencing a new peace and a triumph over sin. A couple of months later I commented, "I have continued to be very much aware that God has filled me with his Spirit and that he has given me the gift of faith."

However, in April of 1969 I found myself in a spiritual crisis. I commented, "Until yesterday I didn't realize how much I've been repressing a long list of worries that have been eating away at me like cancer." The night before, my wrists had swollen and were so painful I was unable to sleep. The next day I had a bout with diarrhea. Worries about the seminary brought me to a new low in June. I commented:

That's life, isn't? From the top of the mountain to the bottom of the valley. Again I realize that looking for fulfillment in anything else but the promises of God is a forlorn pursuit. I was thinking a moment ago about the movie, *Zorba the Greek*, and how it ends with Zorba in a wild dance in the face of utter defeat, saying to his staid English companion, "The only way to survive in this world is to be a bit mad." Sounds like a version of Paul's "foolishness," and Christ's wildly challenging promises concerning prayer and faith. It is that foolishness that makes it possible to smile and be confident when all goes bad -- the impossible certainty that I have died with Christ and risen with him, and that he lives in me and speaks to me and tells me what I must do and that in him there can be no failure.

The seminary continued to provide more than enough raw material for a stressful existence. In March the Mexican members of the faculty surprised me with a long list of demands they planned to present to the Board of Trustees. I felt betrayed. Later they changed their minds, and met with me to ask forgiveness. One of the new members of the Mexican Faculty was turning out to be a disappointment. I'd enlisted him from a successful pastorate, but almost immediately the students began to complain that he came to class unprepared. In August, at the beginning of the new school year, I retired him from classes and made him secretary of the seminary, and he seemed to be doing well at that job.

Then there were the students. A brilliant young man from Mexico City confessed to me that he was being plagued by doubts about his Christian faith. He became involved in the Marxist revolutionary student movement and abandoned the Seminary. In the summer I'd been encouraged by the large number of letters of inquiry, and expected a record enrolment. But we began the year with 62 students, an increase from the enrollment when I assumed the presidency, but not what I had hoped for.

Toward the end of October, many of the students began to meet for late night prayer. Sometimes the sessions would last until 3:00 A.M. I attended most of these meetings, and was encouraged by the fervency of the prayers and the sincerity of confessions of sin. I was convinced we were in the beginning of a revival.

But Satan made his presence known through Juan. This young man had been a drug addict. He was converted in a revival in Monterrey and applied for admission to the seminary. We were doubtful, since it had been less than a year since his conversion. However, his pastor was so insistent that we decided to make an exception. In November he disappeared, along with several hundred dollars from the locker of his roommate. The roommate was so disillusioned that he dropped out of seminary. Within weeks I heard Juan was in jail in Tijuana, and flew up to look for him. I couldn't locate him. On November 26 I wrote in my diary:

Our seminary seems to be in the most severe crisis we have experienced since I took over. I've talked to a number of students who say they're not going to return for the second semester. Besides, the movement toward revival has stopped dead in its tracks. The entire seminary seems to be under a cloud of depression. I've never seen anything like this! It's as if the strong current of a river has stopped dead, turned backward and has now started running in the opposite direction.

Thankfully, a couple of weeks later the depression began to lift, and by the time the students left for Christmas vacation things were almost normal. Six new students applied for the next semester, raising our enrollment to a new record.

I was beginning to understand that the very nature of seminary life creates an atmosphere of continual crisis:

> The students leave their homes, their churches and whatever security they knew before, to be dropped into the midst of the largest city in the world. Most of them have never faced anything like the scholastic discipline required here. They get an average of four or five hours of sleep at night, then on the weekends are required to leave the relative security of the seminary to spend two days in a demanding missionary situation. Add to that the tension of living with a roommate if you're single, or sharing the strains of family life where money is scarce and children are trying to adjust to a scary new lifestyle. No wonder people get discouraged!

In spite of the problems, encouraging progress was being made in plans for moving the seminary to Mexico City. In March we bought a beautiful piece of property on the main thoroughfare of *Lomas Verdes,* an attractive new suburb on the northern edge of Mexico City. We purchased the land from a well-known Mexican comedian, *Clavillazo* (translation: "elbow punch"). Unusual circumstances surrounded the purchase. The property was in a subdivision of recently constructed middle-class homes financed by the Vatican. *Clavillazo* had refused to sell the Vatican his property, preferring to let it go at half price to Protestants! I can see now that this was another stanza in my Caleb poem. God made a commitment to Caleb: "Because my servant Caleb has a different spirit and follows me whole-heartedly, I will bring him into the land he went to (Numbers 14:24). Forty-five years later Caleb reminded Joshua of this commitment: "Moses swore to me, 'The land on which your feet have walked will be your inheritance and that of your children forever, because you have followed the Lord my God wholeheartedly' ... Now give me this hill country that the Lord promised me that day." (Joshua 14:9, 12 NIV). Lomas Verdes means "green hills!

A turning point in our relation to the Baptist churches of Mexico City came in the annual meeting of the Mexican Baptist Convention in April, 1970. Strong opposition was expressed against the Tlalpan Seminary's decision to enter the Theological Community. Many Baptists were concerned because the Community espoused the then popular "Theology of Liberation," a Marxist approach to the Gospel that had as its goal, not the salvation of individual souls, but the reformation of society. The Executive Committee brought a recommendation that the Convention withdraw recognition from the seminary unless they unless they revoked their decision.

At midmorning on the second day of the convention the president of the seminary took the floor and asked everyone who had been blessed by Tlalpan Seminary to come stand at his side. Several dozen went forward. Then he said dramatically, "These are your brothers and sisters in Christ! Are you going to crucify them?" A fierce debate continued all day and well into the night. Finally it was agreed to turn the matter over to the Executive Committee for a recommendation. The next morning the committee reported that at 4:00 A.M. they had arrived at the unanimous decision to recommend withdrawal of recognition from Tlalpan Seminary. The recommendation was approved by a large majority.

That ended the competition between the Torreon and Tlalpan Seminaries. But any hopes that this also meant the end of tensions with the Convention were soon dashed. Many Baptist leaders were still opposed to our relocation.

Plans began to accelerate for the new seminary campus. In June we signed a contract with Josè Valladares, one of Mexico's most prominent architects. In July the Mexico Mission approved a request to the Foreign Mission Board for $100,000 to initiate the construction.

Meanwhile, we continued to deal with the realities of family life. Linda had fallen in love with a fellow student at Louisiana College. We were disappointed that he was not a Christian, but when they came for a visit, we had to agree he was "a nice guy." David began a relationship with a young lady who the year before had been Louisiana College's campus queen. On a visit late in the year she charmed Evelyn and me.

Looking back, I am aware of how limited is the parents' influence over the choices their children make for marriage. And how limited is our ability to predict how a marriage will turn out! We had serious doubts from the beginning about the young man Linda was in love with, but were delighted with David's choice. David's marriage lasted less than two years. Linda's endured twenty-nine years, before it also ended in divorce. In retrospect, I wish we had been more apt at discerning the impending problems. But even if we had, any attempt to break off those two ill-fated relationships would have only opened up a breach between us and our children. The only remedy, it seems, is to keep loving, praying, and trusting in Romans 8:28.

That same principle holds true in relations with others. The seminary year opened in the fall with many tensions. A professor who had joined us the year before turned out to be ineffective. I found myself hoping he'd accept an offer to join the faculty of another seminary, but he opted to stay on. As usual, there were misfits in the student body: a senior who continued the rebellion he had initiated when he was a freshman, another who preached to his fellow students that they could not have fullness of the Spirit unless they spoke in tongues. I found myself spending more and more time in counseling, and often those sessions left me exhausted. On November 26 I wrote in my diary: "The seminary seems to be in the most severe crisis we have experienced since I took over. A dozen students are seriously considering leaving. I have never had to live through so many problems. I am completely wrung out."

As for the relocation of the seminary, there were conflicting currents. We were in the process of closing the purchase of our property, but there were rumors of a growing sentiment among my fellow missionaries against moving to Mexico City. Charles Bryan, our representative with the International Mission Board, would visit us in a few days, and one professor assured me he was coming to tell us we couldn't move to Mexico City.

Dr. Bryan arrived the next week and spent two days as a guest in our home. It turned out to be a very pleasant time. He had come to discuss with us how the Board could help us in the move to Mexico City. Contrary to the rumors, the Board had accepted the relocation as a given.

We closed out the Fall semester on a positive note. Most of the rumored student withdrawals never came to pass. Enough new students enrolled for the second semester for a record enrolment.

I confess that this chapter is an indictment of my weak faith. I had received so many confirmations from the Lord! In June, 1967, God gave me a vision, telling me we must move to Mexico City. In December of the same year, I received another confirmation in prayer, and declared in my diary, "WE MUST MOVE TO MEXICO CITY BECAUSE GOD HAS SAID SO! Yet for years afterward, because of opposition, I vacillated, fell into depression, and looked for other alternatives. I behaved like ten of the twelve spies who were sent out to spy the land of Canaan (Numbers 13: 26-33.) It is interesting that Deuteronomy 1:22-23 gives a version of the reason for sending out the spies that varies from the account in Numbers: the spies were sent out because the people, not God, demanded it. In his commentary on this passage, Alexander Maclaren points out that there was no reason for sending out the spies, because God had promised he would give them the land. That should have been enough! Likewise, God's promise should have been enough for me!

In this chapter I have mentioned a number of experiences that caused me to question God's providence. An incident with one of our young married couples showed me how God sometimes uses unpleasant crises to teach us important lessons. Elda and Gilberto were a tall, fair-skinned couple from Monterrey. In their freshman year Ricardito was born. We watched him learn to crawl, then to stand, then stumble across the green campus. He became God's special gift to all of us, with his long legs, wavy hair and angelic smile. Everybody claimed him, adored him and held him in their arms. Then, a few days before his third birthday, Ricardito died. We were stunned. Gilberto and Elda had taken him to a clinic one night with a cough, and the next day brought back his lifeless little body. Everyone walked about all that day with tears in their eyes, asking "Why?", angry with God. In the classes nobody wanted to listen to the professors' lectures, they just wanted the professor to tell them why they should forgive God for this outrage. It was agreed that Ricardito would lie in state in the chapel in his little bed. All day long Elda and Gilberto were surrounded by their seminary family, weeping with them, praying for them. Nobody wanted to go to the dining hall, just a coffee pot and cookies in the chapel would do. Night came, ten o'clock, midnight, and nobody was interested in going to bed. Around one A.M. the unexpected happened. The conversation and prayers became mixed with songs and testimonies, student after student told of precious moments they had spent with Ricardito. Soon we were sharing a love feast, and tears were spiced with smiles. The anger toward God melted into praise. By the time dawn arrived, the seminary family was united in affection and compassion as never before. Students who had been distanced because of disagreements asked forgiveness, others who had been angry with a professor exchanged the hurt for hugs. Nobody who was part of the seminary family that year ever forgot the miracle of a death that brought the birth of a new life in the Spirit.

*Maclaren, Alexander. *Exposition of the Holy Scriptures, Genesis, Exodus, Numbers.* p.335

Pat with his brother James

Sweethearts

What a beautiful bride!

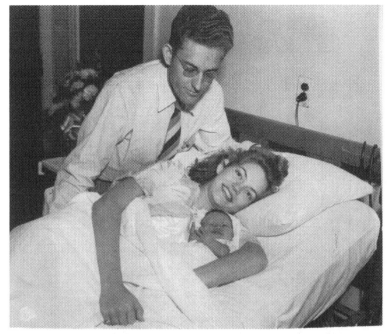

First fruits of our love

Pat's father and mother with their grandchildren

Pat's first student pastorate in Latanier, Louisiana

A new baby arrives in San Francisco

Bayview Baptist Church in San Francisco

Faithful members

Building a new church on one of San Francisco's hills

Our San Francisco home

The church in Palestine, Texas

Missionaries in Mexico!

The church we planted in Mexico's northern desert

The Baptist Theological Seminary in Mexico City

Graduation Day

Missionaries in Merida, Yucatan, Mexico

No lack of people anxious to hear the gospel!

Anastasis, the first church we planted in Mexico City

Celebrating Pat's birthday in the Lomas Church in Mexico City

Vacationing in the country home of Oscar and Betty Franco

How quickly the kids grew up!

Our staff in the counseling center Armonia Familiar, Mexico City

On the staff of the First Baptist Church in Kingwood, Texas

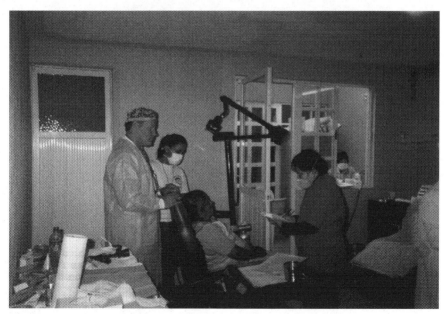

*A medical mission of the Kingwood Church marked the
beginning of a new church in Mexico City.*

Chapter Seventeen
Satan's Victory and God's Intervention
1970-1972

Three years had passed since my assuming the presidency of the seminary.

I'd lived a roller-coaster of exhilarating experiences of God's leadership and numbing experiences of bitter defeat. As 1970 began, I suspected that the stressful days were over. I was wrong! This year would bring a public humiliation, then, the first months of the following year would bring a fulfillment of Isaiah 40:31.

Juan Luna, the ex-drug addict who had stolen money from his roommate and disappeared, was released from prison and requested readmission. He had quite a story for us: the police in Tijuana arrested him for selling drugs. They sentenced him to a year in prison, and were taking him to Mexicali when he escaped and crossed the border into the United States. There he was arrested, and when Immigration discovered his record, they recommended he be sentenced to five years. But the judge, after hearing his testimony of salvation, gave him only thirty days. Although we had our doubts, we agreed to admit him. The area missionary gave him a job in his office, and we rejoiced at the restoration of a prodigal son. (We still had a lot to learn about dealing with drug addicts!)

I was now writing regularly for a new Latin American edition of Guideposts and enjoying a close relationship with the editor.

The year was a mixture of blessings and trials. The seminary was a fertile breeding ground for problems. I constantly received criticism from my fellow missionaries about our budget, the teachings of our faculty, the dress of our students. The projected relocation to Mexico City provoked additional tensions. Though the move had been approved by the Mexico Mission, one missionary seemed to look for opportunities to place obstacles in our path. We were making encouraging progress with Jose Valladares, the architect, in drawing up plans for the new campus, but a representative of the Foreign Mission Board warned us that probably no funds would be available in the foreseeable future.

Early in the year I had an unexpected experience in my personal devotions. One day, as I poured out my heart to God, I experienced a unique filling of the Spirit. Afterward I wrote in my diary: "I felt that I was in control of my tongue, and yet that I wasn't. I felt marvelously happy." Several days later I wrote: Each time this happens, I have afterward the most real consciousness of God's presence, of a profound love for Him. There remains with me for hours afterward a warm, exciting sense of HIS presence.

In July came a stunning surprise. Six months earlier we had met with the leaders of the National Baptist Convention and advised them that the project of the seminary relocation was on track. We were pleased when they assured us there was no problem, they had accepted our decision. But in the annual meeting of the Convention in July the President condemned the move and recommended that, in the light of our obstinacy, the Convention withdraw its recognition of the seminary. The recommendation was unanimously approved. This action was so unexpected that we were left with mouths agape, unable to respond.

I was constantly dealing with problems of the students. We lived out a new chapter of the life story of Juan Luna, the drug addict. Several months after his return he stole money from the missionary who had given him employment and disappeared again. Later he reappeared in Mexico City, and was given the pastorate of a mission. Soon word came that he had stolen money, from the family that had offered him hospitality, and had once more disappeared.

Always something new and unexpected to break the monotony! For example, after numerous warnings, we expelled a student for repeated failures in his exams. The student body went on strike. Nationalism was a constant stress point, especially in regard to the seminary move. The new President of the Board of Trustees was one of those who had angrily challenged me three years before when we first announced the plan to move to Mexico City. Another member of the Board disliked Americans, and expressed his animosity at every opportunity.

I was in a constant private struggle for emotional and spiritual strength to meet these crises. One of my hands tended to swell for days at a time from arthritis and sometimes, because of the pain, I couldn't sleep. In March I wrote in my diary: "Tuesday I had diarrhea. About five o'clock I went home, closed the bedroom door and just sat down and bawled." More than once I arrived at home exhausted and went into bouts of vomiting. Yet, during that same year I mentioned again and again in my diary that I was learning to live in God's peace and not be governed by circumstances. In October I wrote: "I have been incredibly happy most of this week. How can anybody be as happy as I am? I think I have found the key to being happy: fixing my attention only on Christ and letting my fulfillment rest on my relation with him."

In July, on a "mini-furlough" we participated in the wedding of David and Sandy.

Afterward I wrote: "David and Sandy are two unusual young people and I think they have a great future. We love Sandy as a daughter already." We had no inkling of the heartbreak that lay ahead.

Linda's relation with her boyfriend seemed to change monthly. In August she informed us they were deeply in love. In October she complained that they were constantly fighting. In November she broke up with him and began dating others. She wrote us of the peace this decision had brought her with herself and with God. Then on December 26 I wrote in my diary:

We talked with my parents last night by telephone. David and Linda were there, and Charles also. Mama told us Linda would have "something to tell us" when she arrived. That "something," of course, is that they are going to get married. I'm disappointed. I really felt

Linda did the best thing when she broke up with Charles. I'm just going to rest on Romans 8:28. But God only knows how many times someone marries someone else who is "all right" when they should have waited for the person who is just right.

Linda arrived for her Christmas visit with a ring. A few days later, Charles appeared. Linda had told us the breakup had changed him. Spending a few days with him impressed us that he had indeed become more attentive toward Linda and more open to God. Anyway, we had little choice. They informed us they were going to get married in February or March and they wanted me to do the wedding. If I was unwilling, they would stop off at Laredo on their trip home, find a justice of peace and get married. So in February we flew to Louisiana for the wedding.

As the year 1971 began, we had no idea that this year would bring answers to prayer and usher in a new stage in our lives. We were aware that unless some important changes took place, the seminary's future was doubtful. Although we had purchased property in Mexico City, the prospect of moving there was not inviting. The withdrawal of recognition by the National Baptist Convention was the culmination of a decade of growing tensions. Many Mexican Baptists felt they were victims of the rivalry between the two mission boards from the United States. Our acquiring land in Mexico City for a seminary was seen by some as an invasion of a region we had no right to. The Convention leadership resented the fact that Southern Baptists had a program of work independent of their own, and the financial leverage of the Americans was far superior to what the National Convention could offer. Besides the seminary, the Foreign Mission Board sponsored a hospital in Guadalajara and book stores in several cities. Southern Baptist missionaries provided subsidies to churches. I began to hear of plans being hatched to "expel the gringo missionaries." This tension was affecting the work of the churches, and in many respects missionary advance had come to a standstill.

Thirteen leaders of the various missionary programs met in Mexico City on February 5th, 1971 to dialogue about these problems. The morning session was stormy, with numerous complaints and angry confrontations. We recessed for lunch, and when we returned for the afternoon session we were already exhausted. Then something unexpected happened. After a few minutes of silence, someone declared: "I believe the only solution for the crisis we're in is for the Mexico Mission to integrate all our programs with those of the Mexican Baptist Convention." A ridiculous declaration! This idea had been discussed on dozens of occasions, and had always been rejected as impossible, because, we agreed, Mexican Baptists were not mature enough to take over the management of our programs.

But that afternoon the impossible became urgent. We began to talk animatedly about the integration of our programs, most of us with tears. After two hours we, voted 12-1 to recommend this revolutionary action to the Executive Committee of the Mexico Mission. Afterward, I wrote in my diary:

This was truly a miracle, an intervention of the Holy Spirit. I'm so happy -- in fact the more time passes the happier I am and the more I'm convinced that God moved in an unusual way to guide us into His will.

Later someone described our encounter with God this way:

When we returned for our afternoon session an uninvited guest accompanied us: the Holy Spirit. And he whispered in each of our hearts what God wanted us to do.

But there remained two difficult steps. The next day we must convince the Executive Committee of our Mexico mission, and then, if we succeeded, all of the Mexico missionaries.

To our surprise, the executive Committee voted 8-1 to convoke a special meeting of the Mexico Mission. I commented in my diary:

I can't believe it! We are ready to turn everything over to the nationals, including the seminary and our own ministries. This has to be of the Holy Spirit, because it is against human reasoning. If anyone had suggested this ten minutes before we voted, the idea would have been rejected with fervor.

The Mexico Mission met the weekend of March 16. Again, the illogical happened. Missionaries who had repeatedly asserted their conviction that the nationals were incapable of managing our programs, and that, at all costs, we must hold on to our rights, rose to speak in favor of what we were now calling "integration", turning over to our Mexican brothers all our programs, and offering ourselves to cooperate in the work, now as individual Christians, at the invitation of the Mexican entities. Charles Bryan, the Foreign Mission Board representative, surprised us by declaring: "Probably the Board is ready to go even further than what you asking." Not one negative word! I commented in my diary that "all was done on a spiritual level and at the end it became a love feast."

We commissioned our Mission President to travel to the city of Iguala and communicate our decision to Dr. Daniel Garrido, the President of the Mexican National Baptist Convention. Dr. Garrido, a stern military physician, listened to him without comment as he related the decision. When he had finished, Garrido said, "I have only one question, and your answer will tell me if I am to take seriously this offer of you American missionaries: if the Convention decides the seminary should not move to Mexico City, will you obey us?"

"Yes, we will?"

"Then I believe you! Where do we go from here?"

We had anticipated this question in our last meeting. Several declared that we should draw the line at that point. We had spent two agonizing years coming to the decision that the seminary relocate to the Capitol city, and should not take the chance of that decision being vetoed.. I opposed that limitation: "Our decision has been based on the conviction that God has taken the initiative in this relocation. If God worked a miracle in the hearts of us missionaries, are we going to doubt that he will also work a miracle in the hearts of our Mexican brothers?" The group agreed.

The following month we met with the Mexican Baptist Committee on Relations. We were nervous, for this group was very nationalistic, and had been in an attack mode since the decision to relocate the seminary. However, when we presented the offer of the Mexico Mission they received it in good spirit, without accusations or insinuations. Next we met with the *Consejo Nacional* of the Convention, the committee that carried on Convention business between the annual meetings. There were many questions, but all in a good spirit. The pastor known as the most avid critic of missionaries sounded the keynote. He said he had many questions he would like to ask, but would abstain from asking them, for fear of sinning against the Spirit who had moved us to make the decision. Nothing was said about the relocation of the seminary. I noted in my diary: "Patience and dependence on the Holy Spirit must be the key. But I know that the seminary is going to move."

Other meetings between the Convention and our missionaries continued smoothly during the summer. Still, nothing was said about the seminary. In July I wrote, "I have been praying and leaving in God's hands the seminary move, the convincing of the people and the money we'll need. This is surely the most 'impossible' of the 'impossible' things I have been asking of the Lord, and he has given me a deep assurance that he is going to answer." Later that month I went to Mexico City for a meeting with Convention personnel, hopeful that now we'd talk about the relocation of the seminary. Nobody showed up! I wrote,

> Baptists seem so dead and so nearly fossilized, I don't know
> if they're capable of responding to a new leading of the Holy
> Spirit. But I've learned it is not my job to try to figure out
> how to resolve spiritual problems, but to trust in the Lord
> and to rejoice beforehand in the knowledge that he is going to
> solve all the problems.

In August we took Carol to Brownwood, Texas to enter college. Later, we met David and Sandy in San Antonio. David would enter law school at LSU in September. I noted that David and his wife seemed to have no sense of God's leadership, but reminded myself that they were very young.

My own spiritual progress was encouraging. Since the experience of the infilling of the Spirit the year before, I noted:

> There's a greater inner calm, a surer hand on the rudder.
> There is a constant sense of God's presence and a joy in this
> presence. I have made up a list of prayers that are the most

difficult to be answered, and have seen Him answering them one by one. This is truly a new quality of life.

To my surprise, a month later I fell into depression as the result of a series of problems in the Seminary: "The only time I really feel desperate is when I doubt if what I am doing is worth the trouble." Besides, Evelyn's recovery from a hysterectomy a couple of months before was agonizingly slow: "Evelyn is still just up and down, and her emotions are ready to boil over at all times." But a month later I wrote, "Evelyn has almost completely recovered from her operation. I can see that this surgery was good for our relationship. I feel so much closer to her now and love her more than ever."

As the year drew to a close I was feeling optimistic. A meeting with the Relations Committee of the Convention was upbeat. God seemed to be using me as never before. I prayed for a young man possessed by a demon and he was freed. Berenice, the little daughter of a seminary couple, had been paralyzed in her legs since birth. A group of us began meeting each Friday to pray for her, and one Friday as we prayed, she stood up and walked!

I wrote in my diary, "My relation with God continues to be fabulous, and I am enjoying the reality of the fullness of the Spirit. So many complexes and fears that have bothered me in the past have melted away."

Looking back, I can see that the years 1970-1971 were a watershed in my life, in the seminary, in relations with the nationals, and in my relationship with God. Most of what has followed has been the overflow of experiences of grace that God gave me in those years.

The year that followed we saw the completion of the miracle we had been living. When the Mexican Baptist Convention met in April, we had been praying for months that there would be a reversal of the angry spirit that had provoked the withdrawal of recognition of the seminary. Consideration of the seminary relocation was scheduled for Saturday morning, the last day. At Evelyn's insistence, we sat in the second row of the auditorium. At midmorning the president stated: "Now we come to consideration of the relocation of the seminary." After an explanation of the proposal, he opened the floor for a motion. I waited fearfully for someone to move the relocation be rejected.

From far behind us came a loud, "I move the relocation be approved." Then, "I second the proposition." And now that fearful question: "Is there any discussion?" Remembering the angry words in years past when this subject came up, I waited for the storm to break. Not a word!

At last Dr. Garrido declared, "Since there is no discussion, we will vote. All in favor, raise your hand."

I whispered to Evelyn, "I'm scared to look. You do it!"

She looked around, and reported in a hushed voice, "Every hand in the house is raised!"

So came to an end four years of struggle, of conflicts, of secret plots, of sleepless nights, of doubts, of fears, of hopelessness, of battles with my conscience, of upset stomachs, headaches and painful attacks of arthritis. In a most awesome way I saw God teaching me again:

When I respond in faith to God's initiative, the fulfillment of the most impossible dreams is just a matter of time.

Now began a smooth transition to the visible manifestation of what I had many times called an impossible dream. We worked with Architect Valladares on plans for a beautiful chapel. The money necessary for its construction, something I had seen as extremely doubtful, became available. In November we broke ground.

The spiritual breakthrough that had come into my life in April of 1970 seemed to grow month by month. Evelyn and I continued with our regular Bible study together. In January I commented in my diary: "It is interesting that after 25 years together, Evelyn and I are groping for words to explain what we feel. We're finding that, on the spiritual plane, we don't really know each other. Strange. Strange."

I was learning to accept that my wife's approach to personal spirituality was quite different from mine. While I was continually in struggle, she seemed at peace, with no desire for "new experiences." I was still in the process of recognizing as a gift from God the quiet soul that provided a balance for my restless spirit.

I continued trying to comprehend the different ways God works in the hearts of His people. In February I commented:

To what extent is speaking in tongues psychological and to what extent is it spiritual? I do not see any necessary conflict. William James demonstrated that the conversion experience is closely related to psychological tendencies that exist in our mind. It seems to me this applies in the matter of tongues. Take the case of a Christian who has been inhibited in his spiritual life. Overcome with problems, he comes into contact with people who urge him to leave behind his inhibitions. They tell him to let himself go, and he will be filled with the Spirit and speak in tongues. Who am I to say that the Spirit cannot use these circumstances to give that person a legitimate renewal, even though there are problems in finding the words to describe this experience? Here is room for an indictment of "establishment" churches. They have so inhibited the people that when the opportunity is offered to practice an uninhibited religion, many panic. Are our priorities wrong? It appears that the Spirit does not give absolute priority to a 100% adherence to what we conceive as "doctrinal purity" as a requirement for His blessings, because He is using groups that seem to me to have doctrinal problems as instruments in the salvation of thousands. Maybe for God, heart humility is more important than head correctness!

Later that month I lived a disturbing example of the damage that narrow tradition can do. Dr. Herbert Mitchell, a scientist from NASA, came to Torreon to lecture on the American space program and to share his Christian testimony. One Sunday night I was his host for a presentation at the First Baptist Church. After a couple of hymns the pastor announced that, before Dr. Mitchell's lecture, the church would have its monthly observance of the Lord's Supper. "We invite any member of our church or members from another Baptist church who is visiting us to stand and receive the bread and the juice." Dr. Mitchell whispered to me: "Oh my God, is this a closed communion church?" I confirmed his perception.

I remained seated at his side. Later, when the pastor came to the pulpit to present our guest, the scientist whispered to me: "I'm sorry, my spirit is so wounded I will not be able to speak." I had the unhappy duty of announcing to the waiting congregation that our distinguished visitor had suddenly taken ill and we would have to leave immediately.

My opportunities for spiritual growth continued to multiply. During Holy Week I was invited be the chaplain for a youth retreat in Camp Lambdin, near Guadalajara. The thirty young people who attended were unique, recent converts from drug addiction. I had never been in such an atmosphere. They were awake most of the night praising God, singing new songs they had composed to guitar accompaniment, and sharing testimony after testimony of miracles.

I didn't realize at that moment that I was witnessing the birth of a new worship style that now is customary in the majority of evangelical churches in Latin America and the United States. Neither did I have any idea of the conflict this change would produce. I witnessed the beginning of this conflict the next week in the seminary. The next week, the eight students who had accompanied me to the encampment requested permission to lead the worship in chapel. When they played guitars, sang new songs based on the Psalms, and clapped their hands, they provoked a scandal that spread to churches all over Mexico.

That summer spiritual lightening struck the young people of the Baptist churches in Torreon. Carol, who was spending the summer with us, accompanied me to the last night of the associational youth encampment. At the close of the service a teen went forward to confess her sins. Another followed, then another. The procession of repentant young people continued until midnight.

The following week I invited the young people of Calvary Baptist Church to accompany me in witnesssing to the hundreds of youth who always gathered in Torreon's central plaza Friday and Saturday nights. The youth from other churches joined us. Later, we rented a warehouse a couple of blocks from the plaza and equipped it with "psychodelic" lighting. We invited the kids on the streets to our "coffee house," where they were welcomed with wide grins, enthusiastic music and compelling testimonies. Dozens were converted. Later in the year Evelyn and I moved from our new suburban home to an apartment facing the plaza, where we could be closer to the action. This movement in Torreon reflected events in Mexico City and Monterrey, where dozens of young drug addicts were being converted. The effects of this revival produced renewal and church growth throughout Mexico.

This unconventional behavior on the part of a Seminary President began to provoke comments throughout the country, and soon rumors reached me that some were calling me an undercover Pentecostal.

This was also the year of important decisions in our family. As a consequence of her experiences in the revival movement, Carol became convinced that God's place for her was in Mexico. We had removed her from the United States at the age of four, and now, having grown up in Mexico, she felt she was more Mexican than American. Tests by our seminary psychologist confirmed this perception. She was accepted as a seminary student and entered the dormitory. To the surprise of her parents, our spoiled, self-centered youngest child had become a mature, happy servant of Jesus Christ!

As for our oldest child, things were not going well. Midway through his first year in LSU's law school his wife advised him that she and her graduate school speech professor had fallen in love, and that he had separated from his wife and two children. She decided to divorce David and marry the man. David, devastated, came to Mexico to spend a couple of weeks with us. We worked at helping him to survive. In August he moved to Dallas and found a minimum wage job. It would take him years to understand how his own emotional immaturity contributed to choices that were made.

Evelyn and I were beginning to learn a new lesson:

When kids leave home it doesn't mean you've finished with them. You simply enter into a new relationship, which at times can be even more intense than when they lived with you.

Chapter Eighteen
Transition to a Dream Fulfilled
1972-1974

By the beginning of l972, we seemed to have entered into what I had many times called an impossible dream. We had spent several months working with Architect Valladares on the plans for a beautiful chapel. The money necessary for its construction, something I had seen as very doubtful, suddenly became available. In November we broke ground.

The two years leading up to our actual move to Mexico were filled with blessings. By mid-1973 the chapel was completed and money had been approved for the construction of a three-story administration and dormitory building. Soon a nice lot was purchased a few blocks from the seminary for the construction of a five-story condominium for the faculty. So many blessings!

And, as always, there were unhappy people. Now the Mexican Baptist Convention appointed the members of the Seminary Board, and it appeared at times that some of the people they chose were more interested in conserving tradition than in taking advantage of the marvelous opportunities being presented by our move to the largest city in the world. Much time in Board meetings was occupied discussing reports that were circulating through the churches: we were promoting charismatic practices, students were attending chapel improperly dressed, and often we sang songs not included in the Baptist Hymnal. There was never any specific accusation of false doctrine, only rumors of improper music and too much emphasis on prayer and the spiritual life. When I presented a recommendation that we request the funds now available for construction, one member of the Board abstained from voting "because of things they are saying about the seminary."

Sometimes I felt an aching hunger for just one letter from somebody saying, "You're dong a good job." In mid-1973 I wrote in my diary, "There's a lot of criticism against us. But that's nothing new. When this wave of criticism is over, there'll be more criticism about something else. So why wear myself out worrying about such things? God is using this problem to speed my spiritual growth. So thank the Lord!"

One of my most memorable relations came to an end that year. Marian Sanders had been a textbook single missionary. Besides being seminary librarian she was the director of the Sunday School in Calvary Church, an enthusiastic witness -- and possessed a spine of tempered steel. She had been a major instrument in my being named President of the seminary. When the post became vacant, the Board of Trustees nominated another missionary. But Marian was convinced that I was the person God wanted as President, and campaigned against the nomination. This obstinacy on her part caused hard feelings, but when Marian was convinced she was right she put her conscience above pleasing people.

In 1970 she had been diagnosed with leukemia, but the doctor assured her that her case was not acute, and she could well survive for many more years. But the moment arrived when she could no longer work and she left to be with her pastor brother in Louisiana. Finally, they told her she had a month to live. So she returned to Torreon to close her apartment and to say goodbye. On the last day of her visit she and her brother, Perry Sanders, pastor of the First Baptist Church of Lafayette, Louisiana, had lunch with us. After she retired to a bedroom for rest, a thought occurred to me. I knocked on the door, she said, "Come in," and I went over to stand at her bedside. "Marian," I said, "Soon you're going to be with Jesus. When you see him, would you do me a favor? Tell him Pat says 'Thanks.'" She smiled and said, "Sure, I'll be glad to do it.'

And I believe she did!

In June I wrote:

In the States they are in the midst of the Watergate scandal. This week John Dean has been testifying that President Nixon participated in the cover-up and that he lied when he said he knew nothing about it. This is a critical moment in history, and there is talk about impeaching Mr. Nixon. As a result, the value of the dollar has declined and the country is in an inflationary spiral. There is a severe shortage of gasoline and some stations are rationing. There are reports that gasoline may go up to a dollar a gallon.

And in October:

There are tremendous problems in the world! The Jews and Arabs are at war for the fourth time. This time the Jews made the first move and marched well into the Sinai Peninsula. They have driven into Syria, and there are reports that they are only thirty miles from Cairo. Russia has started rattling the saber. U.S. troops have been put on alert. Besides all this, the Watergate scandal seems to be in the process of destroying our country.

How many times in my life have I felt that all I treasured was on the edge of destruction? And yet, it didn't happen! By now I hope I've learned that one of the oldest clichès is really true:

Things are seldom as bad as they seem.

At this time of crisis in the Seminary, in our family, in the United States and in the world, we left Mexico to spend six months on furlough. I had learned that there were many good things about this parenthesis: the opportunity for rest, to spend time with parents, for the children to affirm their identity as American citizens. Most satisfying was the opportunity to report to the churches on God's blessings. On the other hand, beginning with our first furlough I struggled to escape the missionary stereotype. I had the feeling that most people didn't see me as an individual, but as a species of Christianity worthy of being respected, but distanced from the realities of ordinary living. I was interested in communicating my unique life as an evangelist, a teacher, an administrator. But people tended to expect the usual "missionary stories" that seem to bubble from the lips of missionary folk. And many expected the missionary's talk to be long-winded and boring. As a consequence, attendance was poor for the "Associational Missionary Week" that was common back in those days. Most the pastors didn't seek a personal relationship with the missionary his church was hosting. If the pastor ceded his pulpit one Sunday to the resident missionary he often stipulated limits of time, urged the missionary to "just preach a good sermon," and made it his business to find somewhere else to preach that Sunday. Thank God for the exceptions!

However, it felt great to be "at home," and I had many invitations. I began to entertain doubts about whether we should return to Mexico. I had gone through many trials to secure the relocation of the seminary, perhaps my work in Mexico was done. After a couple of months I presented my doubts to Evelyn and she became angry. No, our work in Mexico was not finished. It would be dumb -- and a breach of our commitment to God --if we abandoned the job He had committed to us!

As we returned to Mexico, family again occupied much of our thoughts and prayers. In October, 1973 David married Vicki, an attractive fellow worker with a strong Christian commitment. By now David had been promoted to the financial department of his company, which handled millions of credit cards. Carol had begun a relationship with a fellow seminary student, and in June, 1974 they were married, after a harried week in Mexico City seeking permission for a Mexican citizen to marry an American. Linda and Charles announced the impending birth of our first grandchild!

In the summer of of 1974 the monumental move to Mexico City began. Truck after truck loaded up classroom furniture, books from the library, and household goods. In mid-June I wrote:

> I'm the only one left in my office, everyone else has gone
> to Mexico City. I've started packing my books. We'll have
> to find a furnished apartment until the condominium is
> completed. The main building on the seminary property will

be finished this month. Then they will begin the landscaping
It all seems like a dream.

A dream indeed! I had lived the prophecy of Joel, "I will pour out
my Spirit on all flesh … and your old men shall dream dreams and your
young men shall see visions." The dream had been born one midnight
ten years ago aboard a bus on the outskirts of Mexico City. It had been
resurrected one Sunday morning three years later, the day after the
Board of Trustees pronounced it dead. One by one my fellow workers
had caught the dream, and encouraged me when my faith faltered.
It had survived and prospered during years of unending warfare,
disagreement with colleagues, discouragement, dire pronouncements
of logic. Each time it seemed that all was lost God had provided the
needed miracle. And now, here we were, about to set foot into a new
world, the world of God's dreams!

A month later I was beginning to live the dream fulfilled:

I'm sitting in my office in the new seminary building in Lomas
Verdes. WE'RE HERE! It seems like a dream. I can hardly believe it.
The last week in Torreon, of course, was hectic, with problems with the
movers, and trying to get everything closed out. But we felt the Lord's
presence in the midst of everything.

Chapter Nineteen
Occupying the Land
1974-1976

*And God blessed him and gave Hebron to Caleb the son of Jephunneh as
an inheritance. Hebron therefore became the inheritance of Caleb the son
of Jephunneh the Kenizzite to this day, because he wholly followed the Lord
God of Israel. Caleb drove out the three sons of Anak from there: Sheshai,
Ahiman, and Talmai. (Joshua 14:13-14; 15:14).*

We're not told the details of Joshua's conquest of Hebron.   The
only specific is that he drove out three giants, Sheshai, Ahiman and
Talman, sons of Anak Perhaps that is enough, because forty-five years
earlier the fear of the giants convinced ten of the spies it would be
impossible to conquer Canaan: "We seemed like grasshoppers in our
own eyes, and we looked the same to them" (Numbers 13:33).

There were giants in my own Hebron, Mexico City.   Threats
by leaders among the Baptists had convinced me at first to tell the
Board of Trustees it would be impossible to relocate the seminary to
that city. I saw God drive out those giants, one by one. There was a
denominational giant who declared in an open meeting his disposition
to "shed his blood" if necessary, to keep us out of the city. He came
to a disastrous end, first dismissed from the pastorate of his church on
the accusation of adultery, and later dying of cancer. The theological
education giant, president of another seminary, who moved heaven
and earth to keep us out, simply disappeared.

I'll never forget the drama of a special service in the seminary chapel some months after our arrival. We invited the churches of the area to join us in a service of thanksgiving for God's blessings. The chapel was packed with some six hundred people, representatives of twenty-seven churches. I was asked to bring the message. I simply told the history of God's providence in this monumental accomplishment. The chapel was saturated with goodwill and joy. Not one negative comment. The giants were gone!

Our arrival in Mexico City in the midst of the rainy season reminded us of the enormous contrast to the desert of northern Mexico. I wrote in my diary: "We left Torreon in the midst of a drought. It has been raining here continually. There has been only one day without rain since our arrival, so the workers are unable to do anything outside." We laid boards in the sea of mud, and pushed desks, pianos, beds, and files over them.

We began the new school year with a substantial increase in enrolment, and as the months passed, celebrated the completion of a beautiful circular music building, a library, a five-story condominium and a duplex for faculty housing, plus two buildings with apartments for married students. Month after month I reviewed our construction budget, and marveled. At the time of the approval of the seminary relocation we had no funds for construction, and no specific promises from the Foreign Mission Board. Then the miracle began to unfold, and in the next few years well over half a million dollars was appropriated by the Board. One year after the completion of our construction, a sobering "coincidence" occurred: the Foreign Mission Board initiated a new policy of no more expenditure for construction, except for missionary housing. If we had delayed our decision to relocate, there would have been no money available. A true miracle of God's timing!

Another unexpected miracle was the disposition of the properties we had left behind in Torreon. We were doubtful about the possibility of selling those buildings. Torreon was a farming center with a depressed economy. Who would have use for dormitories, a dining hall, a library, in the middle of a desert? But God made use of the acquisitive capitalistic spirit of a businessman in Monterrey. He wanted to establish a hardware store in Torreon, and after a survey of the city, decided our property was ideally located for his project.

The principal incentive for our move to Mexico City was the mission opportunity. We were pleased when, soon after our arrival, churches began to engage the students for missionary projects. I saw an opportunity for the seminary family to work together on meeting our neighbors. The seminary was surrounded by an attractive middle class community of thousands of new homes occupied by people who had cut ties with their families in other cities and moved to jobs in the capital. Within a few months after our arrival the seminary staff approved a plan for presenting ourselves to these people: we contracted with the local Baptist book store to be their agents in a door-to-door sale of Christian literature.

We were delighted by the friendly reception by our new neighbors. Among these was an attractive red-headed young housewife I met as a seminary student and I were knocking on doors. We found her working in her flower garden, and introduced ourselves. She smiled. "What a coincidence, just a couple of weeks ago I began attending a home Bible study." She invited us in, served us coffee, and listened with intense interest as we explained God's plan of salvation. About a year later she and her husband were baptized into the new church meeting in the seminary chapel.

(The providence of God continued! Tomas, the husband, who had a doctorate in psychology, became Director of Training for American Express in Latin America. They were active in the planting of several new churches. In 2001 he accepted our invitation to join the staff of the Christian counseling center *Armonia Familiar.* Later he became the pastor of a church I helped plant in Lomas of Chapultepec, a wealthy section of Mexico City. More of that later.)

At the end of our first school term, in May of 1975, I felt led to dedicate myself to exploring missionary opportunities in Mexico City. I submitted my resignation. The seminary board refused to accept it. After a month of dialogue, we reached a compromise: I would divide my time between the direction of the seminary and work in the field.

As the months unfolded I could see God's blessings on this new arrangement.

Weekends I worked with a group of students in a project we called "New Horizons".

I enlisted eight students with experience in a variety of skills, such as teaching children with learning problems, diet and cookery, the repair of small electrical household appliances, and family counseling. In a poor subdivision near the seminary we went door-to-door offering our services free to the households, and sharing our testimony. As the weeks passed, a number of people received Christ. At mid-year eighty-five people were present for a service in which six were baptized. Later, a church was organized.

The local Association named me missions coordinator for the quadrant of Mexico City surrounding the seminary, where a dozen Baptist churches were located. Out of this came one of the most exciting missions experiences of my life.

Once a month the pastors of my sector met for breakfast, and we spent a couple of hours in prayer and discussion of strategy for new work. One Saturday in August of 1976 I shared with them a dream born in my heart a few days earlier: the federal government had just completed, about fifteen minutes east of the seminary, a huge housing complex. Known as *El Rosario,* it had been built by the federal Social Security Institute for minimum wage families. Some one hundred fifty thousand people had recently moved into this new facility, and there was no church of any kind. Why not work together as seminary and churches to plant a new work? The pastors agreed to pray about this possibility. In our next meeting they voted unanimously to enter into the project.

In October we convoked a rally of delegates from the churches in my sector. Some thirty people committed themselves to weekend visitation. We initiated the project in November, adding a dozen seminary students to the church volunteers. We followed a systematic plan: beginning at the ground floor of each building, we knocked on the doors of the four apartments fronting the entrance, then climbed the stairs to the five floors one by one, until every apartment in each building had been visited. We offered a five-lesson study on the book of John. Our challenge: if they would answer the questions in the booklet, we would return the following Saturday to review their answers and give them a grade.

As the weeks passed, we could discern a pattern in the response. On an average, one out of ten families accepted our booklet. Of these, in one out of ten families, at least one person received Christ. One convert out of hundred visits is a lot of work! But when your field has ten thousand families, it turns out to be a pretty good harvest.

My co-director in the project was Roberto Mendoza. A layman, owner of a trucking company, Roberto loved God with all his heart and had the gift of an incredible faith. His dream was to pastor the church that would be the fruit of this mission effort. He sold me on an ambitious plan to climax the campaign: we would acquire a large tent, and in March, dedicate an entire week to evangelistic services. The question was, where would we place the tent? We discarded the possibility of having the campaign in the apartment complex, because this was government property. "Just leave it to me," Roberto assured me, "I'll find a place"

By February we gave up on renting a vacant lot next to the complex; its owner was an active member of the Knights of Columbus. When Roberto informed me of this discouraging development he added that God had given him an alternative that was even better. We would pitch our tent in a parking lot in *El Rosario.*

"But Roberto," I protested, "that's impossible, the Government will never give us permission to hold evangelistic services on federal property. The Constitution forbids such a thing!"

"My brother, don't you believe God is stronger than the Federal Government?"

What could I say? We set aside a week in mid-March when we would suspend seminary classes and dedicate ourselves, staff and student body, to the evangelistic campaign.

First we needed to buy a tent. I checked in the yellow pages and contacted a company that manufactured tents. The owner visited me in my office, and informed me that their price for a tent seating 400 people was $2,000. (I did not yet know where that money would come from.) Then he asked a question I had hoped he wouldn't: what did we plan to do with the tent? I had already decided how I would answer that question, if he asked it. My first impulse had been to devise a fictitious answer, but I decided the Lord wanted me to tell the man the truth and trust in Him. So I did.

A voice whispered in my heart, "This guy's a fanatic Catholic and he's going to walk out on you!"

The man sat studying me for half a minute. Then, clearing his throat, he said. "Let me tell you a story. I grew up in the state of Zacatecas, where my father owned a copper mine. Quite often we had the problem of a foreman who mistreated the men working in the mine and took advantage of their wives and daughters. But as time passed I saw that foremen who belonged to evangelical churches were different. They treated their men justly and respected their families. So I promised God that one day I would repay the evangelical community for such integrity. Sir, I believe the time has come to keep my promise. I'm going to let you have a tent free of charge!"

I stared at the man, my mouth agape.

Soon February was half over and Roberto still hadn't secured the permit. Each time I inquired he assured me that he was cultivating the friendship of the director of the housing complex, and the permit would be forthcoming.

The second Monday of March arrived. The campaign was scheduled to begin the following Saturday. That afternoon Roberto came by my office. "Roberto," I told him, "if we fail to get the permit we'll have to call off the campaign. That means that by Friday we'll have to advise the students classes will continue as usual next week."

"Don't worry, Brother. I'll have the permit in your hands by Friday at the latest."

Wednesday came, and Thursday. Still no permit. Friday morning the teachers came to me one by one, brows furrowed, inquiring what we were going to do. When I told them Roberto was sure he'd have the permit before the day was over, they'd leave shaking their heads.

At two o'clock Roberto strode into my office, grinning from ear to ear, and deposited on my desk a document with the letterhead of the federal government, giving us permission to occupy parking lot #5 Sunday through Sunday the third week of March.

The campaign was a resounding success. Each day the seminary staff and student body, plus a couple of dozen people from the churches made follow up visits throughout the community. In the afternoons we had vacation Bible school for the children. Each night the tent was packed, and a gifted young evangelist brought a Gospel message. Every night dozens of people came forward professing faith in Christ.

Saturday night as we were about to leave, Felipe came up to me with a worried look on his face. I had led Felipe and his wife to Christ earlier in the week, and we had engaged him as the night watchman.

"*Señor* Carter," he said, "I cannot stay here tonight."

"Why not, Felipe?"

"Our son Carlos came home from school this afternoon and told us his teacher had warned his class that the priest enlisted people at mass this morning to burn down the tent tonight."

I wasn't too surprised by Felipe's scary report. The priest of the neighboring village of San Pablo had appeared several nights and stood for a while at the door of the tent, his face angry.

Then I heard myself saying: "Don't worry, Felipe, the Lord has stationed angels with flaming swords all around the tent, and those people won't be able to get through!"

The little man turned and made a circuit of the tent, looking for those angels with flaming swords. He returned shaking his head, but said nothing more about leaving.

The next afternoon as I approached the area I checked the sky, wondering if I would see a wisp of smoke. Nothing. But when I arrived at the tent, my pulse quickened. Several dozen women were gathered out front, yelling at the timid young seminarian standing at the entrance. "Take down this tent right now, or we'll tear it down with our own hands!"

I slipped inside and sat praying. A little boy appeared. "Don't worry, *Senor,*" he said, "they're just mad because so many are coming every night."

That night we closed out on a note of resounding victory. Almost three hundred people had come forward during the week.

Roberto did become pastor of the new congregation, and they have prospered through the years. The last I heard they had mothered half a dozen new churches.

Now that we were settled in Mexico City, opportunities opened up for improvement in the seminary's relations with the churches. I was invited to bring a series of lectures on the Holy Spirit at the annual pastors' conference. Each year, before the annual meeting of the Mexican Baptist Convention the pastors met for two days.

This was the largest meeting of Baptist pastors all year, and an invited speaker addressed them on matters that were of interest at that time. I was invited to speak on the Holy Spirit. Because of the accusations that had been directed at the seminary in response to our emphasis on the Holy Spirit, there was a large attendance. I gave three lectures of an hour and a half each, and at the close of each lecture opportunity was afforded for questions and comments. There was intense interest in the question of the gifts of the Spirit. I did my best to show that the Scriptures provide no basis for the commonly held opinion that the so-called "miraculous gifts" were to be discontinued at the end of the Apostolic Age. I affirmed that all the gifts of the Spirit are available for Christians in our day. This includes the gift of tongues. I showed there was no biblical basis for the concept that the gift of tongues is the sign of "the baptism in the Spirit." I gave an exposition of the fourteenth chapter of First Corinthians, affirming the legitimacy of the gift of tongues, and at the same time emphasizing its limitations, affirming my opinion that if Paul were present in today's confused theological world, he would probably recommend that this gift be exercised in private. Also, I shared a truth I had encountered in research for my Th.D. dissertation: Biblical salvation is an integral concept that includes body, mind, soul and spirit,

That same year I preached the sermon at the annual meeting of the Mexico City association of Baptist churches, speaking on the relation between doctrine and tradition.

My experiences in Torreon and Yucatan had convinced me that non-biblical traditions were one of the major impediments to church growth in Mexico. I recounted an experience in Torreon: when I presented to my church three recent converts from the Albia mission, the pastor informed me he was unable to baptize them because he was not ordained. Incredible! He had been pastor of the church for four years, yet he could not administer the ordinances that were a part of the church's regular business because his fellow pastors had not yet laid hands on him. I had also faced this problem as missionary in the Yucatan peninsula. In my sermon I pointed out that most of the practices Jesus condemned had to do with traditions established by the Jewish elders. I used an orange to illustrate the relation between doctrine and tradition: tradition is related to doctrine the same way that the peeling is related to the meat of the orange. The peeling has two purposes: it gives form to the orange and provides protection. But the peeling is disposable. In the same way, when tradition no longer serves the purpose it had when it was established, it should be discarded.

In 1975 the Baptist Spanish Publishing House in El Paso published my book, *Vivamos en el Espiritu Cada Dia* ("Let's Live in the Spirit Every Day"). There were two editions of the book, and it had wide acceptance throughout Latin America.

By this time, I found within myself a deep peace such as I had never before experienced. Not that the problems had ceased. The seminary faculty was engaged in a revision of our plan of studies, with the purpose of reducing our *Licenciatura* program from four to five years. This produced tense moments, as we decided which professor was to give up one or more of his courses. The company making pews for the chapel dragged out their work for nearly a year. An organ donated by the First Baptist Church of Lafayette, Louisiana provoked importation difficulties, then a long search for someone capable of installing it. The federal government demanded $25,000 in taxes on the new buildings. And of course, there were always students struggling with personal and family problems. But these crises didn't produce the desperation that I had experienced in years past.

One reason was the discovery of a spiritual discipline that I entitled, *The Five Dimensions of Faith.* It became part of a seminary course on the cultivation of the spiritual life, and was included in a manual I wrote entitled, *Disciplina Cristiana* ("Christian Discipline"). I have practiced this discipline daily for more than thirty years, and it continues to be a source of peace and inspiration.

I. DECIDE Psalm 118:24; Romans 5:1-5,11
I awake declaring my decision to accept the day as God's gift, and to rejoice in it. This dimension reminds me that, consciously or unconsciously, from the moment I awake, I decide what my attitude will be that day.

II. DESIRE Psalm 84
My day is going to be determined, in large part, by what I desire. From the first thing in the morning, I tune my heart and soul to desire the Lord.

III. DEPEND Isaiah 41:30; Romans 8:28-39
My day will be unstable if I depend on my emotions, my
circumstances, my works, or the opinions of people. But if I
depend only on God's promises and God's love, no care in this
world can touch me.

IV. DARE Mark 11:22-24; John 14:12; 1 John 5:14; Jeremiah 33:3
Christ left a large number of incredible promises. Each day I
program my heart with a number of these promises, and upon
them I hang some impossible dreams that I trust God to fulfill.

V. DON'T DOUBT James 1:5-7; Psalm 103:1-5
No matter what I determine in my heart, and no matter how
pure my desires may be, the devil will try to plant insinuations
and doubts. My human mind is programmed to doubt, but
I can reprogram my mind by so filling it with God's promises that
I trust in as a matter of course. Each morning I end my spiritual
discipline with Psalm 103:1-5, a marvelous song of praise and
affirmation of God's total care.

Chapter Twenty
Wholehearted Obedience
1977-1979

*I, however, followed my God **wholeheartedly**.... You have followed the Lord my God **wholeheartedly**.... Then Joshua blessed Caleb and gave him Hebron as his inheritance. So Hebron has belonged to Caleb the son of Jephunneh the Kenizzite ever since because he followed the Lord God of Israel, **wholeheartedly**. Joshua 14:8,9,13-14. (NIV)*

Three times in the same chapter the word "wholeheartedly" is used to describe Caleb's service to the Lord. The word is used for no other character in the Old Testament. Matthew Henry suggests that "wholeheartedly" means four things: (1) Caleb followed the Lord universally; whatever the Lord told him to do, he did. (2) He followed the Lord fully, sincerely, he was no hypocrite. (3) Caleb followed the Lord cheerfully, without disputing. (4) Caleb followed the Lord constantly, without declining. In all the forty-five years he waited for the fulfillment of God's promises, not once did he join the rebellions that broke out from time to time.

Reading my diary, I can see that my desire has been to serve the Lord wholeheartedly. However, I at times have tended to confuse wholeheartedly with obsessively. Because I inherited the genes of my five foot-seven dad, and not the six-foot-one genes of my uncles, I've always felt the need to prove myself. I remember my freshman gym class at Louisiana College. The coach told us that our final exam would be pushups. Looking at the brawny football guys around me I decided I was not going to let any of them do more pushups than I. Sixteen of us began together, as the coach counted off: "One … two … three …" By fifty only five of us were left. At seventy we were down to three. At eighty it was only me and a huge fullback. Eighty-one … eighty-two ….

"Pat, Pat! … " When I came to, the coach was kneeling over me, shaking me. My first words were, "Did I win?"

I suspect I did a lot of missionary "pushups," trying to be the best missionary since Paul, never quite satisfied with my efforts. A few excerpts from my diary during a six-month period:

This has been a full week. I left Sunday morning and flew to Yucatan, where I preached twice at Merida's First Church. Monday through Wednesday noon I was in Vallodolid at a pastor's retreat. I was the only one on the program, so I was really busy -- spoke a total of seven hours. Flew back Wednesday night. I was very, very tired, but was very busy at the seminary the rest of the week because I had been out so much. When I got back Wednesday Evelyn was in a bad mood. Talked for two days about my neglecting her. The next Tuesday I fell into one of my nervous crises and was in bed the rest of that day and all day Wednesday. I have had trouble getting to sleep at night.… I spent all last week in Costa Rica and returned Monday. Preached about ten times. I came back with the start of two ulcers in my mouth, and one on my lip has been burning like fire for several days.… This past week was very hard. I had meetings every night and never seemed to quite catch up. I received a letter from one of the national professors accusing me of underpaying him, and demanding a raise. There was a lot of sickness among the students. Wednesday night I did the translating both in English and in Spanish at a meeting of the Baptist World Alliance at the First Baptist Church. By the time the week ended I was bone tired. Sunday at 9:00 A.M. I preached an evangelistic sermon at a public bandstand, then on to the church to teach my class.

Still, this "obsessiveness" has had its positive side. There is something in my heart that has never been satisfied just to do the expected. I could have remained for a lifetime as a pastor in Louisiana, but my heart led us to California. I could have been satisfied with a Masters in Theology, but my heart led us to stake everything on moving to the seminary in Fort Worth to seek a doctorate in Philosophy. We could have remained in the States in good pastorates, but my heart led us to Mexico. Once there, I could have settled comfortably into the academic life of the seminary, but I was always being challenged by new missionary opportunities. I could have been satisfied with a mediocre spirituality, but my heart has always been pushing me to penetrate further into the world of the Holy Spirit and prayer. In this pursuit, early in 1977 I began the practice of spending time in heart-searching prayer each night before going to bed:

> A number of times the Lord has spoken to me in late-night prayers in recent months. Twice this week, as I could not sleep, I prayed, and the Lord spoke to me. He reprimanded me for my preoccupation with self. Told me that what pleases him is that I glorify him and praise him…. The Lord is moving in my understanding of how to cooperate with time and reality in my life. I've learned to make a list of things that, if I got them done, I would be satisfied, then another list of "advance" and a third list of "advance plus". I stop every hour or so and just relax completely, reminding myself that time belongs to the Lord, and that he is giving me enough time each day to do what he wants me to do. I finished the past week, a very busy week, without any tension at all.

I also began to receive word from the Lord through dreams. In April, 1977 I read the book *Something More* by Catherine Marshall. One chapter emphasized how, in the Bible, God spoke to his people through dreams, and we should expect the same. The key to understanding a dream, said Mrs. Marshall, is to interpret it as a parable. I was impressed, and asked God to speak to me through dreams. A couple of nights later I had two dreams in succession. In the first I was standing in line with a group of young women, and someone passed by and said with a smile, "Ask them if their dresses are long enough." I smiled back because, in fact, all of them wore dresses that were so long they touched the ground. When I awoke, this interpretation came to me: dress is used in the Bible as a symbol for covering the nakedness of unrighteousness. The long dresses were a parable of my obsession with "doing things" to the point of exhaustion in order to gain God's approval.

The next dream occurred just before I awoke, and was so intricate that I spent an hour working out its interpretation. I was in front of a housing complex playing with a little girl of about three and her younger brother. The little girl said, "I like you and want to marry you." Her little brother said, "Me too." I called over to a group of missionaries standing nearby and told them what the children said, and they smiled and clapped their hands. A moment later I looked down and the little girl was turning blue in the face. I opened her mouth and saw it was filled with paper. I pulled out a big wad and called to one of the missionaries to come and give her mouth-to-mouth resuscitation. He did, but she remained unconscious. I interpreted the dream as follows: the housing complex was *El Rosario,* where we were working to begin a church. The little girl represented El *Rosario I,* where we were doing follow up on the evangelistic campaign we had carried out earlier. Her little brother represented a neighboring complex, *Rosario II*, where we were planning to begin work the next week. When both children say they want to marry me, it represents my wish to continue in charge of the work. My telling other people what the children had said symbolized my desire for applause. The moment they applauded the child began to strangle. Breath is a symbol of the Holy Spirit. The Lord was telling me that the moment I began seeking glory for what He was doing, He would withdraw His Holy Spirit, and no amount of effort I might make would avail to give life to these projects.

In response to those dreams, I turned over the direction of the projects to Roberto Mendoza.

These experiences of God speaking to me through dreams continued for several months. In June I read *God, Dreams and Revelation,* by Morton T. Kelsey. The night I completed the book I had a strikingly prophetic dream. I was driving my car, with my parents as passengers, when suddenly I had to take a detour. I let out an exclamation of disgust. But after a few moments I parked the car and we took a walk up a grassy hill, remarking on how beautiful it was because of the abundant rain. I wrote the following interpretation:

In my journey through life, I am going to have to take a detour because of something that happens to my parents. At first I will be displeased, but after a time I will realize the detour has allowed me to "park my car" and enjoy a very pleasant, fruitful time in which the Holy Spirit (abundant rain) produces fruit.

This dream was fulfilled several years later when, because of a heart attack my mother suffered, Evelyn and I took an emergency furlough. After Mother passed away, we remained for three months so I could serve as interim pastor of the church my father had pastored for twenty-five years.

One summer day, when Evelyn was away on a visit with her sister Georgene in Oklahoma, I decided to spend all day seeking God's presence. In the afternoon, as I waited on the Lord, "words" suddenly gushed from my mouth for some ten minutes, without my being conscious of forming the sounds. At the same time I had the sensation of being touched, bringing healing to my body and my spirit. The effects of this encounter with the Holy Spirit remained with me for days.

These years of spiritual growth, besides bringing a new stability to my life, brought additional confirmation of God's guidance in the seminary. Enrolment climbed to more than 100, the highest in its history. Foreign Mission Board appropriations for building had dried up, and we faced the probability of having to turn down married students for the lack of housing. God placed in my heart the need of acquiring land and building more apartments. I marveled as money accumulated, including a gift from my father, a loan from the church in Krotz Springs, and another gift from the daughters of A.C. Watkins, the missionary founder of the seminary in 1903. By mid-1979 construction was underway.

In September, 1977 we left on a 9-month furlough, without the slightest intuition of the storm that would break at the seminary. We hadn't been gone long when Greg, who had been named interim president, called to tell me he had received a petition from the students demanding he fire Arturo, the administrator. This man, a seminary graduate, was quite efficient, but not gifted in diplomacy. As the weeks passed, conditions worsened. Greg fired Arturo. Arturo protested to the Board of Trustees, and convinced them he had been mistreated. I began receiving different versions from diverse people on the seminary staff. Greg was interviewing students, making recordings of their complaints and presenting the recordings to the Board. I began to dread the headaches that awaited me when I returned.

Meanwhile, I was having many opportunities for preaching and teaching. I gave the Bible study for Foreign Missions Week at Ridgecrest. I was on the staff at Louisiana College, teaching two classes in philosophy and one in Spanish. After preaching at a large west Texas church, the pastor, a friend from seminary days, asked me if I might be interested in the church he pastored. He was in his mid-forties, felt the need to make a change, and was sending out resumes. Discouraged by the problems at the seminary, I entertained the possibility that God might open a door to a pastorate. I had asked myself more than once what would have happened had I remained in the States. I loved the pastorate, had the spiritual gift of preaching and teaching, and wherever I spoke was encouraged by the response of the congregations. For several months I nourished the hope of a new beginning in a challenging pastorate.

But the more alarming reports I received from Mexico City, the more I became convinced that I must return. I had invested so much in that institution. How could I abandon it at this time of need? And if I did, could I expect God's blessing on my new ministry?

In July we returned. A truce had been called in the seminary warfare, awaiting my arrival. I talked at length with all involved, and recommended to the Board of Trustees that we give Arturo a leave of absence. I assured him I valued him, and would like for him to remain at the seminary, but insisted he use these months to examine his personality problems and make changes. Meanwhile, I would find someone to administer the dormitories and the dining hall.

In the first Faculty meeting I had an unpleasant surprise. One of the teachers declared he no longer had confidence in me, that I was a hypocrite and a poor leader. That hurt! But because of having saturated the past months in prayer, I lost no sleep. In the next Faculty meeting my colleague asked my forgiveness and became one of my strongest allies.

In August, when the students arrived, I informed them of the changes that would be made. The underlying problem, I insisted, was spiritual. We were going to give major emphasis during the school year to repentance, openness with one another and prayer for God's healing. We would set aside Thursday nights for an open forum. Both students and staff would be expected to attend. It would be a time for testimonies, confession of sin and prayer for one another. I had opened a prayer room in the administration building, and it would be available twenty-four hours a day. The first Monday of each month the staff would meet together to pray. I would keep my office door open to anyone who wanted to come and talk with me.

The response was remarkable. The Thursday night forums were well attended, by both students and faculty. Within weeks we began to see a great difference. Complaints disappeared, students were talking with one another and with their teachers. It turned out to be the happiest school year of all the twenty years I spent at the seminary. We followed the same plan the next two years, and they were also times of peace. More and more I gave myself to the pastoral role. I found that this practice served to prevent the rebellions that produced turmoil in the student body. For instance, in the spring term of 1979, a rebellious spirit was being created by three student leaders. I called them in one by one, confronted them with the problems they were causing, and each of them asked forgiveness and became elements of blessing.

In later years, talking with graduates of the seminary, many have told me that these were the "golden years" of that institution. Besides a remarkable spiritual unity, we had the blessing of a well-qualified, stable staff, both missionary and national. Dr. Steve Hicks was Academic Dean and professor of Hebrew and Old Testament. Dr. Guy Williamson taught Greek and New Testament, and when he transferred to a seminary in Costa Rica, was followed by Dr. Richard Garrett, an equally qualified man. Dr. Robert Fricke taught Theology. Dr. J.T. Owens and his pianist wife Charlotte did a remarkable job of taking students from all over Mexico, many from very small congregations, hardly any with musical training, and molding them into a choir of some sixty voices. J.T. was a ruthless sergeant who brooked no whispers during the daily hour-long choir practice, and did more than any other of us to instill a sense of discipline into our students. I had the exhausting privilege of accompanying them on tours of Mexico and Texas. They were our best agent of public relations. Dr. Peter Larson, on loan from another mission board, was professor of Church Growth. Missionary Donald Simms was the popular professor of preaching. Missionary James Short taught Pastoral Care. Dr. Don Sewell was with us for several years, before joining the staff of the Texas Baptist Convention. Several missionary wives were invaluable part-time teachers. Besides the missionaries we had a number of nationals on the staff, including Francisco Almanza, professor of Christian education and Arturo Alarcon, Administrator. Half a dozen pastors taught part-time. I consider that the greatest honor of my life was to spend twenty years as a colleague of these dedicated men and women of God, seventeen years their leader. We didn't always agree on everything, but I never had occasion to doubt their dedication, integrity and love.

Evelyn and I found ourselves spending more time in phone calls and prayer for the family. We began to see deterioration in the health of my mother and father. Dad lost the sight in one eye, and had less and less inclination to spend time in the woodworking shop that had been his major avocation. He remarked on one visit that he was just "marking time" until his passing. The children were involved in work, growing families and relationships. We were disappointed when Carol and Mario moved to a pastorate in Juarez. This meant we had little opportunity to spend time with our charming little grandson, David, and later we were not present for the birth of Esther Elizabeth. Linda and Charles, with their two small children, Victoria and Johnathon, were struggling financially, and were not attending church regularly. In 1978 we began to receive reports of problems between David and Vicki. Just before Christmas David called us, talked a long time about the lack of compatibility with his wife, and hinted at a divorce. I exploded and told him that we had already lived through one of his divorces, and in no case would we accept another, that if he divorced Vicki I would no longer consider him my son.

We traveled to Mom and Dad's in Louisiana for the Christmas holidays. Christmas Eve David and Vicki arrived, and we prepared to travel the forty miles to Lafayette, where Linda and her family lived. David suggested I go with him in his car and let the others travel in my car.

As soon as we were on the highway, I apologized for my words on the phone and said, "David, we don't want another divorce, but whatever happens, we love you, and you can count on us."

David slammed a fist into the steering wheel and said with much feeling, "Thanks, Dad. I told Vicki when we left Dallas I was going to talk with you, and if you still felt the same way we'd just turn around and go back home."

Things didn't improve in the marriage, however. A few months later David moved to an apartment. All his phone calls were quite negative until November, when he said Vicki and he were talking more.

As the year ended I was aware that I still had not worked out a healthy balance between my commitment to my work and Evelyn's need to feel that she was important to me. Besides, I had advanced in my journey toward a healthy "wholeheartedness," but still had a long way to go.

Chapter Twenty-One
An Ending and a New Beginning
1980-1983

The Bible gives only faint glimpses of Caleb's family, and most of this is in the genealogical tables of First Chronicles. Caleb's first wife's name was Azubah, "desolation". If Caleb married her in Egypt, as is almost certain, the name probably expresses the desperation of her slave parents. She bore him three sons, of whom we know nothing. His second wife was Ephrath ("fruitfulness"). Their son, born Hur, distinguished himself as an assistant of Aaron the high priest. Ephrath and Hur must have died during the desert wanderings, as did everyone else twenty years or older, except for Joshua and Caleb (1Chronicles 2:18-19).

The early 1980's were a time of endings and beginnings for our family. Evelyn and I were very pleased, when in 1980 David and Vicki ended a period of separation, and agreed to let God be at the center of their marriage. During the separation, with the help of her sister Denise, Vicki had drawn closer to the Lord. Soon after they reunited, she wrote us that she had learned her duty was to give, demanding nothing of others. They became active in church, and in a visit in June 1981, David took me one Saturday morning to a meeting he attended weekly with a group of six Christian men. Soon we were advised of another new beginning: after nine years of marriage Vicki was pregnant.

A beautiful baby, Ashley, was born in 1982.

Late one night in February, 1980 the phone rang. It was Charles, Linda's husband, telling us that Linda had left him. Would Evelyn please come and get the children? The next day Evelyn flew to Lafayette, Louisiana and got Charles and Linda together. Linda told Charles that she was no longer able to take his neglect and verbal abuse. Obviously he didn't love her, so she was giving him the opportunity to begin a new life without her. When, to her surprise, he asked for forgiveness, told her he did love her, and pleaded with her to return home, she agreed. This new beginning seemed to be working reasonable well in the following years. Another son, Andrew, was born in 1982. Charles' photography studio in Lafayette prospered, but unfortunately, the family was not prospering spiritually. Linda was now trying to get into the habit of taking the children to Sunday School and church, but Charles was not interested. As for Carol and Mario, they and their two little children, David and Elizabeth (Liz) were doing well in the new beginning they had made in Juarez. Soon, both of them began what was to be long careers as writers and editors in the Baptist Spanish Publishing House in El Paso.

During this time came the sad ending of the life of one of my parents. In 1981 it became obvious that Dad was beginning the process of passing from this world into the next. He was 84, and becoming ever thinner and more feeble. In July he confessed to mother one morning that he had fallen in his woodworking shop, and that it took him ten minutes to get back on his feet. A few months later he fell again and broke his hip and was admitted to the hospital. For two months mother kept a daily vigil by his bedside, until he passed away in April, 1982. One of the most beautiful memories I have is the all-night vigil in the fellowship hall of the church where he had been pastor for twenty-five years. We sat and nursed cups of coffee while the people exchanged stories of their experiences with Daddy, many of them provoking uproarious laughter. For the tenth time I heard the story of the last funeral Daddy preached: lying in a casket before the pulpit was the body of a notorious hard drinker and womanizer. The church was packed with people who had not been to any church in years. Daddy's first words were: "I'm not going to talk about this monkey whose body lies before us. I'm going to spend my time explaining to the rest of you how not to end up where he has gone."

Evelyn repeats a private proverb every time there's a funeral: "Always after a death a baby is born." Her proverb proved doubly true that year. The day after Daddy's funeral, Linda gave birth to her Andrew.

From the time of returning from a furlough in 1980, I had the intuition that I was moving toward closing out my ministry in the seminary. Now there was no desire to return to the United States. I felt that God had plans for me to enter into a church planting project in Mexico City. On January 5, 1982, I wrote a summary of the previous year, and listed "four spiritual truths that have become very real to me":

1. It is more blessed to give than to receive. I must give myself without limit, expecting in return neither appreciation nor praise, not even understanding. In this I will be discovering the essence of the Christ life and will have fellowship with Him.

2. I am worthy of the job I hold. God gave me that job, and I have no need to apologize for it.

3. If I have God's approval, I already have the best. Anything else that may come my way will be extra, and therefore I should not seek it or expect it.

4. I must see things as God sees them: "God calls the things that are not as if they were." Everything that God wants me to be, the seminary to be, others to be, He sees as already accomplished, and I should see these things in the same way.

By this time, I could count many answers to prayer. In February, 1976 I began a list of answers to prayer, and by April, 1980 the list had grown to forty-eight, many of the answers worthy of being described as miraculous. In my personal life, with occasional exceptions, I had learned how to be at peace in the midst of trials. My work at the seminary had now become mainly pastoral and character-building. God had given me a fruitful ministry of intercession. I had begun to share with Paul his experience of warfare for the souls and lives of men through prayer. Again and again, when I was interceding for someone, the burden became so heavy that I found myself praying with groans and sobs, sometimes for hours. Most of the students had become convinced of the importance of prayer and openness with one another, so at their insistence, the custom of Thursday night round-tables continued.

On the other hand, I found myself feeling like a marathoner who has passed the twenty-mile mark and is longing to reach the goal and an opportunity to rest. I was bone-tired of having to please others, convince others, change minds, bear disappointments with people, feel responsible for the spiritual growth of persons who at times seemed to have little interest in growth. I found myself struggling with the temptation to cynicism. Who on earth was worthy of my confidence? How was I to continue to believe the promises of people when so many who made promises broke them?

For instance, the married student to whom I lent money so he could pay a pressing bill. He promised to sell a camera he owned and repay me. He never repaid me nor even bothered to ask my forgiveness. I watched as he graduated from the seminary and became the pastor of a prominent church ... and wondered .... There was the pastor who was an ardent critic of the seminary. We called him in and made peace with him, and he promised to work closely with us in the future. A few weeks later word came that he had spoken badly of the seminary in a meeting of pastors .... There were colleagues, honorable men, who disagreed with my philosophy of seminary education, and I was never able to convince them. We continued to work together and treat one another with respect, but we were hardly a team.

Then there was the frustration of attempting to improve the financial situation of the seminary. Now that the National Baptist Convention of Mexico was responsible for the seminary, and our subsidy from the Foreign Mission Board was being reduced year by year, I felt compelled to promote a plan for endowment. With the approval of the Convention, we printed attractive "bonds" to be given to donors, and I enlisted men to help in the promotion. Rodolfo volunteered his help. A former high school boyfriend of our daughter Linda, Rodolfo was a brilliant young man who was moving ever higher in the banking world. He sought me out, committed himself to promote the endowment fund, even asked for office space in the seminary. Then Rodolfo simply disappeared, and I never heard from him again. Very similar was my experience with Carlos. A successful businessman, Carlos presented himself to me as an enthusiastic collaborator. He insisted we set a goal of two hundred million pesos, and promised to personally make a donation of a hundred thousand. Within months his enthusiasm dwindled to a trickle, then evaporated completely. By hard work and stubborn promotion, we did secure two million pesos in donations and placed them in a savings account in a Mexico City bank. Within a year there were two drastic devaluations of the peso, and the dollar value of the endowment was reduced by eighty percent.*

As the years passed, the stress of working with the National Baptist Convention never lessened. The situation reminded me of a couple I had counseled. They were in a second marriage, into which the wife brought a child from her first marriage. The stepfather adopted the child legally, but she remained a stepchild, never receiving the affection he gave to his blood children. In similar fashion, before our "marriage" with the Convention, the Convention struggled to support a seminary that had been founded by a beloved elderly missionary of an earlier generation. We, the "other seminary," were seen by many as rich and spoiled. Our seminary was later adopted by the Convention, but was a stepchild that never received heartfelt support.

In retrospect, I have had a difficult time explaining to myself the slow deterioration of Baptist work in Mexico after the decision to unify the work of the missionaries and nationals. As I recounted in an earlier chapter, God's providence in that decision was unmistakable. For a time after the union, the work prospered. But then, many of the old jealousies and criticisms returned. Only a small minority of the churches placed the Convention in their budgets. Several of the nationals who assumed the presidency of the seminary after my resignation were a disappointment. The first was welcomed with great enthusiasm. He seemed to be exactly the person needed because he had experience in education and was great at promotion. Within a few years he was accused of misappropriation of funds, and resigned. A merry-go-round ensued, as presidents endured a year or two and then left.

Then there was the unending stress of trying to keep peace with the students. In 1980 a group of five members of a large church in Mexico City enrolled in the seminary. Their pastor was quite unique, an immigrant from a Central American country, with such a philosophical bent to his sermons that they were often difficult to understand. He created in his young people the conviction that they were the "elite", so they enrolled in the seminary, not so much to learn as to educate their professors. The American teachers were scorned. The first day of her presence in my philosophy course, the only female among the five informed the class that I, as a foreigner, was incapable of teaching a class on the philosophy of Mexico. Before the school year ended we suspended four of the five.

But the major reason for feeling that the time had come for entering into a new ministry was not the problems, but the opening of a door. For several years Evelyn and I had been working with a new congregation a half-hour drive from the Seminary. We helped them obtain funds from the Foreign Mission Board for the purchase of property and the construction of a church building. The pastor was one of my ex-students. As a youth he had been a petty thief, until one day a widow caught him as he slipped into her house and was about to make off with her iron. Instead of calling the police, she talked to him about the Lord. He became her disciple, and eventually entered the seminary. Jose was an effective preacher and had a winning personality. Under his leadership the congregation grew to an attendance of 150. I counseled him on how to become more organized in his daily ministry. His response was spotty. The church became restless because of his lack of leadership. I became so exasperated that Evelyn and I decided to leave the church, rather than be a source of friction. He came to our home and begged us to remain, asking me to become his mentor. At his recommendation the church called me as associate pastor, and we enjoyed a period of peace.

My most satisfying ministry with the church was as counselor of the young people. I had always enjoyed working with youth, and in Torreon had been counselor of the young people of Calvary Church for several years. Here I invested a great deal of my time with the leaders of the youth group, Jorge and Esther. Both were university students, and their enthusiasm was like an electric current in our weekly meetings. Jorge, the praise leader for the Sunday morning service, had an engaging smile and a deep dedication to the Lord. Esther was a pretty, big-boned young woman with a restless personality. She had huge brown eyes that Jorge warned you could drown in. I spent time counseling with her because her heart had been broken by a former boy friend. Discouraged with what he perceived as lack of progress in their relationship, he married Esther's best friend. Esther felt betrayed, and her best friend became a despised enemy.

I also enjoyed the friendship of a dear little twelve-year- old named Iris. Our hearts were joined due to a remarkable coincidence. One weekend I traveled with the youth group to a Veracruz beach for a spiritual retreat. Late Friday afternoon, not long after our arrival, Evelyn called me from Mexico City with the news that my father had died. His death was not a surprise, but I had not expected it to happen so soon. My first impulse was to get into my car immediately and begin the five-hour drive back to Mexico City. But I was to preach that night. As I walked the beach and prayed, the thought came to me: what would my dad have said? I concluded he would have told me to preach my sermon first, and then return home. That's what I did. When I gave an invitation at the close, the only person to come forward was a teary little twelve-year old girl. I was touched, because her father had died of a heart attack just a week earlier.

After our return from the funeral I made a follow-up visit to Iris's home. She smiled happily when I offered to visit her for six Saturday mornings and prepare her for baptism. As I was leaving, a thought came to me. "Look, Iris," I said, "we have something in common. We lost our fathers at the same time. Maybe we could be special friends." She smiled and gave me a big hug. So began a friendship that continued until her marriage fifteen years later.

On one of my visits with Iris I acquired another special friend. Hope, her fifteen-year-old sister asked if she could talk with me. She had just broken up with her boyfriend, and this disappointment, added to the shock of her father's death, had plunged her into a deep depression. As the months passed she became an adopted daughter, and a mutual affection continues until this day.

One Sunday afternoon in July, 1982, in the weekly meeting of our youth group I spoke about witnessing to non-Christians. I closed with a proposition: why not plant a new church? I suggested we try something different. It was a common practice to begin a new work in the home of a church family living in another part of the city. Why not pray that God would open up a home, not of one of our members, but of a person we had never met? The idea excited them. We agreed to pray daily for the opening of a door. We began observing a monthly fast from Friday at sundown until Saturday at sundown, celebrating the end of the fast with a fellowship supper. The last Friday in December we traveled to nearby Cuernavaca for a weekend retreat, and spent the night in prayer. Saturday night I passed out slips of paper and asked each one to write what he felt about the progress of our project. Later, when the leaders reviewed the responses, we were impressed that everyone felt the Lord was about to answer our prayers for an open door.

Early in February Eduardo, a first-year seminary student, came to my office. He lived with his parents in Lomas de Chapultepec, one of the wealthiest areas of Mexico City. A neighbor had recently returned from a six-month stay in the United States, and while there had become a believer. Would I be interested in visiting her?

I accompanied him to a stately stone mansion a block off *Avenida Reforma*, a wide, tree-shaded boulevard that runs from downtown to the western edge of the city.

We were received by Norma, a stolid matron of about fifty and her attractive, smiling daughter Miriam. They told me a story that gave me chill bumps. Six months before, Norma, an interior director, had traveled to the United States under contract to a Mexican industrialist who was constructing a home on the shores of Lake Tahoe. While there she accepted the invitation of one of the subcontractors to a meeting in her home. It turned out to be a Bible study. A month later Miriam received a phone call from her mother: Norma had experienced an encounter with Jesus Christ and her life had been transformed. Miriam was terrified. Her mother had always been a very logical person, her feet firmly planted on *tierra firma*. How in the world had she fallen victim to a religious sect?

Miriam wanted to fly immediately to California and rescue her mother, but she couldn't. She was playing the lead in a production of *The Sound of Music* in a downtown theater. A month later, when the drama closed, she traveled to Lake Tahoe. Her mother invited her to attend the Bible study. To her astonishment, Miriam found herself convinced, and she also became an enthusiastic Christian. Miriam and her mother asked me if I would be interested in beginning a Bible study in their home. Since returning a couple of months before they had been attending a charismatic church, but were excited by the possibility that I, with a doctorate in theology, could become their mentor.

In subsequent visits we prayed together and studied the Bible. I was doubtful about their willingness to accept "Baptist doctrine," but they were convinced God had brought us together, and were ready to subject themselves to my teaching. In March we began weekly Bible studies in their home. From the beginning, the spacious living room was crowded with curious neighbors. Some nights there were not enough chairs, and people sat on the stately stairway that curved upward from the parlor to the second floor. No doubt about it, this was God's work! Not only had doors opened for the beginning of a new church, but this was a strata of society practically untouched by evangelicals.

By the end of the school year, Evelyn and I were convinced it was God's time to leave the seminary and initiate a new ministry.

What had I accomplished in twenty years invested in theological education? Until my entry into the faculty of the seminary in Torreon I had never been attracted by the seminary classroom, and much less by an administrative post. Yet, I'm certain this was God's will for me at the time. Why? For one thing, God had equipped me with a temperament apt for undertaking the risky task of the relocating of the seminary. And very early I had learned two lessons from my parents: first, God has a plan for our lives. We should seek that plan, understanding that we do not have the option of turning it down. Second, personal prayer and prayer support from others bring a dynamic into our lives that makes possible the impossible.

Reviewing my diary, I am impressed by how often I suffered stress, disappointment and feelings of defeat. Yet, aren't those words synonyms for struggle, an inevitable dimension of adventuring with God? Much of Paul's life had to do with persecution, imprisonment, and disappointment.

Was I a successful leader in theological education? The answer is shadowed with nuances. I learned one truth that I treasure to this day:

Theological education is not just depositing information in the mind of a student, but participation with God in the formation of the character of a servant.

How much can be accomplished in three or four years of seminary training? The Son of God dedicated three years of his life to twelve disciples, and at the end he seemed to have failed miserably. It did not take long for me to appreciate the tendency of professors who have spent many years of our lives acquiring doctorates to feel that our major task is to pass the information we have accumulated to the people sitting in our classroom. It's so much more than that!

In the third year of my presidency I spent a couple of weeks as a consultant to the Baptist Convention of Guatemala. They were in the process of a drastic revision of their theological education, influenced by the Presbyterians of that country. Their Christian neighbors had abandoned the institutional approach and gone entirely too theological education by extension. I returned determined to lead our faculty into a more diverse approach. We began to place major emphasis on a non- residential plan, offering night classes to people who worked by day. Also, we appointed a fulltime director of theological education by extension. He led us in preparing guidebooks that could be used both for individual study and in teaching centers in churches and associations. This approach encouraged the multiplication of theological institutes across the nation. Also, I was convinced that the seminary in Mexico City should specialize in offering advanced training for exceptional students drawn from regional institutes. One thing had been evident for decades: it is impossible for one or two seminaries to provide personnel for all the churches in Mexico.

At this time, after more than twenty years since my resignation, I can see three long-range impacts of those twenty years I spent at the seminary. First, the seminary graduates have brought a profound change in worship style of the churches. What was angrily rejected when it was first introduced in the seventies, a more heart- felt worship, is now common across the country. Second, I still hear from pastors that my definition of salvation as including body as well as spirit changed their lifestyle. When I encounter ex-students they speak humorously of my taking them out for a run at 6:00 A.M., and afterward challenging them to join me in fifty pushups. Third, a significant segment of ex-students no longer regard Baptist tradition as of primary importance, and seek rather the rule of the Holy Spirit in their churches. A recent letter from my daugther Carol encouraged me:

> Your influence has a lot more to do than just with the worship and the denomination. I know countless pastors who were your students who now have successful churches that thrive in the freedom of the Holy Spirit. They all talk about the seed that, because of your emphasis on the Spirit-led life, you planted in their life to not be satisfied with a status quo spiritual life; you helped them to be open to the "more," and this has not only blessed them, but thousands of others, since these are growing churches.

* Several years after my departure from the seminary the board of trustees "appropriated" the endowment fund for current expenses. This breach of ethics saddened me. We had promised the donors that the capital would remain untouchable, and only the interest would be used for current expenses.

Chapter Twenty-Two
Wheat Mixed With Tares
1983-1984

Caleb learned not to depend upon men! Of the eleven who had accompanied him in spying out Canaan only one remained faithful to the vision of conquering that forbidding land. Then, for forty years in the wilderness he witnessed the slow passing away of a great horde of unhappy, complaining people whom God had cursed because of their unfaithfulness.

One of the most important skills of leadership is discerning who is worthy of trust and who is not. And not becoming a victim of people who disappoint us. Jesus practiced this from the very beginning of his ministry:

> Now when He was in Jerusalem at the Passover, during the feast, many believed in His name when they saw the signs which he did. But Jesus did not commit Himself to them, because He knew all men, and had no need that anyone should testify of man, for He knew what was in man. (John 2:23-25)

As mentioned in the previous chapter, one of the human motivations of my leaving the presidency of the seminary was the attraction of no longer being in a position of having to please people. But I was leaving an institution where everyone I dealt with   had been nurtured in a

216

Christian setting. Did I expect it to be easier out in the world, where I would work with persons who had never experienced the grace of God?

I entered into this new ministry with abundant signs of God's leadership. A luxurious home in the heart of one of Mexico City's wealthiest *colonias* opened its doors. My first disciples were a mother and daughter whose conversion had been quite miraculous. My co-pastor was a handsome young man reared in that privileged community. From the very beginning curious neighbors overflowed the living room for my Tuesday night Bible studies.

I had no inkling that less than a year later most of my early disciples would have abandoned me and attendance at services would be smaller than it had been at the very beginning. Yes, I had entered a field "white unto harvest," but the "tares" would appear very soon and threaten to overwhelm the harvest!

It wasn't long before I became aware that many of the people who were attending came from a charismatic background. This shouldn't have surprised me, because the charismatics were doing a much better job of reaching people than the traditional denominations. I distributed a letter with a statement of my doctrinal position, but to my surprise there was no negative reaction. Some months later I gave a study on speaking in tongues and the baptism in the Spirit. A few stopped attending, but attendance continued at fifty to sixty in the Tuesday night Bible study. Soon we decided it was time to initiate Sunday services. We signed a contract with the Union Church to rent one of their large salons on the second floor of their building. As the name suggests, this was a non-denominational church with services in English, mostly for ex-patriot Americans and Europeans. The lovely Spanish style chapel is located on *Boulevard Reforma,* one of Mexico City's most traveled avenues.

Early on, I began having problems with Edgar, my co-pastor. A first-year seminary student, he was the person who introduced me to Norma and her daughter Miriam. He had been raised in a wealthy home, but apparently the exclusive schools he attended didn't have discipline in their curriculum. He felt his calling was evangelism, so we named him minister of evangelism. He had an exaggeratedly sanguine temperament, and I never knew what his mood would be on a given day, exuberant or depressed. When I let him occupy the pulpit he had no sense of time. Then Patricia appeared on the scene and matters got worse. Patricia, who had come as a summer missionary from Texas, began attending our services. Soon she was enamored of Edgar, and decided she had found the man God had destined to be her husband. They began talking about marriage.

I spent months looking for an office. I had committed myself to finding a place near downtown. I wanted a non-religious setting, where in time I could develop a counseling center, feeling that this would be a way to contact persons who would never enter an evangelical church. I had begun this new ministry praying that God would show me how to open doors to some of the two million affluent people in Mexico City who were immersed in the Roman Catholic culture that permeated family life, social activities, and even the business world. Home visits were out of the question. Press the doorbell in the stone wall fronting an upper-class home and a maid's voice would ask "*Quien?*" (Who?) Not a chance to be invited in for an evangelistic chat with *la senora!* My hope was that over time we would build up a clientele for a counseling center staffed by Christian psychotherapists.

The Mexico Mission had accepted a proposition I made them: if they would subsidize the rental of my office the first six months, I had faith that, by then I would be receiving enough income from my counseling fees to pay the rent.

On August 13, 1983 I wrote in my diary:

> I've found an office suite! It's more than I had dared hope
> for: reception, a private office, and a salon for conferences.
> Carpeted throughout. I had gotten a bit desperate.
> Everywhere I looked, if it was a decent place, a dozen other
> people seemed to be competing. Jose Moot, a businessman
> from the Yucatan, needed to sublease the office and find a
> smaller place. He thought he had made a deal a week earlier,
> but at the last moment the prospect backed down. He had
> decided that an older person would be more reliable, and
> when he learned I was an American citizen, that sealed it
> for him. The owner of the office was so pleased with my
> profile that he fixed up a contract in ten minutes, without

a background check. Mr. Poot was surprised, because, he told me, the investigation usually took a week. I am sure this was the Lord's moving and His way of saying He wants the best for me. Hallelujah! I've spent the last couple of days completing the packing in my seminary office, and Monday morning I'll make the move.

I had good reason to be excited. The office was located in *Colonia Polanco,* a lovely area of the city known for its wide avenues, exclusive shops and chic restaurants. On the fourth floor of a building occupied by accountants, dentists and physicians, I was across the street from a popular upscale department store. I couldn't have asked for a more ideal location.

I soon was excited about something else. Jose Poot was interested in my friendship! He told me a fascinating story. As a kid, he shined shoes on the central plaza of Merida, Yucatan. One day he did the shoes of a very friendly American, who asked him questions about his family, his schooling and his ambitions. Jose had picked up enough English on the streets to hold a fairly intelligent conversation. Several weeks later he received a letter informing him that the stranger who had asked so many questions was governor of Ohio and that he was awarding him a four-year scholarship to a private college in his state. Jose studied in that college for four years and returned to Mexico with a degree in business.

As the days passed, Jose listened with interest as I shared the Gospel. Soon, he made a commitment to Christ. At the moment I had no idea that, in the months ahead, he would make my life miserable!

I was also mistaken about Marcos. I had become acquainted with Marcos as an adolescent in Torreon. I observed with interest as he completed university studies and established a business downtown. The business thrived. A year after we moved to Mexico City Marcos came to see me. God had called him into the ministry, he told me, and he wanted to enroll in the seminary. I was elated; here was a young man with exceptional promise. Early in his first year I sat him down in my office and opened my heart: we were in need of nationals with graduate studies on our seminary staff. Until now I had refused to send any graduate to a seminary in the United States because I'd observed that, almost without exception, people who went to the States for studies never returned. I made him a proposition: if he would place as his goal a near perfect grade average, I'd see that he received a scholarship for doctoral studies in the United States. Upon one condition: that he make a commitment before God to return to Mexico.

Marcos accepted my offer with enthusiasm, hit a home run in his studies, and we sent him for graduate studies to the Baptist seminary in New Orleans. We had an agreement with the seminary that they would award him a Masters in Theology after one year, then admit him into the doctoral program.

I had placed one other requirement: in order not to lose touch with his homeland, after his first year of studies Marcos would return to Mexico for one year. When that moment arrived, it seemed like God's timing. I invited him to be my associate pastor for that year and he accepted. It would take several years before I realized my error in making an exception with Marcos.

Good things began to multiply in our young congregation. Several times we had baptisms in the huge swimming pool in the home of Norma and Miriam. Among these were Norma and Miriam and Miriam's brother Antonio. Later Antonio's fiancee Ana was baptized. I decided the time had come to form a core group of disciples. Six men accepted my invitation to enter into a bond of absolute commitment to Christ and their church.

Among these was Oscar. Oscar had attended for the first time a few weeks after the beginning of the Bible studies. He arrived at the moment I stood to give my Bible study, accommodated himself halfway up the curving staircase, and fixed his dark eyes on me, never blinking. By the time I had completed the study I was acutely aware of that handsome young man, and suspected that he had a hidden agenda. Did he dislike Americans? Had the person who invited him warned him that I was not to be trusted? At the close of my talk he left immediately, without my having an opportunity to meet him. Miriam told me that she knew him, that some time ago a friend had led him to Christ. But so far he had not found a congregation he was willing to commit to. Oscar became a regular, and more and more I was impressed that he had exceptional promise.

Even with all these encouragements, I was determined to be realistic. I wrote in my diary:

> I continue to remind myself that the Lord is going to have to do it all. We are operating in a stronghold of imperial Catholicism in its most virulent form. I expect more and more opposition and do not doubt the time may come when my own safety will be threatened. But moment by moment I am asking the Lord for the faith I need to behave honorably and valiantly as He leads me forward.

My words were prophetic. We were ecstatic when Libby, a sister of Miriam, received Christ. Libby, a very pretty young woman with a winning smile, became an enthusiastic disciple. Soon she was insisting on baptism. The day set for her baptism, as she was about to dress for entering the pool, her husband appeared. He threatened her with physical harm if she went through with it. After that, Libby attended only a few times and then disappeared. Another attractive young woman came forward one Sunday evening tearfully professing her faith in Jesus. She asked me to visit her husband. He was a writer by profession, not a Christian, but a spiritual man, and surely he would be interested in knowing about Christ. I visited him in their comfortable home just a few blocks from Union Church. He received me cordially and talked with enthusiasm about a script he was writing for a downtown theater. When I attempted a dialogue about Jesus Christ his mood changed. He had seen enough of Christianity and the Church to take away any illusions he might have had, and was now a disciple of an oriental cult. When I attempted to insist that Biblical faith was quite different from the Christianity he had known, he stopped me with a condescending smile and let me know I would not be welcome in his home if I came to proselytize. His wife never returned to our services.

Then there was Rafael. His younger brother José, who had been attending fairly regularly, told me excitedly one Sunday that next week Rafael would arrive. His brother had been in Chicago for a couple of years. He had been converted there and was returning to Mexico with the purpose of evangelizing his *patria*. A couple of Sundays later Rafael appeared. He was a carryover from the hippies of the 70's: long-haired, a shaggy beard, clothes unpressed. He asked for the opportunity to give his testimony, and though it was rather long, it was impressive. He had met the Lord, abandoned the drug culture and now was dedicated to sharing his faith in Christ. He was trusting in God to provide his upkeep, and for the present would be sleeping in his twenty-year-old Chevrolet.

As the weeks passed I became increasingly doubtful that Rafael's presence was a blessing. He preached to anyone who would listen that speaking in tongues was essential to the filling of the Spirit. One day I invited him and his brother to my office for a dialogue. A few minutes after his arrival he suggested we pray. For twenty minutes he spoke in tongues at the top of his voice, so loud that I was expecting that at any moment the dentist across the hall would be knocking on my door demanding we quiet down. Soon people were telling me that Rafael was button-holing our congregation one by one, informing them that I was not faithful to the Bible, that they should dismiss me and install him as the pastor.

In November we went to Cuernavaca for a weekend retreat at a hotel sponsored by a Christian organization. Early Saturday afternoon someone knocked on my door. "Has anyone told you that Gertrude is upstairs in the prayer room conducting a séance?"

"A séance?" I answered, "that's impossible!" Everything I'd heard about Gertrude and her two teenagers confirmed that they were strong Bible believers.

"Pastor, Gertrude has a dozen people with her, and has channeled with a spirit that is giving all sorts of strange advice. Someone told Oscar and Antonio, and they're up there now talking with her."

An hour later Gertrude and her children checked out, and I never saw them again.

By the time the hour came for the six o'clock Bible study, the air was weighted with a strange oppression. I knew that Rafael had been busy propagandizing since our arrival. After an unenthusiastic period of praise, I stood to speak. Immediately I became aware that no one was looking at me, their eyes were fixed on the ceiling above the pulpit. I looked up. A huge bat was hanging from the ceiling, his eyes staring, his throat pulsating. A young woman jumped to her feet and screamed, "It's a demon, we need to pray!"

I answered, "We'll pray later. First, somebody go find a broom!"

One of the men ran out, returned with a broom, and raked the bat off the ceiling. I prayed, opened my Bible and prepared to speak. At that moment Rafael and his brother swaggered into room, grinning.

This was too much!

I pointed a finger at them. "Stop where you are. You are no longer welcome in this congregation. Pack your bags and leave!"

Where had those words come from? They were completely unplanned. I felt as if God himself was speaking through me.

Rafael paused, glared at me, then stomped down the aisle toward me. I was expecting him to come up and grab me by the neck. But instead, he turned and addressed the congregation: "Jesus said we are to go proclaiming the Word of the Kingdom, and if we are rejected, we should wipe the dust of that place off our feet!"

He ceremoniously wiped his feet on the floor and walked out, to a burst of applause.

Exhausted, I somehow made it through my sermon. Afterward, when I reported to the hotel manager about the bat, his eyes widened. "How strange. I've been here for five years, and I've never seen a bat!"

Rafael was gone, but not his influence. Soon after he left, Primitivo arrived. He was, he announced, a man called of God and he was here to help us. He was married, but his wife was not a Christian, and never attended church with him. Primitivo let it be known that God had told him he should divorce his wife. It soon became evident that there was an attraction between Miriam and Primitivo. This became a festering sore, because Miriam directed our praise service, and Primitivo was insisting that we recognize him as one of the ministers. Miriam was in many ways one of the most arresting Christian women I have ever known. She had a gorgeous, open smile, and a soaring, lyrical voice that was perfect for inspiring a congregation to sing from the heart. I had developed a deep affection for her as a Christian sister.

But early in January, 1984 she announced to the congregation that she and Primitivo were engaged, and requested our prayers. I went to Miriam's house and spent until 2:00 A.M. pleading with her and Primitivo, insisting that Primitivo, a married man, should not be pursuing another woman, especially a woman who was the praise leader in her church. Primitivo, very self-righteous, used the Bible to defend his position. In God's sight, he told me, he was no longer married. As far as God was concerned the divorce from his pagan wife had already taken place and he was free to find a Christian companion. At last we reached a compromise: Primitivo would no longer have any leadership responsibilities in the church, and he and Miriam would postpone their relationship until after the divorce was final. Supposedly we were in agreement, but I could see rebellion in the eyes of both of them as we parted.

Miriam informed me a week later that Primitivo was attending another church. Though she did not say so, I was certain they continued to keep company. The situation became a heavy burden on my heart and an object of agonized prayer. I knew that we were headed toward a crisis, and had no assurance of how the matter might turn out.

On February 19, 1984 I wrote in my diary:

> Last Sunday night Miriam told me she had broken up with Primitivo. I went over to her house afterward, and she related the whole story. Primitivo spent all Saturday afternoon trying to persuade her to run away with him. Said they were already married in God's eyes, that he would get her a ring and they would go to Veracruz and join a Pentecostal church and live happily ever after. It was a great temptation for her, because she loved him very much, but God gave her the strength to realize that if she listened to Primitivo her life would be ruined. It was evident that what I had sensed from the beginning was true, Primitivo had a deep, unreasoning streak of self-righteousness, without any commitment to obey God's moral commands.

I knew we were in trouble one evening in March, when Miriam pounded the table and shouted, "Our praise is an offense to the Lord! We've got to get more *loco!*" We were in the monthly meeting of the church council. This group, which was composed of fifteen of the most committed members of our congregation, met once a month to discuss our needs and pray together. Our form of worship had been an object of discussion more than once. About half of the people came from Pentecostal and charismatic backgrounds, and had been nurtured in a noisy praise that meant standing on your feet for an hour clapping your hands, raising your arms, shouting "Praise the Lord!" and occasionally dancing in the aisle. The others preferred more traditional worship styles. I had been emphasizing the importance of our living in love. Those who wanted to clap and raise their hands should feel free to do so. On the other hand the hand-raisers and shouters should not criticize their more restrained brothers and sisters.

So far it had worked quite well. I was grateful for the presence of a trio of young American women who had come to Mexico City to join the National Symphony orchestra. Susan was a cellist, Jessica a violinist and Cathy a pianist. Their participation in the worship tended to tone down the extremes. Also, I was using these young artists to reach out to the musical elite. Sala Chopin, the concert hall of a nearby music store, extended an open invitation to artists to present free-of-charge concerts. The women had given two concerts. I participated also. At the interim period, before people could get away for a cigarette, I invited them to wait just a few minutes for a reflection on esthetics. Using knowledge I had gleaned in my doctoral of philosophy studies, I lectured on the beauty of music as an evidence of a Designer. People had been quite receptive.

I was unprepared for Miriam's outburst. She and her mother had agreed with me that a free worship style that avoided extremes was best suited for the Lomas citizens. Later I realized I had not taken into account the effect of Miriam's months-long association with Primitivo. Besides, there was her younger brother Pablo. Several months before, Pablo, a brilliant agnostic university student, had experienced a rather spectacular conversion, and had immediately become an enthusiastic evangelist, witnessing to his class mates and professors, and exhorting the congregation at every opportunity. Then he decided he had the gift of prophecy. He began reporting visions and revelations that increasingly tended toward the bizarre. One Tuesday night he told me I must give him time the next Sunday evening service to share a prophecy. When I asked him for a preview of what he would say, he launched into a tirade against the people's "coldness of heart and worldliness." I told him we wouldn't have time for him next Sunday, maybe in another occasion. His mother called me the next day, indignant. Later in the week Miriam called and told me she would not be present for Sunday's worship.

The following Sunday I announced there would be a meeting of the church council in my office on Saturday morning. Twelve people attended. I began by expressing my love for each one. Then I told them I had come to the conclusion that our differences on worship style had become irreconcilable. We must make a decision: I was prepared to resign the pastorate and initiate a Bible study in Polanco, if they decided this was best. The other option would be for those who were dissatisfied with our worship style to find churches that better satisfied their needs.

We talked, prayed and cried together for two hours, a group of brothers and sisters in Christ joined by a sincere love for God and for one another. But there appeared to be no solution for the problem that divided us. At last Miriam gave a deep sigh and said, "I want to thank Dr. Carter for what he has meant to me and my family. I believe his approach to worship is probably the best for the people who live in *Colonia Lomas de Chapultepec.* My family and I will go somewhere else." Several others said they would go with her. We joined hands and prayed together. Then, with strong hugs and many tears we said goodbye.

When everyone had left I fell on my knees, buried my face in my chair, and sobbed. How could this have happened? It was so obvious that God had used Miriam and her mother to fulfill my dream of planting a new church. Now they had abandoned me.

"Doctor, please don't cry." I looked up, surprised. Esther was standing at the door, her eyes filled with tears. We sat together for a long time, saying nothing. At last Esther said, "We must not give up. God knew this was going to happen from the beginning. So God has a plan."

In the years following I came to appreciate the wisdom in my young friend's words. As time passed I came to a clear conviction: it is almost impossible for people committed to differing concepts of worship to work well together. I can't remember one person molded in a charismatic congregation who learned to adapt himself to traditional worship. On the other hand, I know of very few people who feel most comfortable in a tranquil worship style who have made a successful transition to another.   I believe I know why: authentic worship is an expression of who we are, of the makeup of our soul and our heart. If I am by nature reserved, if I find it difficult to express my feelings openly, I will be uncomfortable in a praise that requires me to release my emotions. This does not mean I am less sincere in my worship, it only means I am relating to God as I relate to other persons.   My wife has helped me a great deal in gaining this understanding.   She loves God as much as I do, but is uncomfortable with clapping and arm-raising.   It should not surprise me, because we can be sitting side by side in a movie, and tears are flowing down my cheeks, but her eyes are dry.   I have learned to respect her reserve, and the reserve of others like her.

Chapter Twenty-Three
In God's Time
1984-1985

Let's return to God's Poem.

God has written a poem for our lives, and we live that poem by walking in the works he has prepared for us. Doesn't it follow that God has engineered each of us genetically so that walking in those works is the natural expression of who we are?

In the mid-eighties, while on furlough in Louisiana, I traveled to Houston for a seminar entitled *Bi/Polar**. I came away fascinated by what I had learned about myself, and later obtained permission to translate the course into Spanish. It became one of my most valued instruments for group counseling.

The *Bi/Polar* system analyzes one's personality utilizing three "bi/polars": an individual is either a thinker or a risker, a practical thinker or a theoretical thinker, a dependent risker or an independent risker. The seminar revealed that I was strong in independent risking and theoretical thinking. This means that by nature, adventure attracts me, that rather than being content with things as they are, I tend to search for new paths, a better way of doing things. Also, I am attracted by opportunities that involve risk.

Once I came to understand my "bi/polar personality" I understood better why my life has consisted of one adventure after another. The first was my fascinating encounter at eighteen with the pretty blonde who would become my wife. Then, after two years in World War II, and five years of college and seminary, came an unexpected pilgrimage to San Francisco, and four years later, a risk-filled relocation to Fort Worth, marked by two pastorates that seemed to fall out of the blue. Then came God's insistent call to missions in Mexico, our "detour" to Yucatan, and later my election to the presidency of the seminary. Then the agonizing saga of the seminary move to Mexico City. Now I had left the relative security of the seminary and was engaged in a venture aimed at evangelizing the most sophisticated segment of Mexico's citizens.

And I seemed to have failed. The second Sunday after the division of our congregation, I wrote:

> I am still making adjustments to the happenings of a week ago. It has not been easy. We had about 30 present last Sunday and only about 20 on Tuesday. I have struggled against depression and the feeling of "What is my life amounting to -- did I really follow God's leadership when I left the seminary?" I awoke this morning dreading the service this afternoon because of the small remnant that will attend.

A few days later I wrote a seven-page analysis of my situation, dialoging with myself about two possible explanations for what had happened. The first was the possibility that I had made a mistake, and should never have left the seminary. "If this is true, what should I do?" I wrote. "Close out the work in Lomas and my office in Polanco? Try to return full time to the seminary, or opt for some other work somewhere in Mexico? At this moment I have no answer."

The second possible explanation was that God had called me into this work and that the apparent failure was part of a plan that God was going to weave into His purpose.

If that were true, then maybe for the present I should dedicate my major attention to the counseling center I had been trying to establish.

I decided to give my energies to this second alternative. Soon I had four psychologists interested in entering into the project with me. At this time Esther completed her university studies, and instead of accepting an offer of employment in the federal electric company, elected to work with me at half the salary she would have received in that institution. In May I took our staff to Oaxaca, at the invitation of Dr. Saul Cruz, director of the counseling center "Armonia" in that city. He was most encouraging, and offered to coach us. In June I flew to Houston to confer with Roger and Lavonia Duck, who were dedicated to Christian Counseling. I also spent time with Michael Horton, Director of Houston Baptists' Center for Counseling, and we agreed on a three-month internship during my furlough the following summer. In July I began a professional relationship that would continue as long as I was in Mexico, accepting an offer from Lupita Flores, a psychotherapist who worked out of her home near the seminary. She would be my professional mentor, and I her spiritual mentor. During the following years, Lupita was of extraordinary help to me.

Meanwhile, I continued with the group in Lomas de Chapultepec. It became a time for the maturing of men and women who would be our future leaders. In a retreat in April, we baptized Oscar who continued to grow in his commitment to his Lord and his church.

In August we had a call from our children. Mother had suffered a heart attack and was in the hospital. We flew to Louisiana. The first thing she said when I entered her hospital room in Lafayette was, "Pat, don't pray for me to get well."

I answered, "Oh, Mama, of course I'm going to pray for your healing!"

She took my hand. "Pat, I'm serious. You know I've only been half-alive since your daddy died. I want to go on and be with him."

Later I talked with her cardiologist. He assured me Mother would be well enough in a few days to go home. With the medicine he'd prescribe, she would be able to live a fairly normal life. In consultation with our children, Evelyn and I decided we should move up the date for the furlough we had scheduled for the following year, and spend four months with Mother.

We returned to Mexico City and began making hurried arrangements for our absence. A couple of days later, at daybreak, the telephone rang. It was our daughter Linda. "Daddy," she said, "the doctor just told us that Mammaw will not live through the day!"

Shocked, we took the next flight available to Houston. When we arrived at the hospital late that afternoon our three children were awaiting us in the lobby. They informed us that Mother had passed away half an hour before.

I took the elevator to her room, unable to come to terms with the fact that the unique woman who had exercised such an enormous influence on my life was gone. But should I be surprised? Since Daddy's death, every time I called Mother she always assured me she was doing all right, "But I miss your daddy so much. My life has no meaning without him." Mother had decided the time had come to go home to be with her dear husband, had shared her desire with the God she loved, and God had agreed. So it didn't matter what the physicians might say, the Great Physician had opted for another prognosis!

In the hall outside Mama's room I ran into the funeral director pushing a stretcher. He told me he had come for the body, but to take my time, he'd wait. I walked into the room. It was empty, except for Mama's body on the stark white hospital bed. My first thought was, "That's not Mama!" It reminded me of the empty husk a locust leaves behind when it takes wing and flies away.

Evelyn and I passed the night in the little town of Krotz Springs, in the house where Mama and Daddy had spent their last forty years of life. The next day a committee of deacons came to see me. Their pastor had recently resigned. Would I consider being their interim? Evelyn and I talked it over. We could go on back to Mexico City now, but we had already made arrangements to be away for the next four months. Besides, someone needed to be here to dispose of the house and work through the will. So I found myself agreeing to lead the church where my father had been pastor during my eighth and ninth years of life, then again, for twenty-five years before his retirement.

It turned out to be a time of making peace with my memories and ministering to the members of the church, now parents and grandparents, who had been my contemporaries in elementary school. It was a pleasure to stand behind the pulpit of the beautiful little church three times a week, visit the sick, pray for the troubled and hear again and again in the stores in town, "You must be brother Carter's son, you look just like him!"

On December 11 I wrote in my diary: "Thursday we leave. I'm so lonesome to get back to Mexico City! When I think of it a lump comes in my throat and tears fill my eyes. Mexico is really in my heart."

Back in our adopted homeland, I made an analysis of the prospects for the counseling center. The four professionals I had hoped might become my collaborators had departed for one reason or another. Esther was still there, but unsure of how much longer she would remain. Lupita Flores continued to show interest in working with me.

We had named our congregation in Lomas, *Anastasis,* the Greek word for "resurrection." Attendance continued at 30-40. I noted in my diary that more than a hundred people had attended at least two or three times in the previous year, then had disappeared.

In January, Russell Dilday, President of Southwestern Seminary in Fort Worth came to Mexico City for a meeting of seminary presidents. At his request I arranged a breakfast with a group of missionaries. He talked to us about the danger of a takeover of the Southern Baptist Convention by a fundamentalist group. Now seven of the thirty-five members of Southwestern Seminary's trustees were of the "other group", and unless something happened, in another three years the seminary would be in danger of a drastic change. He turned out to be a prophet. But I doubt he dreamed the day would come when the trustees would fire him, place a lock on his office door and forbid him entrance, even to remove his belongings.

Life was interesting. I decided to get serious once more about physical exercise, and began a discipline of running every day, ending with fifty pushups. I was encouraged by the progress of my counseling ministry. Although I had not been able to put together the team of therapists I had dreamed of, most days I was receiving "patients" in my office. And I was still visiting Iris every week. I had begun this practice when she was eleven, and soon she would have her fifteenth birthday. In May she showed me a report card without any failures, so I took her out to a fancy restaurant. We were enjoying a very affectionate daughter-father relationship.

In March Priscilla called. She was no longer living with Eduardo, the man she had married against my advice. He was "messed up," talked constantly about dying, and finally had just disappeared.

In April we had the first of what would be many "Bi/Polar" workshops in the counseling center. Esther and I had worked hard to translate the material into Spanish. Mike Horton came from Houston to supervise. Twenty-two attended, and contrary to our fears that an American seminar on personality might not be applicable to the Mexican idiosyncrasy, everyone left delighted with what they had learned about themselves.

A week later I wrote in my diary:

> I've been battling against depression. Most of the time I'm optimistic, then I find myself in need of being continually busy in order not to dwell on negative thoughts. The thirteen hours in the Bi/Polar seminar exhausted me, and I lost four pounds. It reminds me that I'm not really as young as I feel.

In May the president of the Seminary Board of Trustees came to see me. He had received a letter from some of the students saying that the missionary seminary professor who had been named as interim president had alienated many students, and asking when they were going to name the Mexican president that had been promised when I resigned. I told him the only person I considered capable of occupying the post was Marcos, who still lacked a couple of years before receiving his doctorate from Southwestern Seminary.

That month a miracle from God brought new life to our congregation. I received a call from a missionary friend in Chihuahua: "Pat, last night Porfirio Bas showed up at a Bible study in the civic auditorium sponsored by the First Baptist Church of Houston. He made a public profession of faith in Christ. They're taking him to Houston for baptism, and then he'll return to Mexico City. We don't want him to fall back into the group he ran with before. Will you take him under your wing?"

Would I! Porfirio was a popular singer-actor who had a prominent part in a very popular Mexican soap opera.

A few days later a big-eyed Esther escorted Porfirio into my office. I was struck immediately by his good looks and his contagious smile. He was "at my orders", he assured me, and anxious to be my disciple. But his first option was to find the wife he had divorced a couple of years ago and tell her about the transformation in his life. He did, they reconciled, and I had the joy of baptizing her and their twelve-year-old daughter.

We devised a plan to take advantage of this famous personality that God had drawn to our side. Oscar arranged with the National Association of Manufacturers to lend us their 300-seat auditorium downtown. We printed tickets for a concert, and the members of Anastasis gave them to friends. Porfirio presented a beautiful concert to a packed auditorium and shared his testimony. Then I gave a brief evangelistic message and extended an invitation. Some twenty people responded.

Concerts by Porfirio became the centerpiece of a renewed program of evangelism. We constituted the "Civil Association Anastasis," chartered by the federal government as an agency of social service. Invitations to Porfirio's concerts, and to concerts of classical music presented by our young artists from the National Philharmonic were made in the name of the Association.

I painted the name "Anastasis, S.A." on the door of my office. Most of the people who arrived for counseling had no knowledge that the Ph.D. providing personal and family counseling was anything more than a professional therapist. As time passed, I was learning more and more about how to be an effective counselor and how to use the counseling process to lead people into a personal relation with Christ. I discovered that, as a rule, I gained the confidence of my clients by the third or fourth session. Then I would say to them: "We've completed our diagnosis of your problem, and I've given you some recommendations. If you would like, I can tell you how to receive help from God to carry out those recommendations." Almost without fail, the person would accept my offer. And to my delight, in the great majority of the cases, the session would end with the individual praying the "sinner's prayer". Later, a good number of these became members of Anastasis church.

In July 1985 we formally organized our church. The service was held in the beautiful sanctuary of Union Church with thirty charter members. Among these were Ricardo Almazan, whom we had invited to join our staff as minister of visitation, and his wife Georgina. They were recent graduates of the seminary. Some twenty churches sent representatives. Instead of opening ourselves to questions about our beliefs and intentions, as is the custom in Mexico, we took the initiative. We prepared four work groups to make presentations entitled, Who are we? (testimonies). What do we believe? (doctrine) What are we doing? (our program) and What will we do? (our vision).

By August I felt myself under a threatening cloud. In eight months I would be 60! I could hear a dark whisper in my soul: I was getting old, so my active ministry would soon be drawing to a close.

NO! I wrote in my diary:

> I've decided to begin a discipline to attain the impossible: on my 60th birthday. I'll run a marathon! I've been running for some twenty years now, but I've never gone beyond three miles, because I thought anything more would be fanaticism. But I think that at this stage of my life I need a challenge. Later today I'm going to map out a calendar to increase my distance at the rate of one kilometer per week

In the middle of the month Esther resigned. It was rather a relief. Most of the time she was moody, because the man she loved was not in love with her. She brought her cousin Hope to take her place. Hope was eighteen now, and had just completed secretarial school. Hope always had a smile on her sweet face and her coming was like an invasion of sunshine

September 19 I was taking a shower after a 10-kilometer run. Suddenly I felt dizzy, and leaned against the wall. Almost immediately Evelyn called: "Pat, did you feel the earthquake? The radio's gone off the air." The next weeks were hectic. Seminary classes were suspended so the students could help out downtown rescuing people from the ruins and serving meals to the victims in the basement of the First Baptist Church, which was surrounded by blocks of devastation. I heard more than one story of miraculous escapes from death.

On October 14 I wrote in my diary:

> One nightmare after another! Evelyn called yesterday to tell me that they had just found James Philpot in the street dead. I hurried home and learned that he had been in a minor collision two blocks from home, and a man got out of the other car and shot him in the head.

The Philpots were close friends, and lived in the condominium one floor beneath us. We suspected his murder was related to an incident a couple of weeks before. Someone had knocked at the door of the Philpot's apartment one morning. Jurhee, the wife, was at home alone drinking her morning coffee. When she opened the door, a man threatened her with a pistol and demanded money. She threw her cup of scalding coffee at his face, and he turned and ran.

As is common with the Mexican legal process, we never found out the details of the murder. Mrs. Philpot was advised months later that a suspect had been detained. She never met him, nor was she advised of the dates he would appear before the judge. After a couple of years she heard that the suspect had been sentenced to an unknown number of years in jail.

As 1985 came to a close I had reason to be thankful. Attendance at the church was now averaging 50-60, about what it had been at the time of the division. Now the congregation was united, and I preached often on love. Our theme song was I Corinthians chapter 13 put to music. Two years after the initiation of my counseling center my only staff was my secretary and myself. Hope was still a ray of sunshine. Little by little my calendar had filled with patients. I no longer had periods of doubts about God's will, confident that my striking out on a new pathway had been His leadership. Now I was sure that, in time, I would look back and be thankful that I'd had the courage to take a risk

*Tommy Thomas, Sr., founder of the seminar, later changed the name of his seminar, due to the now common use of "bi/polar" to designate a personality disorder.

Chapter Twenty-Four
"You're As Old As You Feel!"
1986-1987

It must have been frustrating for Caleb to keep the long vigil until God's judgment was completed and the occupation of the Promised Land could begin. But Caleb refused to be a victim of the passing years. On his eighty-fifth birthday he tells Joshua, "I am this day eighty-five years old. As yet I am as strong this day as the day that Moses sent me; just as my strength was then, so now is my strength." (Joshua 14: 10b-11). He went on to conquer Hebron, and then, at perhaps a hundred years old, he began a second family. Caleb proved it: you're as old as you feel!

As I contemplated the coming of my sixtieth birthday I felt the need to do something to prove that I wasn't "getting old". So, as I mentioned in the previous chapter, I decided to run a marathon. As the months passed I was faithful to the discipline of running four or five days of the week, and slowly adding kilometers, hoping that by the day of the marathon the forty-three kilometers would come quite naturally.

Then I added another dream: before the year ended, I would do a sky dive! Evelyn was not enthusiastic about either of these projected adventures, and warned me that my plans were a formula for suicide.

By March I had done twenty kilometers, and In April I did thirty. I calculated that was close enough to the forty-three kilometers that constituted a Mexico marathon. I wanted to do my run as close to my sixtieth birthday as possible, but there was no public marathon scheduled for that time of the year. So I laid out a forty-three kilometer route in the area where we lived. I secured the agreement of Larry, a missionary neighbor, to be my witness.

Finally, I settled on May 10th, six days before my birthday. I chose that date because Evelyn had scheduled a two-week visit with her sister in Oklahoma City. Given the stress my training period had caused her, I feared her presence the day of the event might provoke a stroke. Her last words when I left her at the airport: "Be sure to leave a front door key with a neighbor, in case you're in the hospital when I get back."

On the appointed day, I arose at dawn. Outside, the mile-high atmosphere was quite thin, and chilly. Warming up, I reminded myself that my goal today was not to set a record, but to simply endure the hours necessary to cover the route I'd laid out. The first hours went well. My route involved passing the condominium where we lived every ten kilometers. Without fail, Larry was there, checking his watch and cheering me on. Halfway through, my ex-secretary Esther appeared, gave me a big smile, and shouted, "I'm praying for you. See you at the end of the race."

Five hours passed. I trotted by the condominium and waved at Larry, who assured me, "You're going great. Just ten kilometers more and you've got it made!" I said nothing, but my legs were becoming heavier. Would I make it?

After half an hour, I began to doubt. I'd drained the bottle of water I'd picked up the last time I passed the condominium, and was dying for a drink. A voice whispered, "Unless you get a drink, you're going to pass out!" Another ten minutes, and I collapsed on a strip of green grass beside the street. I'd gone all I could, I wasn't going to make it after all!.

I lay there for five minutes, tears trickling down my cheeks. What a disappointment, eight months of training, and it was all coming to naught. Suddenly, I sat up. No! I couldn't stop now! I got to my feet, mumbling, "Maybe I'm gonna die, but if I do, it'll be on my feet!"

I must have a sip of water! Eureka! There in the gutter was a chunk of ice the size of a softball. Somebody had made a delivery of ice, and behold, God in His providence had sliced off this little piece just for me! I grabbed it up, licking it, swallowing the precious drops, feeling renewed, knowing now that I was going to complete the course. I was no longer running, not even jogging, I was just taking one laborious step at a time.

Larry appeared at my side. "Just a few blocks left, Pat, I'm going to walk with you."

"Okay, just don't say anything!"

Ten minutes later I could see the condominium, and in the street out front a dozen kids waving banners. They'd come for somebody's birthday party, and Susan, Larry's wife, had enlisted them for a welcoming committee. I picked up my pace, feeling like a champion as I ran by to the cheers of "hurray! hurray!" breaking the ribbon someone had stretched across the street.

I still have on my bedroom wall the bright yellow and red poster that another missionary wife, Lorna, did to commemorate that day:

PAT CARTER WINNER AND CHAMP
40 KILOMETER MARATHON
MAY 10, 1986
6:06:42

Since the first of the year, our congregation in Lomas had been looking for a property we might purchase. We were tired of meeting in a rented facility, enduring the tyranny of the janitor of Union Church. By now we had decided the price of properties in the Lomas area was beyond our possibilities. Anyway, we had not enjoyed much success in breaking through the thick cultural-religious crust that enclosed Lomas de Chapultepec. So we began looking in other parts of the city.

One day Evelyn pointed out to me an ad in the paper: a house was for sale in the *barrio Colonia Nueva Anzures,* near downtown, and a dozen blocks from my office. We paid the property a visit.

As soon as we walked through the door, we both had the same impression: "This is it!". A short distance from the front door was a huge living room. To the right of the entry hall was a large bedroom and bath, perfect for an office suite. Upstairs were three bedrooms, plus a spacious salon that had been a recreation room. The gracious lady who received us explained that she had been recently widowed.

Her husband, who had passed away after a long bout with cancer, was a well-known optometrist. She was asking $90,000.

Our building committee visited the house and felt as enthusiastic as Evelyn and I. A couple of weeks later we took the congregation to Cuernavaca on a weekend retreat.

When I presented the project, someone immediately said, "I move we make an offer of $80,000." Surprised, I explained that we should take into account that the sale was for cash within ninety days, a daunting project for a membership of thirty people. To my astonishment, without further discussion, the motion was passed unanimously.

The next three months were an incredible adventure of faith. Evelyn and I had transferred a sum of money to our bank in Mexico City, attracted by the possibility of purchasing an apartment. When the deal fell through, we accepted that this was a word from God that we should donate the money to the purchase of a home for our church.

People sold jewelry, and food, and took out loans. At the last minute the International Mission Board came through with a gift. On the day before the closing date we delivered the $80,000 and took ownership of our beautiful new home. What rejoicing!

Meanwhile, my dream of flinging myself out of a plane was still alive. One day in September Esther came to see me, excited. She had met two young men at the light company where she worked whose hobby was training people for parachute jumps.

She challenged me: was I still gung ho for my crazy dream? My answer: " I'll do it if you jump with me!"

Her brown eyes grew wide. After half a minute's silence she grinned and said, "All right, I'll do it!"

Evelyn had made plans to visit our children in the States the first week of October.

It seemed to me it would be an act of mercy to tell her nothing of my plans, and to carry out the project in the week she was away.

The appointed week we met three nights at a local gymnasium with the young airmen. They showed us how to put on the two parachutes, one that should open when we pulled the rip cord and a spare, just in case. We rehearsed over and over how to jump out of the plane, and how to land.

On Saturday morning we drove to a landing strip beside a beautiful lake in a volcanic crater near Cuernavaca, accompanied by Esther's boy friend and her mother.

Esther went up first, and landed quite well, though she bruised her hip on a big rock.

Then it was my turn. As the little plane gained altitude, I asked myself, seated between the two young men who had trained us for the jump, what in the world was I doing, putting my life in the hands of two guys I had met only a few days before. I was tempted to yell, "Just a minute, I've changed my mind!" But as we continued to ascend, hyped by the thin air, I found myself more and more excited, anxious for the greatest adventure of my life.

After some twenty-five minutes, the pilot cut the motor. The trainer on my right said, "Okay, we've reached ten thousand five hundred feet. Let's go!"

They led me through the door and out onto a narrow strip of metal beneath the wing. They had told me that I was the one to give the order to jump, and that I could back out up to the last moment. But standing there, bracing against the wind, I was surprised that I felt no fear, only an immense excitement. I shouted in Spanish, "On your mark, get set, go!" and threw myself backwards, the two men at my side.

Heaven! I was a bird, flying freely, below me the incredible blue of the volcanic lake, above me the bright blue sky. There was no sensation of falling, only of floating alone in God's immense universe. The thought occurred to me, "If I don't pull the rip cord, I'll enter heaven in less than a minute!"

Then, after forty-five seconds of ecstasy, the parachute opened. I could see my goal four thousand feet below, a round circle plowed in the ground. Recalling the instructions I had received, I pulled on the lines, maneuvering toward the circle.

Oh no! I was headed in the right direction, but clearly I wasn't going to make the circle, I was falling too fast. Where would I hit? Scanning the ground, I couldn't believe my eyes: I was falling toward a herd of cattle!

When I was some twenty-five feet from landing, one of the cows lifted her head and her eyes widened when she saw me. I could swear I heard her yell, "Run, girls, a crazy man is falling from the sky!"

I hit the ground face first, and lay there laughing, laughing, laughing, my sides splitting with a crazy joy.

Finally I gathered up my parachute and headed toward the hanger. Halfway, Esther met me. "Do you know you're bleeding?" I wiped my face with my handkerchief, and it came away stained with blood. I hadn't been conscious of how hard I'd fallen.

Near the hanger one of the trainers met me. "Sir, why didn't you pull your rip cord?"

I stared at him, surprised. "What do you mean? I must have pulled it, or I wouldn't be standing here."

"No, I waited till we passed four thousand feet, and when you made no move, I reached over and pulled it for you."

And I knew why: I had lapsed into such an ecstasy that I was incapable of any thought other than being one with the Creator, very, very near His abiding place.

The next day I went to the airport to pick up my wife. The first thing she said when she saw me was, "My goodness, Pat, what happened to your face?"

"Oh, I had a little fall!"

And she refused to believe I'd been so crazy as to jump out of an airplane until a neighbor confirmed it.

I still remember that parachute jump at sixty years of age as the most exciting human experience of my life. That's why I committed to doing it again in celebration of my eightieth birthday.

1987 began with a pleasing consciousness of significant advance in the church.

From the beginning, my counseling ministry had contributed to the church's growth and now this became more pronounced. Early in the year I began a ministry to the Rivera family. Carla, the wife of a prominent doctor, came to ask my help with a problem: eerie manifestations in her house. Her college student daughter had an apartment in their basement. A couple of weeks before, her little dog awoke her after midnight barking, and she was startled to see a horrible apparition: a huge legless body descending the stairs, the bearded face set in a fierce frown. When she screamed he vanished. The following week the figure reappeared. Could I help them? I made a visit to their lovely home in a fashionable sector of the city. As she guided me through the house, I found in her daughter's apartment an especially revolting monument of a pagan Aztec god. She accepted my recommendation that she throw the sculpture into the garbage. Then we prayed God's blessing over her house. Two weeks later she returned to my office to report that there had been no reoccurrence.

Carla began coming weekly to talk with me about problems in her family. After a month she brought her pretty young daughter for a visit, then her alcoholic sister, a professional singer. After a time her husband, director of surgery at the city's General Hospital, came to participate in marriage counseling.

In January Roberto came for counseling. A strikingly handsome lawyer, he was involved in an adulterous relationship. The night before, when he returned from work, he found a note from his wife informing him she had gone to stay with her mother in Tampico, and would remain there until he was ready to recommit to their marriage. I led him in a prayer of repentance and faith in Christ. That very night he flew to Tampico to bring his wife home. Later that week she called to thank me for the change in her husband, and invited me to lunch in the restaurant on the second floor of the swank department store across the street from where I'd had my office before I moved to the church property.

Paula was a pretty young woman with a charming personality, making me wonder how her husband could have been attracted to someone else. She and Roberto attending a Bible study I conducted in Carla's home. Soon she accepted Christ as her Savior and I baptized her.

But the Devil was not finished with Carla and her family. One night after the Bible study she introduced me to Alfio, a short, dark man with bulging muscles and piercing black eyes. The President's trainer in martial arts, he had recently returned from a year of study in India, where he had received a doctorate in mind control. Carla's husband, who gave a weekly class on physical conditioning to Mexico's Olympic athletes, had invited this martial arts master to present a lecture on the mental control of pain. The master had illustrated the power of mind over matter by passing a knitting needle through his own bicep. Several weeks later I wrote in my diary:

> Something really strange happened in Carla's house last Saturday night. They had invited Alfio for dinner. Hearing the sound of someone playing squash in the court below, they were puzzled, because as far as they knew no one else was in the house. They went down to investigate. They were startled to find the dark squash court empty, with a tiny red light going back and forth, like a ball. Alfio told them to go upstairs, and instructed Carla to bring him a candle and a glass of water. An hour later he came upstairs and told them he had found Ruben, a teenage son who had been killed in an automobile accident several years before, playing squash with his deceased grandfather. And that Ruben warned him the family should call an older brother, Rodolfo, who was in Las Vegas, and tell him to return home immediately, because he was in grave danger. They were unable to communicate with Rodolfo, but he arrived home early the next day saying he had felt terribly depressed and heard strange sounds in his room. I have uneasy feelings about this. Several months have passed since we declared Carla's home freed from demonic influences. Now this guy Alfio appears and wins their friendship. A scenario has occurred to me: Alfio wants control of the Rivera family, and is using black magic to accomplish it. What shall I do? I'll need much wisdom from God to help the family understand what is happening.

In March Oscar married his girlfriend Betty, and they left on a month's honeymoon. By now Oscar's actuary business had begun an aggressive growth that would bring him wealth before he was forty.

A month later I learned of another impending wedding: Esther and her boyfriend Gerardo would be married in October. The news saddened me. Earlier I had jokingly suggested to Esther that God had given her the gift of courtship evangelism. In succession she had begun courtships with three young men, brought them to church, got them converted, and then dropped them. But Gerardo was different. He came to church with her once, and never returned, declaring he had no intention of joining her church. When I reminded her of her promise to God not to marry an unbeliever she let me know her love life was none of my business. In the weeks that followed she vacillated, telling me on her weekly visit that she wasn't going to marry Gerardo, then the next time saying yes, she was going to do it.

On the morning of July eleventh Esther told me the date had been set for her wedding, October 2nd. She knew I'd be in the States on furlough, but she had been counting on me for years to do her wedding. I told her I wouldn't be able to do it, I just couldn't marry her to an unbeliever. She stared at me, then at the floor for a long time. Then she got up and started for the door. I asked her to return and pray with me. After the prayer she kissed me on the cheek and told me goodbye. I asked her if she was angry. She said no, she was hurt. That was the end of a special friendship that had lasted some six years. Esther married Gerardo, and since then we have spoken to each other less than half a dozen times.

Evelyn and I returned to the States in September for furlough. In December I wrote:

> I've just finished reading *The Prince of Tides*, by Pat Conroy.
> It is a beautiful, haunting novel. At the end, the hero leaves
> New York City to return to South Carolina and his wife and
> children. Back home, he affirms his love for his family and
> the South, but every night on the way home from work,
> he drives up a hill and looks north, whispering the name of
> the city he has abandoned. In less than a month I'll return
> to Mexico City and in the next three years it'll be decided
> if I leave and come back to my own heritage. This book
> reminded me to the depths of my soul how profoundly, how
> completely I love that smog-ridden, beautiful, murderous city
> and how completely I am in love with the people. Returning
> to my heritage is the right thing to do. Here is security, peace,
> and there in Mexico City is worry, uncertainty, adventure,
> promise, fear, love. I feel this moment what I feel often, and
> with such passion it tears my heart. What I really *want* is

to go to that city I love, get an apartment and day after day
open my arms to the people who so much need my affection
and God's love, and live there and suffer there ... die there.
I don't know if I'd be happier there than here, but I do feel
... feel ...feel ... that there is my destiny, there I truly belong,
there I am truly alive. Oh God, my Father, I feel that you
placed that destiny in my soul. For the rest of the years that
I'll be here on earth, please let me live that destiny -- please!

*In the years following our purchase, property values sky-rocketed.
Within four years the church had an offer of $400,000 for the house.

Chapter Twenty-Five
Time To Lower the Curtain?
1988-1989

The Bible doesn't tell us how Caleb felt when he concluded his conquest of Hebron. Was there a letdown? Did the old warrior have a problem putting his sword aside? Reading my diary, it's interesting to see how my own attitude toward retirement began to change.

In January we returned from furlough. I saw immediately that Ricardo's interim pastorate had not gone as well as I had wished. This was worrisome, because in three years I would be leaving, and he would probably inherit the pastorate. Ricardo still had much to learn in terms of pulpit skills and relationships. On the other hand, he possessed two qualities I considered most important, and had found lacking in many pastors. He had integrity; there was no doubt about his love for God and for the church. And he was loyal. I had the impression he looked upon me as his spiritual father, and would never betray me. Besides, he had the blessing of a consecrated, intelligent wife, who herself had felt a call from the Lord for the ministry. It would take a while, but I was confident that he would become an effective pastor.

By May we were bringing in extra chairs. A concert by Profirio in a public auditorium resulted in forty-three professions of faith. Most of these accepted our invitation to a Sunday morning breakfast, and a month later we baptized twenty-three.

In June a surprise visit from Marcos and his wife brought a resounding disappointment. They traveled from the Seminary in Fort Worth to inform me that they would not be returning to Mexico. Marcos had become disillusioned by the jealousy expressed toward him by a number of his colleagues in Mexico. Besides, he had written the Director of the Seminary in Mexico City inquiring about an opportunity to teach, but had received no reply. As for my suggestion a couple of years before that he return as pastor of *Anastasis* church, he doubted that the church would want to pay him the salary he would require. I looked at this young man for a long time in silence before speaking, and decided it would do no good to point out to him that he was breaking a contract with me, a contract that he had sworn to before God.

My heart was crushed, I had been wrong to deposit my confidence in Marcos! He would not, after all, become the exception to the problem that had prevented me from sponsoring anyone before him for studies in the States, knowing that most visitors from Latin America become addicted to stateside comforts and refuse to return home. This disappointment produced a wound in my soul that remained for years afterward.

Meanwhile, my counseling ministry was returning to the success it had enjoyed before our months in the United States. By mid-year my calendar was full. Among these was the return of Carla What I had foreseen as a consequence of her friendship with Alfio had came true. She spent three hours telling me a chilling story: her daughter had fallen completely under Alfio's spell. Her son had threatened her with a knife when she forbade him to continue seeing the *maestro*. At my recommendation she began looking to God for strength to confront her enemy. A week later she invited Alfio to her home. She rebuked him for his betrayal, and warned him he was to have no more contact with her children.

By July I was very much aware that we were only three years away from retirement. I wrote in my diary:

> The entire world belongs to God, so I cannot accept the idea
> that being an American means I must return to my own
> country when I am 65. Is retirement a law from God? Or

shouldn't I insist that God's will has nothing to do with dates and ages and men's traditions?

But by November there came a change in my thinking:

> Our time for retirement has been set for July 31, 1991, but I'm beginning to wonder if we may leave before then. I have realized all my goals here, and don't want to continue for three more years doing more of the same.

A surprising development this, the very success of my work producing in me the feeling that there was nothing new ahead. The church was indeed prospering. The last Sunday of July we had celebrated our third anniversary, with an attendance of more than 200. What I had written in my diary at that time weren't the words of someone ready to pack up and leave: "I'm amazed at what's happening. There are stirrings in every area…where are we headed? What does God have in store?"

My counseling ministry had reached a saturation point. Most days, after spending six or seven hours dealing with people and their problems. I returned home late, exhausted. And more and more I became aware of the limitations in achieving permanent changes in people's lives. Paula was a case in point. I wrote in mid-September:

> We had baptisms yesterday. Among these was Paula. Her father's death about six weeks ago seems to have brought things together for her spiritually. Her husband refuses to come to church because of problems with one of the men in our church, but she attends regularly.

A week later I wrote:

> I had lunch with Paula today. We've become good friends. We seem to have a lot in common in our way of thinking. I'm excited because within three weeks we begin a Bible study in her home. Paula took me to her home today. They moved in a couple of months ago, and it is beautiful.

To my surprise, the Bible Study in Paula's home brought negative consequences. In December I wrote:

> I don't know what I'm going to do about continuing the
> Bible study in Paula's house. She has not attended a service
> in Anastasis since the Bible study began. Her husband insists
> that since they have Bible study in their home she doesn't
> need to go to church. We spent two hours together yesterday,
> and she admitted that throughout her marriage she has been
> under the complete domination of her lawyer husband, and
> that she has little hope of being able to break the cycle.

As 1988 came to an end, I was aware of a striking contrast. Five and a half years before I had left the seminary with a dream burning in my heart: I would drop into the world of the wealthy and influential with the purpose of giving a testimony of Christ. I had achieved a success, as far as I knew, beyond what any one else had experienced. I had won a significant number of people to faith in Christ, and God had used me to mold them into a vibrant church. I had built up an upper class clientele who filled my days seeking help with personal and family problems. December 31st I wrote a summary of that year's accomplishments:

Explosive growth: Average church attendance in January, 65, in March, 70, in April 75, in May, 95, in July, 122, in August, 170, in November, 190.
Sixty-five baptisms.
Attendance of young people grew from eight to 32.
I had a full counseling schedule all year, and presented a number of Bi/Polar seminars, including four with the cosmetic company *Modelo*.

Yes, remarkable successes. But a sobering discovery: at this level of society there seemed to be a certain inflexibility that brought frequent disappointments.

The year 1989 began with a revolution in the federal government. My early morning runs took me by a huge estate enclosed in high stone walls, with a fortress-like watchtower at the entrance. This was the home of *"La Quina,"* head of the petroleum union, known as one of the most powerful and corrupt men in Mexico. On January 11th I was surprised to see the gates thrown open and the streets filled with soldiers. *La* Quina and forty-six of his cohorts had been arrested. The next day I wrote in my diary:

> Very interesting, because Carlos Salinas Gortari was elected president a few months ago with the smallest percentage of votes in fifty years. There has been a lot of opposition to him, and some have predicted his assassination. Yet he has dared to depose *La Quina*. Everyone fears there will be a strike of the refinery workers, so yesterday and today the lines at the filling stations have been horrible. No one knows what will happen, but the army is backing the President.

Thus began a battle that lasted for six years and ended with President Salinas fleeing to Scotland, accused of stealing millions.
In March I wrote of a vision that I would not fully understand until many years later:

> Tremendous moments of vision such as I experienced yesterday leave me with a feeling in the depths of my soul that I'm not going to leave Mexico. Sometimes the retirement date, July 31, 1991 seems a certainty, but I'm committed in my heart of hearts to the vision that the Lord has given me and repeated so many times.

One strong impression stays with me about the years 1983-1991. I was startled by, entertained by, inspired by, an incredibly rich and varied parade of people who became a part of me, some of them for the rest of my life, others for a few months or a few years.

Manuel de La Flor was one of these. Early in the year he made a counseling appointment for himself and his wife, Corinne. Manuel's first wife had died a couple of years before, and six months ago he had married Corinne. She was fifteen years his junior. As we worked together, I learned about their backgrounds. Corrine was Catholic, part of a close-knit German family. Manuel shared with me an interesting testimony: some six months before, on a business trip to Veracruz, he dropped into a Christian book store and the proprietor chatted with him about his spiritual condition and sold him a book. As a consequence, Manuel invited Christ into his life. I had the privilege of baptizing him, and he became a faithful member of *Anastasis* church.

One Sunday afternoon, after a fellowship lunch at the church, we lingered to share testimonies and talents. When Manuel offered to play a piece on the piano I was surprised, because he had not told me he was a pianist. Seated in front of me was Benito Rios, now retired, who for most of his life had earned his living giving piano concerts in the dining rooms of five-star hotels. He had been baptized a year before, and was now our church pianist. As Manuel began playing a composition of Beethoven, Benito edged forward in his seat and began drumming his fingers in time with the music. At the conclusion he rose to his feet, shouted "*Bravo*," and led the congregation in a resounding applause.

Only then did I learn that Manuel de la Flor was a well-known concert pianist, and that he was featured quite often in concerts of the National Symphonic Orchestra. Some months later, under the sponsorship of the church, he presented a concert in one of the major auditoriums of the city and gave his personal testimony. As a result, we baptized a number of new converts.

Every Sunday new people appeared. I remarked midyear, "I can't remember the last time I preached when there weren't decisions". In July we celebrated our anniversary in a downtown hotel, with 300 present. Our church auditorium was no longer adequate, so we hired an engineer to prepare plans for an expansion that would accommodate 350. Meanwhile we began having two services each Sunday morning.

God knew that Satan wasn't pleased with the growth of Anastasis Church, so He sent a special person to support me in the trials that lay ahead. One morning a stately German lady of some forty-five years of age appeared at my office and informed me that God had appointed her to be my intercessor. I was somewhat skeptical at first, but as the weeks passed I thanked God for this special gift of His grace. Gisela never missed a service, and once a week we spent an hour together in prayer. I learned that, as a child, she had lived through the Second World War in Germany. When the war ended she emigrated to Mexico to attend the national university, met a Mexican student and married him. When Christ came into her life she joined a Baptist church. Years later she became convinced that God had called her into the ministry of intercession. She shared this with her pastor and offered her prayer support. His response surprised her: God was capable of carrying out His sovereign plans without her prayers, he told her, but she had his permission to pray for him and the church if she so desired.

For the past nine years she had been asking God to lead her to a church where the pastor would welcome her ministry. Finally, God had directed her to Anastasis. She continues to be blessing for me and for my ministry!

In September construction began on our expansion. We had received the verbal consent of the city authorities, with the promise that within a few days they would deliver us the documents. Days became weeks. Then, in mid-October, city officials appeared and placed seals on our doors. The reason: we had begun construction without permission. We contracted a lawyer, and he presented our case before the *Delegada*, the chief officer of that section of the city. She informed him that the week before she had received a protest in the name of eighty block captains, saying that our Sunday meetings constituted a problem for the community and demanding that that they shut us down. We began meeting in a downtown hotel, and though our attendance was close to what it had been before, the accelerated growth ended.

The year ended with a number of discouraging family problems. Evelyn fell into a depression, in part because of the church problems, but mostly because of stress over crises in the lives of our children. David's wife, Vicki, had fallen ill with a rare blood disease that baffled her doctors and threatened her life. Carol's husband had advised her he no longer loved her, and that as soon as the children graduated from high school he would divorce her.

Disappointment with people. I had experienced so much of that! But had I the right to expect that my experience would be different from that of others who dared to enter into the arena and challenge the world system? When Christ died on the cross he was abandoned by most of his followers. Paul knew what it was to be betrayed by people he had trusted. From prison in Rome he writes to Timothy:

Do your best to come to me quickly, for Demas, because he loved this world, has deserted me.... Only Luke is with me.... Alexander the metalworker did me a great deal of harm. At my first defense, no one came to my support, but everyone deserted me.

And yet, for every person who had disappointed me, a dozen had remained faithful! I learned a lesson:

I should not stop trusting people, but neither should I choose certain people to be "stars" in my ministry. I am incapable of discerning those who are going to be special. Anyway, why should I place such a burden upon anyone? And upon myself! It is God's job to choose his "special people," not mine!

Chapter Twenty-Six
End of an Era
1990-1991

I suppose that reaching the age of retirement is an unsettling experience for most people. And for one who has spent most of his adult life in another country there is an added stress, because it involves, not only leaving a workplace, but also a culture, a way of life. For the wife there is a unique problem. Ordinarily, a husband's retirement requires adjusting to the fact that he is going to be at home every day. But in the case of expatriots, there is no home to retire to; they together have to find that home. All this was in our minds in 1990, as Evelyn and I approached the end of our missionary service. I wrote on January 14:

> Evelyn has problems with tension and high blood pressure, and more and more she talks about retirement. I still don't see how all this is going to work out, given my key role in Anastasis, and the fact that I feel better and stronger than at any other time in the last thirty years. But that's in the Lord's hands and I'm content to leave it with Him.

Our church began the year with the confidence that we would soon return to our building. An influential man in the federal government talked with the *Delegada* and informed us she had agreed to remove the seals. But we would soon discover that this optimism was misplaced.

A January trip to Dallas brought home just how serious Vicki's sickness was. She had received, the day before, the bimonthly injection of radioactive isotopes into her marrow, and was shut up in her room, in too much pain to communicate. Her sickness baffled the doctors. Twice a week she had to go to the hospital for the removal of two pints of blood! They had not yet found the way to stop this overproduction. However, the next day:

> Vicki took us out to eat. Very cheerful and pretty. It came to me that she has little hope of recovery. They are constantly moving to other parts of her body to draw off the excess blood, because her veins keep collapsing. She is a remarkable woman.

I didn't realize how much this had impacted me until we returned to Mexico. The next day I awoke with the feeling I couldn't breathe. At breakfast Evelyn talked about Vicki and I began to cry. Later, at the office, midway in my first counseling session I felt so bad I excused myself and went home. I slept all afternoon, got up for a few minutes, went back to bed and slept all night, got up for a while, then went back to bed and slept another hour and a half.

As the weeks passed, we continued looking for ways of pressuring the *Delegada* to remove the seals. Her superior, the *Regente,* wrote her a letter instructing her to revoke her order. She ignored it. Roberto, the husband of one of my clients, was the pilot of the President's helicopter. He promised to speak with the President. A week later I heard news that dimmed my hopes: for two years the *Delegada* had been Roberto's lover, and when he was converted and broke up with her she became an enemy of Christianity.

In spite of our being "in the wilderness" the church continued to prosper. Attendance returned to what it had been before the placing of the seals. New people came every Sunday, and each time I preached there were professions of faith. In April the young people had an evangelistic breakfast and ninety attended. It was a busy life! The last Sunday in June I wrote:

What a weekend! Yesterday the young people had another evangelistic breakfast, and I was the speaker, then I visited Iris. She's twenty-one now, and very enthusiastic about the fact that her church (the sponsor of Anastasis) has gone charismatic. A group of about 20 people helped me move my office to a new location, because the *Delegada* has been threatening to close the one I have at present. Then I went to a reception for several graduates of the American School. Today I taught my Sunday School class, preached, and baptized fourteen people.

In July I wrote in my diary:

The annual meeting of the Southern Baptist Convention in New Orleans turned into a rout, and the takeover by the fundamentalists is complete. There is talk of a purge of our seminary faculties and the possibility of a split in the Convention.

By September I was into the fourth month of a training program to run another marathon on my 65th birthday.

After so many failed attempts at having the seals removed from our building, we decided to sign a lease with the downtown Maria Sheraton Isabel Hotel. We had toyed with the idea of purchasing a property quite a long way from our present location, but now we felt that God was telling us to rest from the crisis and take advantage of this five-star hotel on Avenida Reforma.

Great news came from Vicki. The hospital that was treating her received a million dollar grant to experiment with a radical new procedure. They removed a portion of her bone marrow and subjected it to a special laboratory procedure for several weeks. Then they re-injected it. A couple of weeks later the doctors advised Vicki that she was in remission. She would need to go in once a week for a blood check, but until further notice her blood was in the high range of normal. Halleluja!

But bad news from Carol:

We called Carol last night, and she said she and her husband are definitely going to divorce, that she had found some cards he had written to "that woman", and others that this person had written to him. He tells her he knows he is messed up but that he doesn't want to change. Given her lack of income and fragile health she may end up living with us. Evelyn is worried about Carol, and that is affecting her sleep. There are so many uncertainties! What a blessing it is in these difficult times to remind myself that the only unchanging joy is loving Christ and being loved by Him!

In mid-November Evelyn and I decided to take a trip to Houston and Dallas. I needed a rest, I couldn't remember a time when I'd had so much trouble with exhaustion. A part of the problem was the smog. I had reached twelve kilometers in my training program, but often it left me tired for the rest of the day. So I decided to abandon the goal of running a marathon to celebrate my sixty-fifth birthday. In Houston we visited the town house we had bought a couple of years before. The man who was leasing it offered to buy it, but we refused. Kingwood, with its quiet wooded streets and beautiful greenbelts, seemed a paradise. We were encouraged by the prospect of a future church home. The real estate agent who is managing our house took us to her church and we received a hearty welcome from the pastor and the Minister of Education. However, when we returned to Mexico City it still seemed like coming home. I wrote "I accept that we indeed are going to retire, but I feel stronger than ever that we are going to continue with a ministry here."

As we moved into the new year, everything we did was under the shadow of our approaching retirement. I saw no other alternative to leaving the pastorate of the church to Ricardo. Our relationship had matured, and there was no tension between us. On the other hand, he was beginning to draw lines of separation. When our church council discussed the possibility of my making return visits, he emphasized that I would be returning as a "friend" of the church, not as the pastor.

On January 16, 1991 the long-awaited war with Iraq began. Saddam Hussein had invaded Kuwait. President Bush had worked successfully at uniting most of the nations, and the U.N. had set a deadline for withdrawal. When Saddam ignored the deadline, the war began with fierce air attacks. I was surprised at the reaction in Mexico. People were depressed, and the papers were filled with predictions of gas warfare, and thousands of deaths. I wrote:

> The ground assault hasn't begun, but will probably begin within a week. Everyone is dreading it because it will surely mean fearful losses. There are more than half a million soldiers on each side. Nine allied planes have been shot down. Hussein has poured 300 million gallons of crude into the gulf. They are now saying they expect the war to continue for at least two or three months.

In February the church had a weekend retreat at an estate in Cuernavaca that Oscar had recently purchased. The purpose of the retreat was to lay out plans for a reorganization on the basis of my leaving. Afterward I wrote: "I continue to feel quite strange about my future. The July 31st deadline is like dropping off a cliff." The invasion of Kuwait began February 24th. Two days later I wrote:

> There had been awesome predictions: a terrible air war, disaster from the dug-in fortresses, gas warfare, a stubborn resistance by the Republican guard, terrorism worldwide. None of this has happened. At this moment Kuwait City has been occupied; the U.S. army has encircled the Republican Guard, and everywhere the Iraq army is surrendering, already there are 30,000 prisoners. Everyone, including the generals, has been surprised.

As the date for retirement drew closer, I found myself struggling with conflicting impressions. I had more counseling patients than ever, and many invitations to preach in other churches and citywide meetings. An invitation had come to travel to Austin and preach at the annual meeting of the Texas Hispanic Convention. Plenty of energy. In April I commented, "So many doors are opening I can't believe I'm leaving the country for good."

On the other hand, I complained about the pollution "getting completely out of hand". Most of the time the green hills surrounding the city were shrouded in a gray cloud. I suspected that this atmospheric poison was beginning to affect my health.

Besides, my patience was exhausted with attempts to have the seals removed from our church building. After seventeen months there had been no movement. In March a lawyer told me he had arranged everything and it would cost us $1400. A month later the price was raised to $7,000.

In May Evelyn and I drove to Houston. We stayed in our townhouse, which was now unoccupied, sleeping on cots. We bought a new car. After returning to Mexico City I wrote:

> I fell in love with Kingwood. It is beautiful and peaceful. The people were very friendly. I had the opportunity to try out the greenbelt and it was fantastic -- tall pines and oak trees, birds singing. Reminded me of Ridgecrest.

Meanwhile, Carol called to tell us she had given up on trying to save her marriage and agreed to sign the divorce papers her husband had brought home. He has an obsession for a married woman, with whom he talks for hours on the telephone. He has resigned the church he pastored, in preparation for the divorce. Carol has been having grave problems with depression, and this is affecting her health. On the advice of a friend she sought counseling from the pastor of a church in Juarez. I wrote in my diary:

> Carol has been attending *Vino Nuevo*, a charismatic church in Juarez. Her pastor is a prominent figure here in Mexico and this past weekend was with a church here in the city. I talked with him and his wife and thanked them for their personal interest in Carol.

Late in June we attended our last annual meeting of the Southern Baptist missionaries in Mexico, our spiritual family. The meeting was held in the context of developments that would bring radical changes to Southern Baptists and their way of doing missions. I wrote:

Keith Parks, Executive Director of the Foreign Mission Board, was our Bible study leader and his interpretation of trends in the Southern Baptist Convention was rather depressing. The tendencies that started more than a decade ago have radically changed what the Convention is, and there seems to be little hope for a reversal. I'm glad we are not going to be part of what will happen to the Foreign Mission Board in the next decade. A committee presented a plan for basic changes in the way mission work will be done in Mexico. There was a lot of debate, some of it bitter.

In the midst of the tensions there were unforgettable expressions of love and appreciation on the part of our fellow missionaries. I gave an interpretation of our thirty-one years in Mexico. There was a celebration of our retirement, presented as a graduation.

Our last week in Mexico City the Baptist Association sponsored an elegant testimonial banquet in a downtown hotel, attended by many pastors and the leaders of the Convention and the Association. Many kind words were spoken. Oscar read a touching testimonial to our ministry and the blessing we had been in his own life.

And thus an era came to an end. On July 31st we closed the door on the fifth-floor "penthouse" condominium we had occupied for the last seventeen years and headed for the airport, wondering what awaited us in the United States after more than thirty-three years away. We would have no friends to greet us when we arrived in Houston, no church home, no work to do. About the only concrete hope we nurtured was that we would live for at least nine years more so we could welcome in the new millennium. Realistically we figured we had about fifteen more years of life, and we hoped they would be years of health and peace.

Chapter Twenty-Seven
A New Beginning
1991-1997

And Hebron therefore became the inheritance of Caleb the son of Jephunneh the Kenizzite to this day, because he wholly followed the Lord God of Israel... Then the land had rest from war. (Joshua 14:14-15)

We're not told what Caleb did after his conquest of the city of Hebron. We do know that afterward, Hebron was designated a city of refuge, and was given to "the sons of Aaron" (1Chronicles 6:57). Caleb retired to the hill country surrounding Hebron IChronicles 6:56).

The last day of July, 1991 we boarded a plane for Kingwood, Texas and that night occupied the town house that was now our home. I wrote in my diary:

> We're very pleased with the living conditions. Kingwood
> is a planned community, a paradise for retirees. The houses
> and lawns are well kept, And the "green belt" is fabulous, a
> football field wide band of forest reserved for   walkers and
> bikers that continues for some fifty miles. All I have to do is
> step out my back door, and there it is! It's impossible not to
> go jogging every morning.

The first Sunday we attended Forest Cove Baptist Church in the morning and First Baptist at night. Dr. Dearing Garner, pastor of First Church, visited us Monday night and talked about the need for a counseling ministry in his church.

The next week we went to Dallas. David and Vicki had just entered a new home and had it "fixed up like a palace". Linda and her family were in an apartment. The next week Carol had a stopover in Houston, and was a bit more optimistic about her marriage.

A week later she called and said Mario wanted to work things out so they would not have to divorce. This pattern of withdrawing and returning! It had been that way since the beginning of the marriage.

We continued to pray about which church we should join. The Minister of Education at Forest Cove took me to lunch and spoke enthusiastically about the possibility of my being a teacher in a seminary for lay people he planned to establish. They had just purchased sixteen acres on nearby Highway 59 and were making plans for a megachurch.

In mid-September I made my first return visit to Mexico City, spending eight days in the home of Oscar and Betty. Ricardo was very optimistic about the future of the Anastasis church.

In October we began to define our future as retirees. First we needed to decide what church we'd join. One Wednesday morning I awoke and a thought came to me: if Evelyn should speak a positive word concerning First Baptist before the next Sunday, this would be God's word that we should join that church. Friday morning at breakfast she said, "Pat, I think you'd get along much better with Dr. Garner." So the next Sunday we joined First Baptist.

Forest Cove church had attractions, with exciting plans for the future. But there was something about the dynamic of the leadership that set off warning bells in my soul. As the months and years would unfold, I'd have occasions for giving thanks for our decision, as one by one the staff members were dismissed. Ten years later, after building an enormous church plant on their new campus, the congregation divided, and the pastor formed a new church a few blocks away.

Then a pleasant surprise: since I did not possess a Texas professional license as a psychologist, I had discarded the possibility of joining the staff of the Union Baptist Association's Center for Counseling.

Then one day in October I had lunch with Dr. Charles Wisdom, a former teacher at our Mexico City seminary, and now pastor of First Baptist Church of Katy. Jim Herrington, Director of Missions for the Association, accompanied us. Dr. Herrington introduced me to Miss Neal, Director of the Center for Counseling, and she was very encouraging. The next week I was interviewed by the psychologist in charge of approving staff members, and behold! he decided to make an exception to the professional requirements in my case. I was left speechless. No doubt about it, God had plans for me in Houston!

This became even more evident the next week, when Pastor Garner took Evelyn and me to lunch and invited me to join the church staff. The next week, at his invitation, I spoke in the Wednesday night service. Afterward he said, "I don't know what we have done for the Lord to send us a man like Dr. Carter." A couple of weeks later we agreed I would join the staff in January as part-time Associate Pastor, and give most of my attention to counseling. I also formalized my alliance with the Associational Center for Counseling.

In November I spent ten days in Mexico City and occupied the apartment that Anastasis church had bought for us. I found myself quite busy, with a large number of counseling appointments and preaching at both Sunday services. On my visit the following month I was discouraged by reports of dissension in Anastasis Church, and began to feel that, in the light of the ministry that had opened up to me in Kingwood, my visits to Mexico City would soon become less frequent.

I closed out the year 1991 giving thanks to God for the many unexpected blessings since arriving in Kingwood. By now I had no doubts about God's having led us into retirement in that beautiful city. I wrote:

> One desire I mentioned upon projecting this year was that by this time "I will have defined the general thrust of my retirement ministry." That has been fulfilled. Praise the Lord!

In their January business meeting the church extended me a formal invitation to be Associate Pastor, with a generous part-time salary. The

church was in a pattern of growth, with a Sunday School attendance of
700 and four staff members besides myself.
Later that month came an unpleasant surprise:

> Evelyn has had trouble for the last week or so with insomnia
> and depression. She has an appointment with the doctor
> tomorrow. Don't know what's behind it, maybe this dark,
> rainy weather.

My mid-February visit to Mexico was encouraging. Ricardo
seemed to have worked out his problems with the church, and now
Oscar had become very active, almost an associate pastor. He had
purchased a house a few blocks from the church for a counseling center
and contracted a staff of Christian psychologists, baptizing the center
Armonia Familiar (family harmony). I had no inkling of the important
place the center would occupy in my life in the years ahead.

Evelyn and I were living a surreal drama. She had dreamed for
years about returning to live in the States. We had a home in an
exceptionally beautiful city, and were active in a church very much like
the one in which she had spent her high school years. Who would have
guessed she would fall into depression! I wrote:

> Evelyn worries me; she doesn't have any joy in life.
> Sometimes I feel she has sentenced herself to die, she's so
> apathetic about everything. I feel like I'm living with a
> stranger.

As the months passed her depression deepened. Some days she
stayed in bed most of the day, and talked about wanting to die. She
had always enjoyed TV, but now had no interest in it. In June we
traveled by automobile to Mexico City. The month we spent there
in our apartment was pleasant and productive, but Evelyn continued
with her problems. She had frequent appointments with the dentist,
complained continually about a pain in her side, and was sure she had
cancer, until a doctor did a barium enema.

Upon returning to Kingwood I entered into what was becoming a
full ministry. The pastor had me fill the pulpit for three Sundays while

he was away, and the number of counseling clients continued to grow. That month I began teaching a young marrieds Sunday School class, a ministry that would bring me much satisfaction in the years ahead.

Evelyn continued with her depression, and in October, I began taking her each week to a Christian counselor. I had been invited to give the Bible studies at an emeritus missionaries' conference in Richmond, but she fell into such a panic about going that I had to leave her at home. After eight weeks the counselor said he could find no psychological basis for her depression. He recommended she ask her physician for a prescription for an antidepressant. She did, and within a couple of weeks was feeling fine!

Later that year I received a clean bill of health on what I feared was a problem with my heart. I commented that I felt the Lord was telling me that I'd live until 93 without any serious health problems.

Among the encouraging things that happened in the early months of 1993 was the progress in my writing. I completed a novel entitled *Atchafalaya,* a story of my boyhood in South Louisiana. Joyce Farrel, a book agent, reviewed the manuscript, liked it and entered into a contract with me to market it. Immediately I began working on a novel based on experiences in Mexico, and gave it the tentative title, *The Serpent and the Lamb.* By July the *Atchafalaya* novel had been turned down by various publishers who said there was no longer a market for "the traditional Christian novel." That did not discourage me in my work on the novel about Mexico. I was discovering that writers write because they have to, not because they get applause from the publishers.

I was busy in my associate pastorate, working with a steady stream of counseling clients, preaching often at the church, and every Sunday teaching a class of 50-60 young marrieds. Besides, I continued periodic visits to Mexico City. As 1993 ended, I was filled with satisfaction.

The most memorable event of the year was a three-week preaching ministry in the month of November as a guest of the Baptist Convention of Hungary. The trip was sponsored by the Virginia Baptist Convention, and I was invited to speak to churches and associations on the Holy Spirit. Many Baptists were abandoning their churches for charismatic groups, and they hoped my lectures would be a corrective. It was quite an adventure, staying in a Budapest hotel in a room overlooking the

Danube, traveling across the snowy countryside by train, sleeping in the homes of pastors, enjoying great Christian fellowship. It began with a surprise: the President of the Convention picked me up at sundown on Sunday, and on the way to a downtown church informed me that I would preach that night. I had no sermon notes, because I had thought I would be attending as a spectator. When we entered the large stone building I saw it was packed with some 400 people, most of them middle-aged men in staid gray suits. I preached with liberty, feeling empowered by the prayers of my intercessors back home.

Our third year of retirement my agent sent my *Atchafalaya* manuscript to other publishers, without result, but I still did not let that affect my commitment to writing. By the end of the year I had written 400 pages on my novel about Mexico. I pushed myself physically, reaching ten miles in my determination to at least run a mini-marathon. I traveled several times to Mexico City, preaching at *Anastasis* Church and participating in a marriage retreat. In May I did the unthinkable: I traded in our Buick for a three-year-old Cadillac! I felt like anything but a retired missionary, driving such an exotic automobile. It took months to overcome my discomfort when I visited churches. But I kept telling myself I had as much a right to own a luxury car as any other Christian. The pastor took a number of trips to orphanages in Europe, and left me the pulpit. A very satisfying life!

The year 1995 brought continued problems with Evelyn's health. In February I had to cancel a trip to the Holy Land at the last moment because she was in the hospital with severe pain in her side. It turned out to be nothing serious, but I was concerned about her facial spasms and occasional difficulty in speaking. By the end of the year she was feeling better.

1996 was not an encouraging year for our children's' marriages. David separated from Vicki and rented his own apartment. Carol and Mario were still living together, but with the agreement they would divorce as soon as the children finished high school. Linda complained continually about her husband's verbal abuse. Her daughter Victoria married a drug-addicted boyfriend, and by the end of the year had separated from him and moved to Philadelphia with her baby, Zeke.

As the New Year began, Evelyn's health problems returned. I wrote in my diary:

Evelyn seems to be moving toward being a semi-invalid. I mentioned to her the other day that maybe we should think about having a caretaker live with us. I still like to be on the go, and have a number of engagements lined up for next month. But her health problems throw a shadow over my plans, knowing I may have to cancel them.

Much of our prayers were invested in our children. David and Vicki continued apart most of the year. David frustrated us, one month talking about returning to his marriage and the next month very skeptical. We would learn later that there was another woman involved. Finally, in November he moved back home and we visited them in December. Things seemed much calmer and they were planning a Caribbean cruise.

We were relieved to learn that David was finally determining where his priorities needed to be and, in fact, had been going to psychological counseling in an effort to address his continuing commitment issues.

And I was learning that it was impossible to deny the reality of an aging body, In April I wrote:

> Thursday I return to the Mann Eye Clinic for a follow-up on a visual field exam they did four months ago. I'm expecting them to tell me that my eyes are deteriorating and that I face blindness. This is because in the last couple of months I have had increasing problems with "floaters". Facing any kind of light makes black spots float over my visual field, and sometimes they are almost like a web. So I am asking myself what life would be like without eyesight.

In June and July I acted as interim pastor while Pastor Deering was away on a sabbatical. It was a busy time, one week I had three funerals. I enjoyed the preaching opportunity, but was glad when the two months were over. Upon his return, I did not receive any word of commendation on my interim ministry, but was grateful to be working with a man whose integrity was unquestioned, who gave me complete freedom and showed me in indirect ways that he appreciated my presence.

In September a magnum event: Evelyn and I celebrated our 50th wedding anniversary. Our children were present, plus Evelyn's brothers and sisters.

My only brother James had died three months before of a stroke, but even if he had been alive, he would probably not have attended. A tragic life. He and I had never been close. Four years my senior, he had always seemed resentful of me when we were kids, and after we both married, years would pass without any communication. He never attended church and was a chain smoker. I wrote about his funeral in June:

> Had the opportunity to spend a lot of time with Jana (James' wife) and with Jimmy and Diane (his children). G'ana talked to me about how hard it had been to live with James. Diane said she had never felt loved by her father. I saw no tears in the three days we were with them. Yet quite a number of his friends attended the funeral and spoke highly of his friendship. Seems he could express affection to those outside his family, but not to those within. Yet I am sure that he loved his wife and was never unfaithful. My brother was always an enigma. I tried to remember good things about our boyhood together, but could hardly remember anything positive.

January, 1997 began with the promise of a pleasant continuance of my retirement schedule. The church had completed a magnificent $3,000,000 Administration building, and I now had a beautiful office with a waiting room. I spent the second week of January in Mexico City and preached at the 25th anniversary of the *Primera Iglesia Bautista* (First Baptist Church) of Satellite City, a prosperous northern suburb. This church, which met in the chapel of the seminary, was averaging 1400 in its five services. I now had a long-standing loving relationship with them and their pastor, having participated in a number of their annual marriage retreats.

Later in the month I went on a twelve-day trip to the Holy Land with a group from our church. I had not visited Israel before, because I feared the Christian shrines had become so commercialized I would be a disappointed. The opposite occurred. When I returned I described in my diary three "encounters" with Christ, one on Mount Megiddo, overlooking the site of the future Battle of Armageddon, one in the praetorian where Jesus was whipped before His crucifixion, and one on the shore of the Sea of Galilee:

> This morning I arose early to watch the sunrise. As it came over the mountain, on the other side of the Sea, the sun painted a golden path completely across, from shore to shore. In the middle there seemed to be a fire kindled, moving out in waves like a flame. A true *shekeina* encounter!

I have over my desk a photo of this phenomenon. I don't know if I took the photo, or someone else, but as I grow older it has become a symbol of my walk toward heaven and inspires me every day.

Meanwhile the writing on my novel continued. I was counseling people every day, some with really miraculous results. My young married's class was also a great enjoyment, and I noted that fully half the people who joined the church were from my class. In June our granddaughter Esther (Liz) came to visit us for a week.

We thoroughly enjoyed her visit:

> She is 18 now, pretty, charming. We talked a lot, and I filled her in on family history. The best day was Tuesday, when she and I spent most of the day at Astroworld, enjoying a lot of the rides, including the bungie jump. Turns out she has inherited my adventurous genes and likes to do the crazy things I like. Wish I could spend more time with her!

In September I mentioned in my diary the first indication of a crisis that was to bring a revolution in my life, a tightness in my chest while running. A thalium test at the cardiologist's revealed a partially blocked blood vessel. A catheterization showed 90% blockage. They scheduled me for a bypass at St. Luke's hospital. I was half an hour away from surgery when another cardiologist came in, looked at the x-rays and said he could solve the problem with a stint. I had to make an immediate decision. I made a mistake, opting for the stint.

Had a rough recovery, including a return to the hospital with urination problems.

But, unknown to me, my feeling of weakness and my conviction of attacks by Satan initiated a relationship that would become a special blessing. I called Linda Vogel and asked her to come over and pray for me. She did. We agreed this was a satanic attack, and removed from the house a number of demonic souvenirs we had brought from Mexico.

In the following months I never had the conviction of a complete recovery, and there was a feeling of tightness when I ran. The cardiologist had told me that stints were successful 80% of the time. Was I going to be one of the unfortunate 20%?

Chapter Twenty-Eight
An Unexpected Renewal
1998-2000

The Bible does not tell us how long Caleb lived in Hebron before it was declared a City of Refuge and he was forced to move to the hill country outside the city. Whom did he have as family? As we have noted earlier, Azubah died in Egypt, and during the forty years in the desert the second wife, Ephrath, along with the sons of both wives, passed away. Did his grandchildren live with him? We are not told, but that is likely. In later life, Caleb took to himself two concubines, Ephah and Maacha (IChron. 2:46,48). Why did he choose to have concubines, rather than marry another wife? We don't know, neither Moses nor Joshua had concubines. Of these, seven sons were born. Francine Rivers, in her novel, The Warrier*, suggests that these sons were bitter at having been uprooted from their home in Hebron. She believes that the one bright spot in his life was Achsah, his only daughter (she is called, not "a daughter," but "Caleb's daughter," as if she were the only one) and that she alone shared his devotion to Jehovah. Caleb gave her as wife to Othniel, his nephew, who was the most valiant of his warriors. It's obvious she had her daddy wrapped around her finger! First, she persuaded Othniel to ask her father for a choice piece of land, and then she convinced her father to give her two water springs (Judges 1:12-15.)

What happened after Caleb's retirement? Joshua 15: 14-20 is very similar to Judges 1: 8-15. Both recount the taking of Hebron. Some commentators suggest that both passages are taken from the same earlier document. However, the first verse of Judges makes that impossible: it declares that the invasion recorded there occurred after the death of Joshua. I must agree with Francine Rivers that this second account in Judges describes a reconquest of parts of Canaan by Caleb, years after his retirement. Many of the Canaanites had remained in the region, and as time passed they occupied Hebron, so Caleb had to put on his armor again and complete the conquest that had been left half-done.

This is the moment to tell you how I discovered that my life poem rhymes with the life of Caleb.

As mentioned in the last chapter, some months after the placement of a stint in one of my heart arteries, I began to feel again the same tightness in my chest that had provoked the earlier crisis. This became the basis of a spiritual struggle. In January I wrote in my diary:

> Last week my doctor told me he was sure my chest pains were angina, and booked me an appointment with the cardiologist. The strange thing is that I feel I hear God telling me I'm healed. I have committed myself to believing this, but doubt interferes. Last night. I saw doubt as black roots clogging my heart and mind. I visualized the roots being pulled out and wrapped around the cross, then melting.

A few weeks later I wrote:

> Tomorrow morning at 6:00 I'm to enter St. Luke's Hospital for a bypass. An angiogram showed a 90% blockage. The stint did not work! I had expected the angiogram to be negative. I was disappointed, but I had told myself it was a no-win situation, because even if it showed no blockage I would still have to find out why these feelings of pain continued. I had tried every spiritual means I knew and there had been no improvement. I had decided I'd need to go to someone with a gift of discernment. I have no explanation

for why it came out as it did, except that God has not promised to exempt us from suffering.

When I awoke in ICU, my wife Evelyn told me it was Wednesday. I blinked. The operation had taken place Monday morning, but I had no recollection of Tuesday. She explained something had gone wrong in the recovery room. I'd begun bleeding and they'd had to go back in for repairs.

So there I was, flat of my back, without the strength to turn over, even if they'd let me. They brought me food, and I struggled for ten minutes trying to swallow a teaspoonful. A heavy depression pressed down on my chest, clogged my thoughts, enclosed my feelings in a thick darkness. What reason did I have for hope? I'd already lived two years beyond the biblical threescore and ten, and this nightmare was a portent of a future without meaning, without peace, without joy. They placed me in a private room Thursday night.

"Pat," Evelyn told me, "Linda asked permission to spend the day with you tomorrow." It was Friday, visiting hours were over and Evelyn was standing beside my bed, purse in her hands.

"Linda? Oh, I don't know, I don't feel like talking with anybody. I just want to be alone."

"I'd hate to tell her no. She seems so sure it's something she needs to do. And she told me to tell you she doesn't expect you to say anything."

What choice did I have? Linda was practicing a ministry I'd helped her to discover. Some years before, I'd noticed Linda's commitment to prayer. One day I asked her: "Have you considered the possibility that you have the spiritual gift of intercession?"

"I've never heard anyone say that intercession could be one of the gifts of the Spirit."

"It's not in Paul's lists of the gifts, but I'm convinced God has equipped some people with intercessory prayer as a special gift. And I suspect you're one of those people." Later, Linda became a leader in intercessory prayer, and God had used her to bless many lives, both in our church and in the Near East.

So the next day Linda was in my room early, in one hand her Bible and in the other a cassette player. At the close of the day she gave me a word from God that would change my life. She read me Joshua 14:6-14, where Caleb reminded Joshua of the visit of the twelve spies to Canaan and of a promise Moses had made him:

> On that day Moses swore to me, "The land on which your
> feet have walked will be your inheritance and that of your
> children forever, because you have loved the Lord my God
> wholeheartedly." Now then, just as the Lord promised, he
> has kept me alive for forty-five years since the time he said
> this to Moses, while Israel moved about in the desert. So here
> I am today, eighty-five years old! I am still as strong today as
> the day Moses sent me out; I'm just as vigorous to go out to
> battle now as I was then. Now give me this hill country that
> the Lord promised me that day ... Then Joshua blessed Caleb
> son of Jephunneh and gave him Hebron as he had promised.

Linda closed her Bible and said to me: "Dr. Pat, you spent most of your adult life in Mexico. When you retired you took for granted that your ministry there had ended. But God has other plans. He wants you to know that you are his Caleb and that, just like Caleb, he has prepared a Hebron for you in Mexico's hill country."

I was grateful for Linda's ministration, but at the moment I was too weary to appreciate the significance of her words. Still, a seed had been planted in my spirit that afterward would bear fruit, and that would become the inspiration for this book.

After I returned home, Evelyn fell ill. We were blessed by the ministrations of Linda and her prayer partner, Donna. They were both convinced that God had a special plan for my life, that He had made Mexico City my Hebron and that great opportunities lay ahead for me. We began meeting weekly to study the Word and to seek God's will. At the moment there was no indication of any future in Mexico City. I had gone there only three times the year before, and now with my physical limitations the future was doubtful. Looking back, I can see how God was moving, but very slowly, so slowly that His hand is seen much more clearly in retrospect than at the moment.

In June came the first sign of God's providence. Due to the physical problems of both of us, Evelyn and I decided to move to a one-story house. We had noticed that town houses were slow to sell. One just a couple of doors down had just been sold after nearly two years of a For Sale sign in the front yard. We contacted a real estate agent one Friday and she came over for us to sign a contract. The following Monday a man and his wife came to look at the house. The next day their agent called and asked us how soon we could vacate, the couple wanted to purchase our townhouse! Shell-shocked, we got busy looking for another place, and within a few days, to our pleasant surprise, found an attractive four-bedroom home not far away.

Later I realized that name of our new Kingwood "village" was a prophecy. Thirty months later we would plant a new church in a home in Mexico City, my Hebron. The home was located in a section named *Lomas de los Bosques*. And guess where we had bought our new home? In a section of Kingwood named Woodland Hills, an exact translation of *Lomas de los Bosques!*

We spent the months of September and October in Mexico City, where I taught in the Seminary. Besides preaching every other Sunday in the Anastasis Church, I had more invitations than I could accept. We enjoyed those two months, but there was also a feeling of sadness. The seminary was in such a desperate financial crisis that some of the Convention leaders were talking of selling the property.

1999 was in many ways a parenthesis year. My health slowly returned to normal.

Evelyn was enjoying her best health in a decade. My Sunday School class prospered, with an average attendance of seventy. The church was averaging over 800 in Sunday School, with many Sundays close to 900.

Thank God, the year 2000 began without a major disaster! Most of the "experts" had predicted that the entry into a new millennium would bring weeks, maybe months of crisis. Telephone lines would be shut down, public buildings would be in chaos, food and water would become scarce, there would likely be no electricity. All because the computers that controlled everything had not been programmed for the new millennium. We stored food and water, bought battery-powered lamps and a camp stove. What a relief that none of the dire predictions came true!

On the other hand, the year 2000 was pivotal in my life and in my post-retirement ministry. God never gets in a hurry! In March of 1998 God had given through Linda an exciting prophecy. But more than two years had passed, and I had not seen any concrete confirmation. Meanwhile, life went on. In March our daughter Linda, after twenty-nine years of marriage, left her husband and rented an apartment. She'd decided she could not take any more of his negative outlook on life and his inability to show affection. I was also learning to adjust to a new development at church. A new minister had been added to the staff, and although he had another title, was now functioning as associate pastor, having taken over the preaching assignments that I had before fulfilled In May a crisis threatened to split the church. The pastor had decided we should begin a Saturday night service, in spite of the opposition of a significant portion of the members. Thankfully, in the last staff meeting before the vote was to be taken, the staff convinced him the church was not ready for this change.

In June of 2000 God spoke again! I spent a week with Carol attending a week of "revival, prophecy and spiritual warfare" in her church in Juarez. We were in services twelve hours a day Monday through Thursday. The last night, her pastor stood to make closing announcements to the crowd of about 4,000. At that moment the Spirit whispered in my heart that the pastor was going to mention my name. I prepared myself for an invitation to direct the closing prayer. Suddenly he paused, fixed his eyes on me where I was seated with Carol in the second row:

"Dr. Carter, you have had a fruitful ministry. Here on the platform are several ministers that you prepared in your seminary. But the Lord wants you to know that your best years are yet to come. You are going to be surprised at how long you live, the health you enjoy and the fruit you bear." He continued in that vein for some three or four minutes, then pronounced the benediction.

I had a hard time going to sleep that night. Two years before, in the most difficult moment of my life, my intercessor Linda declared that God had made me His Caleb, and that my best years were yet to come. Tonight, Carol's pastor had repeated that same prophecy, in almost the same words!

In the following months Linda and Donna and I met each week for prayer. We talked of God's plans for me in Mexico City and awaited the opening of a door.

In August that door opened. I led a group from our church on a medical mission to Mexico City. The first day of work was Thursday. Friday morning at 6:37 I wrote the following:

"Time of Harvest." That's the word the Lord has given to me. I awoke this morning at 4:30. Had slept a good five hours, and couldn't go back to sleep. Then, almost imperceptibly, God's Spirit began speaking to me. Since then it has been very strong. I haven't had an experience like this in a long time.

At 7:30 I went down to where the group was having breakfast and told them I wouldn't be going out with them that day that the Lord had told me I should remain in my room all day because He had a word for me. During the next ten hours I wrote on fifteen sheets of lined yellow paper what God was saying to me. It boiled down to the following: God was telling me that I was at the beginning of the fulfillment of the prophecies, and that He wanted a commitment from me. I pledged to the Lord my absolute obedience, and my readiness to do whatever might be necessary to respond to His Time of Harvest.

After two years of drought, this was the year of abundant rain! The very next month came a sign from the Lord that blew my mind, and also that of Linda and Donna. In our weekly prayer session I shared a surprising discovery. The day before I had searched in a Bible dictionary for the meaning of the name Caleb. I was shocked to discover its Hebrew root: "dog."

For the Hebrews, the dog was the most despised of all animals. Deuteronomy 23:18 says, "You shall not bring the wages of a harlot or the price of a dog into the house of the Lord your God." It was an insult to call a person a dog.

"Why do you suppose Caleb's parents gave him that name?" I said.

Linda answered, "Maybe they didn't. Maybe it was a nickname."

"Why of course," Donna said, "You know how mean kids can be to one another. Imagine this little Gentile stranger showing up one day in a world of Hebrew children. It's not surprising they gave him an insulting nickname."

I mused, "Well, if they did, it stuck with him, and after a while, it must not have mattered. Like a boy I knew who moved from Louisiana to Philadelphia. The kids there called him 'Reb'. Later, when he became a baseball star, they still called him "Reb," no longer as a put-down, but as an affectionate nickname."

We were silent for a moment. Then Donna turned to me and asked, "Dr. Pat, what's your middle name?"

I looked at her for a moment, surprised by the question. "My middle name **is** Harold. In fact, my mother wanted that to be my first name, until --"

I jumped to my feet and began pounding on the desk. "No! Oh no!"

Linda and Donna were staring at me.

Finally I caught my breath, and sat down slowly. After a while I said, "Guess what: I was named after a dog!"

And I told them a story: my father for many years traveled the world as a sailor. Finally, he decided it was time to return home, claim Marie, the red-headed French girl he loved, and settle down. In Belgium, the last port of call, he bought a handsome German shepherd. All the way back to Port Arthur the dog slept with Dad's Irish buddy, so Dad and his shipmates, as a joke, named the dog "Pat".

Daddy and his new wife settled in Port Arthur, Texas and he went to work at the Texaco refinery. Three years later James was born. James and Pat became inseparable friends. James was four years old when, just a few days before my birth, a tragedy occurred: Pat disappeared. Every day after school James wandered the streets looking for his beloved playmate, and every night he cried himself to sleep.

The day I was born James announced to his parents that that they must name his new brother "Pat". They laughed. Name the new baby after a dog? Impossible! Months ago they'd agreed that if the baby was a boy he'd be named "Harold."

But little James was stubborn. Every night when he said his prayers he thanked God for sending his new brother, Pat, to take the place of the precious friend he'd loved for four years. Each time Daddy told Mom he was going downtown to register my birth, Mom would insist they give James' heart one more day to heal. Finally they decided they could wait no longer. They resolved the problem of the name in the only way open to them at the moment. On the wall above my desk I have a framed copy of the birth certificate:

Father's Name: James Alec Carter
Mother's name: Mary Monteilh
Baby's name: a blank

The date of the registry of the birth, June 21, reflects the gravity of the battle that had been going on in the Carter household. Five weeks had passed since my May 16th birth date, and still the name problem was not resolved!

Many times my mother told me how little James finally won the war. One day he returned from the corner grocery with a red lollipop in his hand. He went to the cradle and placed it beside the baby's head, saying to his mother, "When Pat wakes up, give him this sucker." Touched by the gesture, my mother gave in and began calling the baby "Pat". Though the two names were never registered, it was taken for granted after that that my legal name was "Pat Harold".

After Linda and Donna stopped laughing, we bowed our heads and gave thanks, because this "Caleb" poem was not of recent origin. More than seventy years ago, God had been present when my dad bought a German shepherd dog and named him Pat. And it hadn't been an accident when, seven years later, Pat disappeared just a few days before the arrival of a new baby, a baby for whom God had already set apart his own Hebron in Mexico's hill country.

Pat = "dog". Caleb means "dog". Pat = Caleb. Of course God has a sense of humor!

"Before I formed you in the womb I knew you; before you were born I sanctified you; I ordained you a prophet to the nations." Jeremiah 1:6

Now the three of us were certain that God was about to doors for me.

In October I returned to Mexico City, this time to participate in a marriage retreat with the First Baptist Church of Satellite City. My heart was open for a word from the Lord. October 13 I wrote in my diary:

Yesterday I preached the opening sermon. Just before I spoke the group sang a chorus: "I'm going to possess the inheritance that God gave me, I'm not going to be afraid." It struck my heart, and I shed many tears. What does the Lord have prepared for me? I wonder!

In November Oscar accompanied me to Merida, where we presented together a "Bi/Polar" personality seminar. He urged me to make plans for extending a helping hand to the Armonia Familiar counseling center the next year. Christina, the Director, had already talked with me about the disarray in the staff. Several of the psychologists were rebellious, uncooperative, and continually complaining. Changes needed to be made. Oscar proposed that I set aside one week a month January-March to spend in Armonia Familiar, making an analysis of the problem and proposing solutions. He would pay my plane fare and hotel. Upon our return I spent the night in Betty and Oscar's new home in Bosques de las Lomas. Betty showed me a recreation room downstairs where she dreamed of planting a church. The next night a group of five couples invited me to dinner. They all lived in the Lomas district of Mexico City and attended different churches. Now they wanted to begin a church in their area. Would I help them?

They gave me some statistics: The Lomas area was composed of half a dozen *colonias,* or burroughs. The population was in the top 1.7% of income in Mexico. This was the most unevangelized area of Mexico City. Half a million people lived there, and there was not a single evangelical church.

I told them I could not accept their invitation to be the pastor, but if the five husbands were willing, I would work with them according to the New Testament pattern: I'd train them, each according to his gifts of the Spirit, to be the elders, or lay pastors of the congregation. They agreed. We decided we would have our first service in January, in the home of Oscar and Betty.

*Tyndale House Publishers, Inc. Wheaton, Ill., 2005

Chapter Twenty-Nine
New Beginnings
2001-2003

As I have mentioned, Judges 1:9-15 appears to describe Caleb's reconquest, after his retirement, of the city of Hebron and his defeat of the three giants Sheshai, Ahiman and Talmai .

What reconquests awaited me in my own Hebron? There was, indeed, a need for reconquest! The seminary had serious problems. In the seventeen years since my resignation seven men had been named president and had resigned or had been terminated. Enrolment had decreased and there were critical financial problems. *Armonia Familiar,* the counseling ministry, was in trouble. Oscar Franco had revived this ministry after my departure, but there were problems with the staff. Then there was the matter of the abandonment of *Lomas* de *Chapultepec.* Anastasis church had been organized there, but had later moved to another area. Finally, Anastasis Church, which I had founded and pastored for eight years, was in crisis. Many members had left.

As the year 2001 began I entered into a new lifestyle, very much aware that the "Caleb Prophecy" of three years ago was being fulfilled. I agreed with Oscar to make monthly visits for three months. My assignment was to work with the staff of *Armonia Familiar,* with the purpose of resolving conflicts and training them to work as a team. It was soon clear that three months would not be sufficient, so I continued my monthly visits. Besides, in January we initiated a Monday night

Bible study in the beautiful new home of Betty and Oscar in *Bosque de las Lomas*, an extension of Lomas de Chapultepec. I was to lead the Bible studies the Mondays I was present, and Oscar the other nights. The first Monday night twelve people attended, and there was a lot of enthusiasm.

Meanwhile, I decided the time had come to end my ten-year stint as associate pastor of Kingwood First Baptist. However, two hours after I placed a letter of resignation on the pastor's desk he called me in, insisted he needed me, and urged me to continue. Surprised, I agreed.

In my visits with *Armonia Familiar* I spent most of my time interviewing the staff. By April I felt I had a good grasp of the problems. Months before, Cristina had been elevated from Business Manager to General Director. Anita, Director of the division of psychotherapy, felt she should have been named to that post. She was resentful, and refused to submit herself to Cristina's authority. Several of the other five psychotherapists were also unhappy, each with his own reasons.

In March Evelyn and I lived a scary scenario. The seminary in *Lomas Verdes* was celebrating its Centenary. A part of the celebration was to be a weekend visit by the staff and choir to Torreon, six hundred miles to the north, where the seminary had been founded. The seminary Director had invited me to preach in two Torreon churches on Sunday morning. Evelyn accompanied me to Mexico City the previous Monday. We stayed in the home of Betty and Oscar. By Wednesday, Evelyn was feeling ill. On Thursday she was admitted to the hospital, and the doctor diagnosed a blockage of the large intestine. By Friday we had to make a decision: if the antibiotics did not reopen the intestine, they would have to operate. Should I cancel my commitment in Torreon? We talked and prayed, and finally decided that I must go because a cancellation on my part would destroy plans that involved three institutions and hundreds of people. So Saturday morning I took the flight with fear and trembling.

Late that night I called Evelyn's room in the hospital. *Hermana* Ruth answered. I had baptized her and her two teenage children some twelve years earlier. A retired military nurse, her stern discipline masked the heart of a dedicated servant. She told me Evelyn's abdomen was so swollen she appeared pregnant. The doctor had warned that if the large intestine did not begin to function by 6:00 A.M. the next morning he would have to operate, and the surgery would be extremely risky. A group from Anastasis church had surrounded her bed for hours that afternoon, praying for her healing. I knew that people in Kingwood were also praying. I slept little that night.

Glory to God! I called again at six the next morning and *Hermana* Ruth told me the blockage had cleared. The doctor had just left, declaring that the only explanation he could find was that God had answered the prayers of all the people who had surrounded Evelyn with so much love. Ruth had stayed all night, forcing a complaining, tearful Evelyn to her feet again and again to walk the hospital aisle.

In June, a pleasant surprise: Dr. Tomas Garcia visited me in *Armona Familiar*. I had witnessed to Tomas' wife Patty back in 1976, as I led the seminary students in door-to-door visitation of their community. Within a year Tomas and Patty were baptized and had been active in several churches and missions. Tomas was a gifted Bible expositor, and had pastored two congregations. He held a doctorate in psychology and for the past eighteen years had been Director of Training for American Express in Latin America. He explained that he was frustrated with the limited success of his training program, and longed for an opportunity to put into effect a Bible-based curriculum.

His words excited me. Years before, when I began my counseling ministry, I had invited him to partner with me. After a week of prayerful consideration he had declined. I informed him that the opportunity he desired was available in *Armonia Familiar* and its projected program of training for business personnel. Maybe his dissatisfaction with his present position was God speaking to his heart! He said he would pray about it. Of course, we could not offer the salary Tomas was receiving in American Express.

In September I arrived in Mexico City a few days after the 9/11 disaster in New York City and was surprised by the impact it had made upon the Mexican people. They worried that at any moment something similar might occur in Mexico City. We initiated a monthly Sunday night service in the home of Betty and Oscar. Seventy people attended the first service.

In October surgeons in Houston's Methodist Hospital removed ten inches of Evelyn's large intestine. What a change for her! Soon she was enjoying foods that had been forbidden for a decade or more.

We had been impressed by the peace our daughter Linda enjoyed since her separation and divorce. The depression and lowered self-esteem that are commonly the fruit of a divorce had not happened in her case. She had a well-paid job, so there were no financial worries. At midyear she informed us that she was dating David, a person she had met in the singles department of her church. They had been friends for a year, and had decided they were ready to go beyond friendship. In November they were married. It was obvious they were a good match. Like Linda, David seems innately cheerful. He adores her, and surrounds her with the emotional support she desired for so many years.

As the year drew to a close there was good news and bad news in *Armonia Familiar*. Eleonara Roque joined our staff. She and her husband, Daniel, an executive in the Roche Pharmaceutical Company, were members of the new congregation in Lomas. Then, the Federal government came through with their promise of $216,000 for the purchase of a new property a block away from where we were presently meeting. On the other hand, little progress was being made on the staff problems. Anita remained obstinate in her refusal to cooperate with Cristina. Besides, she still lacked her diploma from the university, because she had not completed her thesis. She promised this would soon be accomplished, but I saw little reason to believe her. I brought in three businessmen from the United States for a seminar on team work. There was a superficial enthusiasm on the part of the staff, but knowing the resentments boiling beneath the surface, I was not optimistic about a permanent impact.

In 2001 I made a discovery that changed my life: for the first time I came to understand the meaning of the blood of Christ. All my life I had heard about and sung about -- and mentioned in my preaching -- the blood. Yet, I had never felt comfortable talking about the blood. I remember as a child that when the congregation sang, "Are You Washed in the Blood?" I sang along with them, but when we came to the words, "Are your garments spotless, are they white as snow, are you washed in the blood of the lamb?" I shuddered. Wash my clothes in blood? Ugh! I never quite got away from that feeling.

This attitude left me with a guilt complex. The Bible is filled with references to blood. The sacrifice of animals began with Abel, and under Moses was established as a system of obtaining pardon for sin. Paul built his theology of redemption upon the blood, and John declares that "the blood of Jesus Christ cleanses us from all unrighteousness." But through the years the blood continued to be for me merely a theological concept that had no real impact on my daily life.

About the turn of the century I decided I must find a way to change my attitude. I felt like a hypocrite, preaching a key Biblical concept that had no real place in my life! I began asking God to give me a fresh insight.

One day I was reading a newspaper account of a four-alarm fire that had placed a dozen people in the hospital. An urgent call went out for blood donors. This reminded me that for medical science the blood was not just a theoretical concept, it was a matter of life or death! I grabbed an encyclopedia and began reading about what the blood does for the human body. As I read, it occurred to me why I had been having difficulty relating to the blood. The Christians of the New Testament were familiar with the temple sacrificial system, so the concept of Christ's blood as a sacrifice was easy for them. But, in all my life, I had never seen a sacrifice. No wonder this concept was so hard for me to apply to my daily living!

I soon came to see that medical science's discoveries about the role of our blood in health and healing provides a striking parallel to the place of Christ's blood in our salvation.

First, medical science helps us understand that the washing in Jesus' blood is not an outer washing, as in the sacrificial system, but an *inner washing*. A patient is desperately ill. The doctor orders a pint of blood from the blood bank, transfuses this blood into the veins of the patient, and a marvelous thing happens: the desperately ill person's life is restored!

Back in the 1940's the RH factor was introduced. Physicians discovered that if one parent had RH positive blood and the other RH negative, death was almost inevitable for the baby they produced. The only solution was to drain out the blood of the newborn and wash clean the circulatory system with another's blood. Paul speaks of something similar in the "washing of regeneration" in Titus 3:4-6. John tells us that Christ "washed us from our sins in his own blood (Rev. 1:5 KJV). Paul explains in Romans 5: 18-19 that we have inherited the "bad blood" of our father Adam, and this blood inevitably brings death. But when we receive a transfusion of Christ's blood the curse is removed. Imagine! When I received by faith a transfusion of the blood Christ made available on the cross, His DNA became my DNA!

There is a second parallel. The function of the red blood cells is a metaphor of how, when we confess our sins, the blood of Jesus Christ "cleanses us from all unrighteousness." Forty-five per cent of our blood volume is composed of red blood cells, tiny rounded discs with indented centers that are constantly circulating throughout our bodies. These absorb the poisons accumulated in the body's tissues and transport them to the lungs, where they are removed. In the lungs the red blood cells receive oxygen, and then circulate through the capillaries, sharing this life-giving oxygen with the tissues. Similarly, when we confess our sins, Christ's blood cleanses us (John 1:9,7) and provides an infusion of the oxygen of the Holy Spirit to renew our heart and soul with love, joy and peace.

There is a third parallel. Medical science has discovered that the white blood cells heal our bodies. The white blood cells are soldiers. When an infection threatens, a trumpet sounds and these warriors by the thousands rush to the site of the invasion and destroy the enemy. Isaiah 53:5 make clear that the blood of Christ heals us, not only spiritually, but also physically. In the New Testament the same Greek word *sotso* is translated, at times, "save" and at times, "heal" (see Acts 13:31 and James 5:14-15). This is a reflection of the Biblical concept that the healing Christ provides is integral: spiritual healing, mental healing, and physical healing.

This discovery of what it means to be washed in the blood has enriched my prayer life. Each day as I pray I live again that transfusion of Christ's blood that brought me salvation. Each day as I confess my sins, I picture Christ's red blood cells taking away my unrighteousness. Every time I feel a pain, or an illness threatening, I close my eyes and invoke Christ's white blood cells for healing.

Christ's blood is God's miraculous instrument for cleansing and for healing.

As the year 2002 began, we moved ahead with plans for the future of the *Lomas* church. Some thirty members of the congregation spent a weekend in the Cuernavaca weekend home of Oscar and Betty, participating in a relationship seminar and a study of the gifts of the Spirit. Each one identified the ministry he would be part of. We made plans for initiating Sunday evening services. Later in the month seventeen people were baptized.

In February we dedicated five elders, defining their ministries in accord with their gifts of the Spirit. The next month Gabriel Cesar, pastor of the church in "Satellite City," met with us and committed himself to collaborate for the one year in the preparation of the elders, and to preach once a month. I was pleased with the progress of talks with Tomas Garcia. He was feeling more and more that God was preparing the way for him to become a part of *Armonia Familiar*. American Express was in a program of reorganization, and had mentioned the possibility of eliminating his department. Meanwhile, a solution for the problems in our counseling center was slowly unfolding. Eleonora Roque was working with the staff in a program of professional growth, and as I interviewed our personnel month after month a concept of who should remain and who should be let go began to emerge

As the year progressed we could see more evidences of God's providence. In April we had our first evening service in the sanctuary of Union Church. Sunday mornings an English-speaking congregation worships in that beautiful colonial chapel. It is located in the heart of the *Lomas* district on Reforma Avenue, an elegant boulevard that sweeps from downtown some fifteen miles westward to the edge of the city. In our first service, I was very conscious of God's "Caleb" providence. Eighteen years before, the nascent Anastasis church began a period of substantial growth in that very building. After two years we bought property near downtown and moved away. And now Caleb returns to continue an uncompleted conquest!

There was also an encouraging development in *Armonia Familiar*. Tomas Garcia informed me that in August American Express would terminate his twenty-year employment, and that he was convinced God was leading him to work with us.

And there was more. I'd had little relation with the seminary since my resignation nearly twenty years earlier. Now was a critical time for the seminary because its president had fired five teachers and taken an aggressively negative attitude toward the *Satellite* Church, which occupied its chapel on weekends. For years I had been praying that this church, one of the fastest-growing congregations in Mexico, would become a working partner of the seminary. At the moment, the opposite seemed to be happening. So I was pleased when the president invited me to bring Linda and Donna to the seminary for a two-day ministry of prayer with the staff and the student body. The first day, entering the seminary campus, Linda said, "Wait a moment, do you smell what I smell?" We did! a strong, sweet fragrance of honeysuckle. We paused, searching for flowers. There were none. We agreed that God had given us a sign.

Tomas began his work with us, dividing his time between Armonia Familiar and the church, which had recently agreed on a name, "The Christian Church of *Las Lomas*." The leaders of the congregation spent a second weekend in the home of the Oscar and Betty in Cuernavaca mapping plans for the future. Pastor Gabriel began a 12-month study of "The Purpose Driven Church."

In September another scare for Evelyn and me. I was in Mexico City at *Armonia Familiar*, preparing to leave on a retreat. The phone rang. It was Pastor Garner in Kingwood: Evelyn had suffered a heart attack and was in Emergency. I caught the first flight out and arrived back in Kingwood at midnight. Evelyn was in Intensive Care, but apparently out of danger. Later, knowing the full story, I realized how near I had come to losing my beloved life partner. That morning Evelyn began to feel very weak, and had pains in her jaw and her arms. She called the church office, asking for help, telling them she suspected a heart attack. Two of the secretaries came at once, dialing 911 on a cell phone. An ambulance arrived, they placed her on a stretcher, and before they reached the ambulance, she suffered a cardiac arrest. They revived her with a defibrillator.

The doctor told me later that if the ambulance had arrived ten minutes later it probably would have been too late. The medical term, "home death" describes 90% of the cases of elderly persons at home alone when a heart attack occurs. Most do not have the presence of mind to call for help. Evelyn said later she still doesn't know what prompted her to call, she had never had such symptoms before and could easily have passed them off as insignificant.

Two near-death experiences in the span of two years! Evidently God still has plans for Evelyn. She tells me now that she has no fear of death because she died on that stretcher and it wasn't bad at all!

Slowly, painfully, the new profile for *Armonia Familiar* was unfolding. We decided that Anita was not functioning adequately as Director of Psychotherapy, so we turned over the administration of that department to Eleanora. Anita was indignant. I explained to her that we wanted her to continue in personal counseling, because she was very good at that. Eleanora talked with her regularly, encouraging her to remain, but at the same time moving ahead with urgently needed administrative changes. I was pleased with the emerging professionalism and commitment to Christian principles in our institution.

The seminary, after so many frustrating years, seemed to be on the verge of important changes. After his financial rescue of the seminary years before, Oscar Franco had been named to the Board of Trustees. Now he was president of the Board and was advocating a partnership with the Satellite City church. He was in favor of the church's proposal to buy a portion of the seminary's property for the construction of a 3,000 seat sanctuary, and to assume responsibility for its financial support. This would put an end to the perennial economic crisis that had haunted the seminary since breaking off its relationship with the International Mission Board. I was ecstatic, because for many years I had been convinced that God's destiny for the seminary was a partnership with this church, one of the most dynamic Baptist churches of Mexico.

As the year 2003 began, we were impatient for the completion of the renovation of the building purchased for *Armonia Familiar*. Instead of being ready for occupancy in January, as we had hoped, it was obvious we were months away from that event. A third floor was being constructed, and there had been disagreements with the contractor over a number of details. We had recently added two new psychotherapists to our team.

In February Evelyn accompanied me to Mexico City. It was immediately obvious that her heart attack had left her with a deficiency of energy at higher altitudes. She spent most of her time in bed. One day we were walking down the street and she stumbled and fell. I was holding her arm, and she took me down with her. Both of us landed on her arm, and for months afterward she would be seeking relief for the recurring pain.

The following month saw the publication of my book, *Charming the Serpent*. I had tried to explain in my novel a paradox that had bothered me since my first years in Mexico: how is it possible that Mexico, a country blessed with abundant natural resources and an intelligent, energetic people, has never been able to move up from third world status? Why are the majority of her people poor and her government perpetually corrupt? I had become convinced that at the root of these problems is a demonic presence carried over from pre-colonial days and incorporated into the theology of the Roman Catholic Church. The more I lived and worked in Mexico the more I became aware of this presence, like a dark shadow hovering over the people's subconscious, provoking in many a dark passivity, a depressive spirit, a prevalent black humor.

The media center of Kingwood First Baptist sponsored a book-signing, and several hundred people purchased copies. It was a great day for me! That same week an article on the book was published in *The Observer*, Kingwood's weekly newspaper. Later, I was interviewed on a Christian radio station.

Meanwhile, Oscar moved ahead with his dream for the seminary. He presented his recommendations to the National Counsel, the Convention's governing body, and they were approved. Oscar, along with Gabriel Cesar and Gilberto Gutierrez, President of the Mexican Baptist Convention flew to Waco as guests of Dr. Robert Sloan, President of Baylor University. For two days Sloan laid out a red carpet for them, and expressed a strong interest in establishing a Christian university in Mexico City. Oscar began talking about a "Baylor University of Mexico." But the President of the seminary continued to give headaches. He imposed on the Satellite church a sharp increase in rental of the chapel, and informed them that they could no longer use the music building. This saddened me, because I had hoped that the decades-long animosity between the seminary and the church would end. An evil spirit was at work!

Later that year the beautiful new home for the counseling center was dedicated. On the first floor was the reception area and the office of the Director. On the second were the counseling facilities and a room and bath reserved for me. As a third floor we had added an attractive auditorium with a capacity for a hundred people. At the back of our property was another three-story edifice with offices for the counseling personnel, a library and a warehouse.

In December a Christmas concert was presented by the Lomas church. The building was packed and the concert inspired in us a spirit of optimism and advance. By the time the year ended, I was ready to declare it the most satisfying year of my life. With one exception: I had decided the time had come to publish my novel in Spanish. When in August I was invited to preach at the annual meeting of the Hispanic Baptist Convention of Texas, I had the opportunity for fellowship with Jorge Diaz, Director of the Baptist Spanish Publishing House in El Paso. Jorge and I had nurtured a friendship for several decades. I presented him a copy of my novel. He told me they had been looking for a good Christian novel to publish, and encouraged me to believe that *Charming the Serpent* was the answer to his prayers. A month later I received a surprising letter from the book editor of the Publishing House. He informed me that he had read my book with much interest. It was well-written and absorbing, he could not put it down. However, they would not publish the book because it was "charismatic." Several exchanges of letters were not sufficient to change his mind. I was puzzled; because hundreds of traditional Christians had read my book and nobody had expressed such an opinion. I concluded I would translate the book myself and self-publish it, just as I had done with the English version.

Meanwhile, I began a new project: my memoirs. I had been keeping a diary since 1951, recording through the years the story of God's providences, of my inner battles, of miracles of God's grace. I wanted to leave this story as a legacy for my family and for the Christian community.

Chapter Thirty
Unpleasant Surprises and New Beginnings
2004-2005

Caleb's life was marked by unpleasant surprises. The cowardly report of ten of the Canaan Exploration Committee must have broken his heart. He lost one wife in Egypt and another in the desert. During Israel's forty years in the desert, how many times was he, along with Moses, disappointed by the failures of the people? We're told little about Caleb's conquest of Hebron, but we can be sure there were many difficulties. Then imagine how he must have felt, after battling to conquer the territory God had assigned as his inheritance, when he was told he must give it up, because Hebron had been designated as a City of Refuge. Finally, it was his fate to live his last years in the epoch of the judges, when the Israelites were abandoning the God of their fathers, and adopting the corrupt ways of the pagan society that surrounded them.

God had rhymed my life with Caleb's and had brought me again to Mexico City to complete the poem He had written for me. However, disappointments are the dark side of bright dreams. The year 2004 had more than its share of these dark moments.

A misadventure one chilly Sunday afternoon in January was a parable of the year that awaited me. I flew into Mexico City from Houston, excited about an occurrence that had all the marks of a special divine providence. In December, Dr. David Harms and his wife had arrived in Mexico City from Honduras. Thirty years before, after graduating from medical school in Guadalajara, they had gone to serve in that country. For twenty years they worked in small villages among the poor. Then they decided to spend what remained of their missionary career in Tegulcigalpa, the capital city, trying to reach people who had the future of the country in their hands. They perfected the art of small groups, and planted three churches. Now they wanted to spend their last six months before retirement doing the same in Mexico City.

David and I had been in contact off and on during the past thirty years. I admired his work, and he had mentioned more than once his appreciation for my ministry. David and his wife came to visit me soon after their arrival in Mexico City. When I learned of their intentions my heart accelerated. I had commented to Tomas just the day before that small groups might be the key to reaching people in our area. It was very difficult to bring the affluent people in our community people to a church service, but they would likely accept an invitation to a neighbor's home. I asked Tomas to join me in praying that God would send someone to lead us in beginning small groups. And here, the very next day, David and his wife appear! David shared my feeling that this looked like God's providence. He agreed that he would pray with me that if it were so, God would make it clear to him. So as I flew into Mexico City that January afternoon I felt certain that we were about to step into a new stage in God's plans for Lomas.

I took a taxi to *Armonia Familiar,* walked a few blocks for lunch at my favorite taco restaurant, unpacked my suitcase and dressed for the afternoon service in Lomas. A little after five Tomas rang the doorbell downstairs to let me know he was there to take me to church. I stuck my head out the window and yelled, "I'll be right down." I turned, my foot caught in the telephone cable, I left my feet and seemed to sail through the air. Landing hard on my right hip, I lay there a moment, stunned by the impact, surprised by the sharp pain.

They were waiting for me! I pushed myself up and struggled downstairs. Later, as the church service progressed, the ache in my hip grew more acute. When the time came for the sermon I stumbled to the pulpit and for half an hour forgot what had happened. But when I'd finished I found myself unable to move, and Tomas had to help me to my seat.

Ricardo and his wife Priscilla, a couple from the church, drove me to the ABC hospital. A physician took X-rays, studied them and came back shaking his head. Because of my age, he had been sure that the fall had fractured my hip. But he had found nothing! He took more X-rays, and the same result. By this time I was unable to move. Ricardo and Priscilla put me in a wheel chair and took me to spend the night in their home. Several days later when I returned to Kingwood, I was still using a wheel chair. The orthopedist took more X-rays. Afterward he congratulated me for my forty years of daily exercise. That was the reason, he told me, for no broken bones During the next six weeks I progressed from the wheel chair to a walker, to a cane, and finally I was able to move about unassisted. But like Jacob, I was left with a recurring pain in my hip, a reminder of my own frailty and of God's grace.

Just as I had hoped and prayed, David Harms joined our church and began a training program for cell groups. The people welcomed him, but only a few committed to opening their homes for small groups.

In April came a development that I was certain God would use to give a big boost to our cell groups. Mel Gibson's film, *The Passion of Christ,* came to Mexico. Oscar rented a theater for nine presentations of the movie. A large number of our members were there every night to welcome the people as they arrived. A ten-minute intermission provided an opportunity for the presentation of the Gospel. At the end of the movie, as the people moved out of the theater, we provoked personal chats. In the literature we gave them was included an invitation to attend meetings of dialog in the following three weeks.

Weeks later we weighed the results: not a single person had been added to our congregation as a result of our concerted, prayer-saturated evangelistic efforts!

Later I found that other congregations had sponsored presentations of *The Passion of Christ and* had experienced the same disappointment. It dawned on me that, unlike people in non-Catholic countries, the citizens of Mexico had constant reminders of Christ's death. There were crucifixes in their churches, they wore crucifixes around their necks, and every time they went to mass they ate Christ's body and drank His blood. So *The Passion of Christ* was not a fresh experience for them. What they needed was not more about the crucified Christ, but an encounter with the risen Christ!

And our small groups? David Harms worked tirelessly until his retirement in August. Several groups were formed, and a number of people came to Christ. But this movement that has impacted enormously in some parts of Mexico did not work for us as we had hoped.

The biggest disappointment of the year had to do with the seminary. But the word "disappointment" is not strong enough, "disaster" would be more appropriate.

By the beginning of the year, Oscar had taken on the seminary as his special project and was determined to bring it out of the role of neglected child. He personally intervened more than once to supplement the seminary's budget in times of crisis. He had gained the support of Gilberto, the President of the Mexican Baptist Convention for a project that he was convinced would bring a transformation in theological training and in the financial status of the seminary. He named this project "Seminary at a Distance". The seminary would offer training to church leaders through the internet. Any church in the convention, for fifty dollars a month, could subscribe to this service. The seminary would help the churches purchase the electronic devices necessary. Each church would form classes, and the seminary professors would give lessons by means of the computer screen and afterward engage the class in dialog.

Oscar and his group planned a demonstration for the annual meeting of the National Baptist Convention. I would act as a professor, speaking to the Convention from Kingwood. We were very excited about the project, certain that we were on the brink of a revolution in the preparation of leaders and in the impact of the seminary upon the churches of Mexico.

A technician set up the necessary equipment in the First Baptist Church of Kingwood. At the appointed hour I sat before the camera, ready for action. Half an hour later a face appeared from the media center at the seminary. They informed me that Oscar had not been able to set up the necessary equipment at the theater where the Convention was meeting, but that our successful hookup was proof that the plan was viable. Already, more than fifty churches had signed up.

But later that day a call from Mexico City relayed heartbreaking news: in a business session of the Convention, Oscar and the other members of the seminary Board of Trustees had been dismissed and another slate of candidates installed in their place. It turned out that for weeks a *coup d'ètat* had been brewing, promoted by the deposed seminary President and one of the professors. Their legislative assault was so sudden and so well engineered that the Convention President did not recover from his surprise in time to defend Oscar and his Board.

Oscar was devastated. Not only had he been thrown out on his ear without a word of thanks for all he had done for the seminary, but the "Seminary at a Distance" had died. Lunch with him on my next visit was a dreary wake. He had washed his hands of the seminary, and would have nothing more to do with it. Ever! Daniel Jimenez, who had been named interim President of the seminary, informed me that he had made frequent calls to Oscar's office, but Oscar refused to speak to him.

As the year ended I completed a Spanish version of my novel, *Charming the Serpent.* And fought against depression. And meditated on a grim lesson I had learned:

When everything seems to indicate that you have joined God in an unbeatable project, be careful, Satan has a strategy for defeating you!

This inexplicable heartbreak reminded me of the years 1967-1971, when events seemed to have undermined God's plans for moving the seminary from Torreon to Mexico City. I encouraged myself to believe that, just as in the past God had moved to counter Satan's strategies, He would do it again.

The year 2005 began without risky dreams, and there was a certain comfort in walking on solid ground. The most solid was my home fort, *Armonia Familiar*. Here indeed was proof that dreams do come true. For more than a year now I'd had the blessing of my personal apartment in *Armonia Familiar's* beautiful headquarters. I always arrived to a comfortable bed, clean towels in the bathroom and two young women, Juana and Lupita, ready to prepare my meals. Most important, we had a staff of seven mature Christian psychotherapists, plus three competent administrators, two of them with graduate degrees in psychology. So the original task that had motivated my monthly visits could be stamped with a bright, bold seal: "accomplished!"

The seminary, though, returned to the precarious situation it had experienced before the intervention of Oscar. Enrollment was the lowest in forty years, so income was very limited. By the end of the year they were pleading for help to pay utilities, cover salaries and buy food for the dining hall. On the other hand, God blessed with an excellent administration. Daniel Jimenez's title was changed from "interim Director" to "Director." On most of my visits to Mexico City we found time to have lunch together. I was pleased that, for the first time since I'd resigned from the seminary twenty-three years before, the Director sought my counsel. I grew to respect Daniel for his competence and integrity. Tomas Sanchez, a retired CPA, was named Administrator. Immediately, changes were evident. He trimmed the row of tall, stately cypresses facing the street that I had planted thirty years before. These had been neglected, and some had died. Each time I visited the campus, they seemed to me a parable of the state of the seminary. A year before I had donated money for pruning the trees, but the former Director had appropriated the donation for the purchase of office equipment. *Senor* Sanchez hired a maintenance man, and soon the plumbing was repaired and the walls were painted. Now when I arrived for a visit my heart swelled with pride because the campus I had poured out so much love upon was beautiful again: green grass, well- attended shrubbery and bright flowers. What of the future? My hope now was anchored, not in any current projects, but in the vision from God that had motivated the epochal move of the seminary from Torreon half a lifetime ago.

The *Lomas* church, as the year progressed, settled into a pattern that was both comforting and worrisome. On the positive side, its roots were firm. The Christian Church of *Lomas* was here to stay. On the other hand, growth was slow. Nearly every Sunday new people arrived. Some returned, and became regular in attendance. But the ebb of those who moved away kept the attendance more or less the same, between eighty and a hundred. Was it God's plan that the Lomas church simply be a witness by its presence? Or would there come a time of substantial growth? In moments of discouragement I reminded myself that the church began, not as my own dream, but as the dream of five families. I had simply responded to their request for help. And I thanked God that we were blessed with the pastoral leadership of Tomas Garcia, a man of integrity, love for the flock and an exceptional gift of Biblical exposition.

Of course, like every other family, Tomas and his attractive, dedicated wife Patty, encountered problems. A year ago they had entered into a period of trial with their son Pablo. Some ten years before, Pablo had married. Three children were born. Then, at the age of thirty-five, Pablo suffered a severe heart attack. The doctors informed him he would need to severely limit his activities. After a couple of months he was dismissed from his job.

Then his wife left him. He and his three children moved in with his parents. He fell into depression and renounced his faith in God. By the end of the year Patty was so depressed that she announced she was taking a sabbatical from all her church activities.

She no longer attended the Sunday services. This was an incredible change in the life of a person distinguished by her sunny smile and deep devotion to God and His church.

It looked like Satan was attacking the church leaders. Oscar and Betty discovered that their daughter Valeria had eating problems. They placed her in a clinic. After two months she was released. I attended a "welcome home" meeting one Saturday night at the Franco's house. Nearly a hundred people were present, mostly aunts and uncles and cousins. A DVD was shown of Valeria's life. Then Valeria spoke. She confessed that she had drifted away from God, and felt that this was God's judgment. But now, she declared, she was making a new start. The next night at close of the service she gave the same testimony to the church.

Then came upsetting news from Eleonora and Daniel Roque. Eleonora was the Director of Psychotherapy for *Armonia Familiar,* and Daniel treasurer of the church. Daniel, a top executive for Roche Pharmaceutical in Latin America, was notified that his company had been bought out by Bayer and he would be one of the victims of a downsizing. After several months of tension he was offered a job in Switzerland. They would have to sell the beautiful home in *Lomas* they had bought less than a year before and of course, leave the church.

How we would miss them! But the day they were leaving to look for a house in Switzerland, Bayer offered Daniel a post as Senior Vice President for Latin America. We celebrated the news like a reprieve from a prison sentence.

I was beginning to ask myself if the time had come for retrenching. Perhaps I needed to recognize that the major purpose of my monthly visits to Mexico City had been realized, and consider an interim pastorate. It seemed like a sign from God when Daniel Acuna, pastor of a Hispanic Church in Stafford, a suburb of Houston some forty-five miles to the south, called and asked to meet with me. We had coffee, and right away I liked him. In his mid-fifties, Daniel and his family had immigrated to Houston fourteen years before, fleeing an economic crisis in Argentina. Daniel supplemented his salary selling insurance. He was tired, and felt the need to take a three-month sabbatical. Would I fill his pulpit during this time?

I agreed, and in July began a very pleasant three-month relationship with "*La Iglesia del Amor*," ("The Church of Love.") Average attendance was 150, the members were from a dozen Latin American countries, the lively worship was accompanied by half a dozen instruments, and smiles and hugs abounded. It was a great three months, and when Evelyn and I left we were sure we had begun a permanent friendship with Daniel and his sweet wife Ana Maria.

Plans were made for a final service the last Sunday of October. Daniel would be present, and afterwards there would be a meal. But the Tuesday before the scheduled service, Evelyn and I found ourselves on the highway to Dallas, part of more than a million people fleeing the advance of a hurricane named Katrina. What an adventure! We tried half a dozen different routes, came close to running out of gasoline, and after twelve hours arrived at the home of a very anxious son and daughter-in-law. We spent the rest of the week with them, and it turned out to be a very pleasant visit. When we returned home we found the yard filled with tree limbs, but thankfully our house was intact. In spite of the tension-filled trip, we didn't regret it, because our section of Kingwood had been without power for four days.

Surprise! Demons are not limited to Mexico; they are also busy in the United States. Mark and Myra, a handsome young couple just turning thirty, were members of my young marrieds' class. Mark, in spite of his youth, had advanced quite far in the construction business, and now specialized in the supervision of high-rise condominiums. Myra always had a sweet smile. Some six months after they joined my class Mark came to see me.

"Dr. Pat," he said, "it took a while for Myra and me to agree on this visit, we don't want you to think we're crazy."

I listened, fascinated, as this intelligent young professional told me their story.

From the moment he was born their son Jacob, now five, had been had manifested an uncontrollable temper. He came out of his mother's body screaming and continued his screams as the nurse took him to the nursery. An hour later they returned him to his mother, informing her that they had been unable to get him to stop crying. Myra would have to look after him, because he was disturbing the other newborns. That was the beginning of days, weeks, months, and years of stress. Jacob seemed angry most of the time. He screamed, slapped his mother, sassed her, slept little. As the years passed they tried specialist after specialist, each of whom prescribed drugs that had no effect. Finally they secured an appointment with a noted team of pediatrics in Houston's famed Children's Hospital. Many visits and a variety of drugs yielded little results.

"That's why we decided to come see you, Dr. Pat. Myra and I suspect Jacob's problem is spiritual. We believe he is being oppressed by an evil spirit." Mark told me that since he was very small Jacob had awakened them frequently at night, complaining of scary creatures in his room.

"Myra and I have been recalling the history of both our families. Going back to my great-grandparents there have been problems with alcoholism, nervous breakdowns and suicides. My father died in an accident when I was in my mother's womb. My mother has struggled all her life with depression and alcohol addiction. There have been many problems in Myra's family. She and her mother have always had a very bad relationship. When I was young I was becoming an alcoholic, then decided I would not be a victim of my genetic inheritance. I stopped drinking and turned my life over to Christ. Tell me Dr. Pat; is it possible that Satan, since he could not have me, is seeking vengeance through my son?"

I told Mark it seemed likely to me that that indeed his little son was the victim of demonic oppression and we agreed we would meet weekly for prayer. The following week Mark and Myra arrived accompanied by Jacob. In the past Jacob had been friendly to me, but now he looked at me with open hostility. His parents set up a video for him in a corner of the room, and as we talked and prayed together, he seemed to be totally absorbed by what he was watching. We had agreed we would pray for Jacob without trying to draw him into our circle, until we felt the Holy Spirit's prompting. This continued for some six weeks. The script was always the same: the arrival of Jacob with his parents, refusing to acknowledge my greeting, remaining absorbed in his video as we prayed, refusing to say goodbye when they left.

One morning when I awoke I sensed a whisper of the Lord: this was God's day for a confrontation! When they arrived, I told Mark and Myra of my impression and they were in agreement. After some minutes at prayer Mark went to his son, took his hand and brought him to sit on the couch at his side. Jacob sat mute, eyeing the floor.

"Jacob," I said softly, "you don't like me, do you?"

He shook his head vigorously.

"Is it because you're afraid I'm going to ask you to do something you don't want to do?"

"Yes!"

"Look at me, Jacob."

For the first time, the little boy looked me in the eye.

"Jacob, I'm going to make you a promise: I'll never ask you to do anything you don't want to do. Do you believe me?"

The hostility melted from Jacob's face, he gave me a half smile and said, "Yes."

At that instant I sensed a separation between Jacob and the spirit of fear, and knew that it was Jacob himself who had responded.

I turned to his father. "Mark, as Jacob's father and as a man of God you have authority over the demonic spirit that has been oppressing your son. You speak the word of liberation."

Nodding, Mark placed a hand on his son's head and declared, on the authority of Christ's blood, that his son was set free. Then he thanked God for hearing his prayer.

Jacob raised his head, opened his eyes and gave me a smile.

"Got a high-five?" I asked him, extending my hand.

Still grinning, Jacob slapped my hand with all his might.

From that day, Jacob's parents noted a decided difference in their son. His fits of anger were less frequent. Sometimes he would go for weeks completely at peace. We did follow ups, and continued the learning process. Mark and Myra noted that when the grandparents visited, Jacob's conduct worsened, and concluded it was because they had yet to be freed. Myra did a video telling her mother what she had never been able to say face to face, and her mother responded positively. We prayer-walked the upstairs of their home, because Jacob still didn't like to go upstairs alone.

This experience gave me a fresh awareness of the reality of "familiar spirits," and I prayed the Lord would help me to create this awareness in the minds of other young parents.

In April, an unexpected adventure: Evelyn and I went to Hawaii! Ten years before I had suggested we celebrate our fiftieth wedding anniversary by vacationing in Hawaii, but Evelyn didn't like the idea of spending ten hours or more on a plane. So I'd given up the idea. Then one Sunday night we ran into Dale and Maria Theresa on the church parking lot. "Guess what," Dale said, "I'm taking Maria Theresa to Maui Wednesday. Come with us."

"Thanks," I replied, "I'd love to go, but Evelyn refuses any flight that lasts more than above a couple of hours."

On the way home I remarked, "Well, it would've been nice."

I was startled when Evelyn replied, "You know, maybe we ought to go."

As soon as we got home I dialed Dale and asked him to check it out. Dale is a Continental Airlines pilot and that means he and his family have special travel privileges. His being a pilot was what tipped the scales in Evelyn's mind. If any emergency came up on the flight she could put her fate in the hands of someone with experience. An hour later Dale called and told us he had made reservations for us. "And look, I hope you won't mind, but Maria Theresa and I want to make this trip our Christmas present for you."

The trip was marvelous, not only because of the beauty of the island and the adventure of traveling the ocean floor in a submarine, but especially because of the fellowship with Dale and Maria Theresa.

Some six years before Dale, a member of my Sunday School class, came to see me. Soon to celebrate his fortieth birthday, he was concerned that he had yet to find the person he would be willing to spend the rest of his life with. "I don't know what the problems is, Dr. Pat. I've gone out with a number of nice girls, but I haven't fallen in love with any of them.

Dale had grown up on a farm in Indiana, the child of Christian parents. Quite handsome, he was a committed Christian. For years he had been a sponsor of a Christian orphanage in Guatemala. And of course, as a pilot, he drew a good salary.

Then he asked me a question: "In your opinion, would it be a sin if I tried a matrimonial bureau?"

"A sin? I don't think so. But dangerous? You bet! If you decide to go that route, you need to pray a lot."

Months passed. I saw Dale only occasionally, because most weekends he was on flights to other states, or to Latin America. Then one Sunday he appeared in class, accompanied by a slim, very attractive young woman. "Meet Maria Theresa, my wife."

The next week we had lunch with the newlyweds and they told us their fascinating love story. Dale had indeed signed on with a matrimonial bureau, not in the United States, but in Colombia. This agency was dedicated to bringing together young Columbian women interested in the possibility of marriage to an American, and American men with a corresponding intrerest. Dale dated several *señoritas*, but none of them met his requirements, especially because one of his first questions had to do with the other person's relationship to God. Things changed when he was matched up with Maria Theresa.

While in Hawaii I asked them that inevitable question: was it love at first sight?

With a wide smile, Maria Theresa answered with her charming Latin accent, "Absolutely. The moment I saw him I said, 'That one's for me!'"

"I turned to Dale. "And you also, love at first sight?"

To my surprise, Dale shook his head. "No, it took a while. I kept telling myself, 'This is too good to be true.'"

I could understand his hesitation. Maria Theresa, in her mid-thirties, was a professional and lived with her family. She had never married, refusing several proposals. Though she had not attended an evangelical church, she had an affirming testimony of a personal faith in Christ.

Our class gave the newlyweds a warm welcome. I expected them to ask me for counseling, sooner or later. After all, they were adults of long standing who had become accustomed to making their own decisions, and their cultures were very different. Dale had acquired a working knowledge of Spanish, but Maria Theresa knew no English.

However, as the months passed, then the years, Evelyn and I marveled at the beauty of their marriage. They seemed to be on a perpetual honeymoon. Maria Theresa, always smiling and upbeat, traveled quite often with Dale. Both families accepted the marriage enthusiastically. She enrolled in English classes in a nearby university and within a year became quite fluent.

We had already formed a pleasant friendship before the trip to Hawaii. The week we spent together in that island paradise deepened our friendship. There were many highlights, but the most unforgettable one for Evelyn and me was the luau we attended. It turned out we were longest-married couple, and they presented Evelyn a gorgeous lei.

Unpleasant surprises are an inevitable part of living. But God's pleasant surprises always outnumber the disappointments. That's the promise of grace.

Chapter Thirty-One
New Adventures
2004 - 2008

In 2003 I had published my book, *Charming the Serpent,* a novel based on Mexico's demonic history. I knew I must publish it in Spanish, because, after all, the book had been lived out in Spanish, and I had learned that the people in Mexico were largely ignorant of the demonic history of their country. When the Spanish Baptist Publishing House decided not to publish the book, I began a search for a translator and contracted a young woman with considerable experience. But when she delivered the first fifty pages, I was disappointed. Being a novel, the book is crammed with figures of speech. The translator's rendering of these was inadequate, in some cases ludicrous. I paid her, gave her my thanks and began looking for someone else. Now I realized I must find someone who had lived sufficient time both in the United States and in Mexico to feel at ease in the idiom of both. After months of frustration it dawned upon me that the only person I knew who filled that description was Pat H. Carter! Besides, I now realized I didn't want a translation, but an interpretation. As I wrote *Charming the Serpent* I had placed myself in the shoes of the American citizen reading the book. Now I must place myself in the shoes of the Mexican reader, avoiding stereotypes that might offend him, and winning his acceptance of my interpretation of the history of his country.

Early in 2004 I completed my work. I was encouraged when Ruby, a member of our church in Lomas, offered to read the book and recommend revisions. Ruby, a brilliant young mother of Iranian descent, is a convert from Islam. She spent three months with the book, and when she had finished I accepted her recommendations practically intact. She suggested a title, *Desnudando a la Serpiente,* and I liked it. Carol, my youngest daughter, agreed to be the editor. I felt very fortunate to have her help, because she had more than twenty years of experience in the Spanish Baptist Publishing House in El Paso, Texas.

Late in 2005 the book was sent to a publisher in Columbia, and in December 900 books arrived in Mexico City and 200 in Houston. I prepared a lecture to lay out the background of the book in meetings of promotion, entitled, "In Search of the Soul of Mexico". My novel, I explained, had as its purpose an answer to the conundrum that is Mexico: "How is it possible that a nation with abundant natural resources, populated by an intelligent, disciplined people, has continued century after century, year after year, as a third-world country? Why has Mexico not been able to realize its dreams?" The frustration produced by this puzzle is mirrored in the soul of the Mexican people, a soul described by its psychologists as depressive, masking its unhappiness with black humor.

I suggested that the key to understanding Mexico can be found in a study of its ancient god Quetzalcoatl. For thousands of years Mexico and middle America worshipped dozens of demon-gods. Only Quetzalcoatl was common to all the cultures. I dwelt on a surprising phenomenon: Quetzalcoatl was endowed by his theologians with the seven key attributes of Christ: Water of Life, Light of the World, salvation through his blood, Conqueror of Death, Creator of the new man, incarnation of God, and a Second Coming. Amazing! How can we explain the fact that these characteristics were applied to Quetzalcoatl centuries before the knowledge of Christ arrived to the Americas? My thesis: Satan, after God thrust him out of the Garden of Eden, found another garden, middle America, and there he placed Quetzalcoatl, an incarnation of Satan himself. Satan's purpose was to mock God by giving this serpent, which God had doomed to crawl on his belly, wings to fly, plus all the attributes of God's own Son. Though

Quetzalcoatl's temple was destroyed by Hernan Cortes, he remains active in Mexico's ubiquitous superstitions and witchcraft.

A second influence on the soul of Mexico is the syncretistic religion introduced by the Roman Catholic Church. When the early Franciscan missionaries found they were unable to replace the pagan religion, they incorporated it into Christianity, baptizing its gods with Christian names. The crucifix and the Virgin Mary are the two major symbols of this syncretism.

In February, 2006 I traveled to Mexico City and presented my Powerpoint lecture in two churches. In March I presented the study to the students of the Mexican Baptist Theological Seminary, and the book was placed in the Seminary library and book store.

In April a turning-point came in the promotion of my novel. Mexico City's Christian University of the Americas sponsored a breakfast on my behalf in the Hotel Del Prado. Some two hundred people attended, leaders in half a dozen different denominations. After my presentation a pastor introduced me to a tall, handsome gentleman named Manuel Moctuzuma, along with his father, his wife and his teenage son, explaining that they were descendents of Emperor Moctezuma II.

I was stunned, because the lecture I had just presented was centered on the reign of Emperor Moctezuma. I accepted their invitation to join them at their table, preparing myself for a negative critique of my talk. To my surprise, *Don* Manuel congratulated me for an accurate presentation of his distinguished ancestor. In the months that followed a friendship developed, and each time I went to Mexico City I had breakfast with Manuel, accompanied by his wife and half a dozen others.

Señor Moctezuma had graduated from the national university as an ecologist. He was engaged in the development of a section of an eastern jungle that he had inherited from his family. He had been a Roman Catholic and a follower of the Aztec religion until his conversion nine years before. Now he was an ardent Christian and Professor of History at the Christian University of the Americas.

As the months passed, Professor Moctezuma adopted *Desnudando a la Serpiente* as a textbook in his class on the history of Mexico and placed several hundred copies of the books with his students. He encouraged me to write a sequel. The old gods, he assured me, continue active in Mexican politics. As I read half a dozen books on Mexican pre-conquest history that he lent me, I learned more about the fascinating story of Moctezuma the Second and the sophisticated world he created on the island of Tenochtitlan. One of the books Professor Moctezuma placed in my hands was written by an uncle, a professor in the national university. Like some of the characters in my novel, his ambition is to return Mexico to its pre-conquest glory. He challenges the concept that Moctezuma's kingdom was superstition-ridden and oppressive. To the contrary, he insists, Moctezuma ruled over an ideal society.

One of my biggest surprises was the acceptance of my novel by Baptists. Because of the negative reaction of the Baptist publishing house, I had prepared myself for a crisis in my relation with my denomination. The opposite happened. The Executive Director of the Mexican Baptist Convention sent me an e-mail in April. He had read my book, and was convinced it illumined a serious omission in the evangelism being practiced in Mexico. At the moment of inviting Christ into one's life, he suggested, the convert should be required to renounce the demonic culture that he has inherited. He asked my help in correcting this omission in a program of church planting he was promoting throughout Mexico. In subsequent months we met several times, he promoted my book in the denominational newspaper and included a leaflet about the novel in a monthly letter to the Baptist churches of Mexico.

In March I presented my novel to several hundred leaders of the First Baptist Church of Satellite City, one of the largest churches in the country. In May I spoke at a national retreat of the leaders of the Baptist denomination's church planting movement. In July I was the featured speaker at a meeting of the Regional Baptist Convention in Toluca, a state capitol, and in October at the Central Baptist Convention in Mexico City. In August I presented nine hours of conferences at the annual Baptist Pastor's Retreat in Monterrey. Again, my novel was well received.

In addition, the promotion of my book provided the opportunity to become acquainted with Christian leaders in the larger evangelical community. In May I was the featured speaker at the monthly breakfast of the Christian book stores in Mexico City. There I met the president of the ministerial alliance, who later wrote an endorsement of my book. I contracted an announcement on the back cover of the Christian journal, *Vida Màs Familia* (Life Plus Family). The Director of this publication, who also edits five other Christian magazines for the Assembly of God Church in Mexico, offered his friendship and his collaboration in the promotion of my book. Without charge, he placed a full-page advertisement of *Desnudando a La Serpiente* in a journal sent monthly to more than six thousand Assembly of God pastors in Mexico. In September, at a breakfast with Manuel Moctzuma, I met Eduardo Marquez, a pastor and "Apostle" in one of the charismatic movements. He spoke enthusiastically of how he had used my novel in the conversion of the owner of a *Salòn de Fiestas*.

Every October book publishers and book stores cooperate in the "*Expo Cristiana.*" They contract a floor of the World Trade Center in Mexico City Thursday-Sunday and rent booths to more than 300 Christian agencies. I wanted to take advantage of this opportunity to promote my book, but became discouraged when I found that the cost of a booth, plus the rental of a hall for a promotional speech would be $2300. However, a few weeks before the event, *Armonia Familiar* and the Christian University of the Amèricas invited me to share the two booths they had rented. I spent four days with them, and Saturday afternoon presented my talk, "In Search of Mexico's Soul" to an overflow audience.

By the end of October my stock of books had dwindled to less than 100. A friend of Ruby did a fresh revision of the novel, Carol again did the editing, and we contracted the publishing of one thousand more copies.

Meanwhile, life continued to unfold. In March Evelyn celebrated her 80th birthday, then I also in the month of May. On a visit to Dallas later that year Evelyn and I looked at houses and apartments. David was insisting that we begin thinking of moving closer to him and his sister Linda. He pointed out that my frequent Mexico trips meant that Mom was often at home alone. How could we be sure there would not be a repetition of the heart attack several years before? However, when we returned to our Kingwood home it was like folding ourselves into the arms of a very dear friend, and we agreed we were years away from a resettlement.

In May, Carol and her husband declared an end to their troubled marriage of more than thirty years. We were saddened but accepted it as inevitable. Her husband had become involved with a woman he met on the internet. A few months after the divorce he married her. Carol, on her part, experienced a renewal and the emotional freedom she had longed for.

In October, a year after the retirement of Dr. Dearing Garner, we had the experience of calling a new pastor, Dr. Kevin McCallon. He and his wife Erin came for a four-day get-acquainted visit, and by the time he preached on Sunday morning the church members were enthusiastic in their agreement that he was an answer to a year of fervent prayers. Also, beginning that month, after fifteen years as teacher of a young marrieds class, I moved into a new arrangement of team-teaching. Because of my trips to Mexico City, plus other preaching opportunities, I was seldom in my class more than two Sundays per month. Now I was finding satisfaction in mentoring, preparing others to carry out ministries I had done alone before.

In late October Evelyn and I had an adventure that had been on our calendar for more than sixty years: we went on a Niagara Falls honeymoon. It turned out to be all we could have dreamed, with a room on the twentieth floor of the Sheraton Hotel, overlooking Horse Shoe Falls. But on the return trip the dream turned into a remarkable imitation of a nightmare. We were due to leave Niagara Falls very early Friday morning and drive fifty miles to Buffalo for our flight home. Thursday morning snow flakes began drifting down. By dark the flurries had turned into a steady flow, but people assured us there was nothing to worry about. Winter was still weeks away, they said, so the snow would melt as soon as it hit the ground. Friday we awoke at dawn to a heavy snowfall. It took me ten minutes to identify our little red rental car and defrost the windshield. At the Canadian customs they warned us that one of the highways to Buffalo was closed and the other was covered with heavy snow. We talked it over and decided we couldn't take a chance on missing our flight. Soon we found ourselves in a white wilderness. Only a few vehicles were on the highway, and the flurries raised by the eighteen-wheelers roaring past blinded us. I saw right away that I must, at all costs, stay in the ruts made by the preceding traffic, or we'd end up like numerous cars we saw stranded in enormous drifts. Scary!

The fifty-mile trip took nearly two hours, and to our dismay we found the airport shut down. The city was buried under twenty-two inches, the heaviest October snowfall in history. There was no power, and because of live wires that had fallen into the streets, the city prohibited taking out your car. I called a dozen hotels and they were all filled. So Evelyn and I found ourselves marooned in a terminal with no heat, only emergency lighting, and the restaurants closed.

Sounds terrible! But isn't it interesting that we end up remembering most disasters as fascinating adventures? That night Evelyn demonstrated her unique gift for shutting out the world. She found an abandoned wheelchair, bundled up in her coat, and slept peacefully for several hours. I stretched out on the floor with a coat for a pillow, but couldn't sleep, because of the people around me who who preferred chatting to trying to get a few winks. About eleven I resolved that I was not going to be a victim of my circumstances. "Lord," I said, "by faith I receive your grace, so that tomorrow I will be as alert and rested as if I had slept eight hours." It worked! The next morning we got a 9:00 o'clock flight to Newark, and from there a flight to Houston, arriving at our home port at ten. Our baggage had not accompanied us. But the next day after church I went to the baggage claim, delivered my receipts, the attendant consulted her computer and within five minutes delivered the two missing bags. I was impressed! At noon Evelyn and I, enjoying Kentucky Fried Chicken in our warm breakfast room, agreed that life is good, and that appropriating God's liberty frees us from being victims of our circumstances.

In November I fulfilled another dream, this one twenty years old. After my sky dive at sixty I had promised myself I'd do another at eighty. But I encountered a problem. Half the fun of a sky dive is being accompanied by a partner, and as the months passed I couldn't find anyone interested in throwing himself out of an airplane. Finally, in October, the most macho guy in my Sunday School class agreed to do it with me. I was sure he'd have a great time, because Matt had demonstrated his adventurous spirit by traveling on his Harley Davidson all over the United States and in Mexico. But the following Sunday, shame-faced, he told me his wife had turned thumbs down.

What would I do? We were less than two months from the end of my eightieth year! Thank the Lord, the next week Tom, one of the most *macho* men in our class, volunteered. His wife had set only one condition: before the jump he must double his life insurance!

It was great. At 14,000 feet, you fling yourself into a roaring hurricane (remember, when you leave the plane it's going 150 miles an hour, and then you fall at 120 miles an hour!) I'd spent a hundred dollars for a photographer to accompany me on the way down. The last time I'd jumped the photographer's camera failed, and I had no lasting proof of that wild adventure. But this guy was very professional, his camera was attached to his *helmet*, and he made half a dozen jumps every day. Halfway into my fall he floated over and shook my hand. As I said, it's a great adventure: you fall eight thousand feet in less than a minute, pull the rip cord, and then float slowly down for the last six thousand feet, enjoying an incredible view. And this time I didn't run the risk of repeating what happened in my Mexico jump, forgetting to pull the rip-cord. I was hooked up to a trainer who had already jumped 4,752 times.

No, Evelyn wasn't there, but she did agree a couple of days later to take a look at the DVD. Years ago Evelyn and I came to an understanding: she lets me do anything I want, as long as she doesn't have to go along. After so many risky adventures, she has learned the technique of just tuning them out.

In mid-December 1,000 copies of the second edition of *Desnudando a la Serpiente* arrived, and I began laying plans for promotion in a number of the major cities of Mexico. The next eighteen months were filled with carrying out those plans. I was invited to present my book in a number of churches in Puebla and Guadalajara. I gave a study on spiritual warfare to several hundred church leaders at an annual retreat near Mexico City. Upon registrering, each of those attendending received a copy of *Desnudando a la Serpiente.* In May, Manuel Moctezuma, accompanied by his wife and son, took me on a tour of a large segment of eastern Mexico. Beginning in San Luis Potosí, about 250 miles north of Mexico City, we drove eastward across the arid countryside. The trip provided a distressing specimen of Mexico's economic crisis. We passed through dozens of small villages practically abandoned by *campesinos* that had migrated to the United States. Manuel explained that this area had for centuries been the bread basket of Mexico, but a generation ago had become sterile. He is convinced God placed a curse on the countryside because of the people's idolatry. We spent a part of two days in *Ciudad del Maiz*, Manuel's home town. From this county seat town the Moctezuma family, for more than a century, ruled over hundreds of thousands of acres that stretched from the Gulf of Mexico almost to the Pacific. In the main square is a statue of an ancestor who was President of Mexico. He was assassinated in 1847. Across the *plaza* from the statue is the cathedral. Inside, near the altar, is a plaque on the wall that reads: "Here lies an eye of President Felipe Barragan." Manuel informed me that his ancestor's heart is deposited behind the altar of the cathedral of Guadalajara, and his head behind the altar of the National Cathedral in Mexico City.

Adventuring with God! My promotional tour of Mexico stirred many memories of years past, and introduced me to realities I had not known before. Here I was in my eighties, and life was more exciting than ever. When would these adventures end? The greatest adventures of the Biblical Caleb began when he was eighty-five. In God's poem for His second Caleb, has He reserved the biggest adventures of all for eighty-five and beyond?

Will I see the end of this age? As I meditated on the possibility of fulfilling Manuel Moctezuma's dream of a sequel to *Desnudando a la Serpiente,* I discovered a fact that set my creative juices to boiling. In the year 3550 B.C. the Mayans initiated a calendar. From the very beginning they set the date for the calendar's end: December 22, 2012. Just one year after my eighty-fifth birthday! That discovery gave me the key to the sequel: between the two last chapters of *Desnudando a la Serpiente* I had left a space of some fifteen years. My sequel would cover those fifteen years, and its ending would coincide with the end of the Mayan calendar.

I have just completed writing that sequel. Except for the last chapter. I have yet to decide if the ending of the Mayan calendar should usher in the End of the Age, or a new beginning. Either way, I suspect that, like the Caleb with whom my life's Poem rhymes, my own biggest adventures lie ahead.

Epilogue
The Greatest Adventure

At the end of the book of Job we are told: "Now the Lord blessed the latter days of Job more than his beginning." I'm thankful that I can say the same about my own life.. God has blessed the latter days of Evelyn and me with health, peace and joy. Like Job, our principle joy is our children, grandchildren and great-grandchildren. Our son David's partial retirement coincided with the marriage of their daughter Ashley and the birth of Kamdyn and Jacob. David and Vicki consecrate a large part of their time to the care of their grandchildren while Ashley works as an executive of Clinique, a cosmetic firm. Linda and her husband are at a period in their careers when her responsibilities as a personnel trainer for Palm Harbor Homes, and his as manager of a restaurant occupy most of their time, but they continue to be two of the happiest people I know. Carol is excited about the freedom she now enjoys to explore the unfolding of Romans 8:28 in her life. A freelance writer and a popular speaker for women's retreats, she is re-locating to Phoenix and an exciting new ministry that awaits her.

I still remember a surprising event that occurred toward the end of my dad's life. Evelyn and I were visiting my parents, and with them were driving the seventy miles from Krotz Springs, their little South Louisiana hometown, to Alexandria, the frontier city between Cajun South Louisiana and Anglo-Saxon North Louisiana. When the conversation lagged Mama, in the back seat with Evelyn said, "Why don't we talk about heaven?" Dad, seated at my side, grumbled, "Heaven? I don't even know if there is a heaven!" Mama voiced an indignant protest, but we *didn't* talk about heaven. Of course Daddy did believe in heaven, but he wanted Mama to know it wasn't something he felt comfortable talking about.

I've never forgotten Daddy's words. I regret he didn't feel comfortable dialoguing about that awesome place he would be entering in just a couple of years. But from what I've observed, the majority of people seated in heaven's waiting room feel the same way as my daddy.

It doesn't make sense! Trudy Harris concludes her delightful book, *Glimpses of Heaven,* reminding us that everyone dies, dying is a very natural part of living. It is not an ending but a beginning. A transition into the life God has promised to all of His children.

When I turned eighty, I made a resolution to begin preparing myself for heaven. My life has been a story of adventuring with God. Now, as I await other adventures that the Lord has prepared for me here on earth, I have begun my orientation for the greatest Adventure of all. By accelerating my participation in God's plan to mold me into the image of Christ. By reading books on heaven. By keeping my heart tuned into the "Heaven Channel," for any word from the Lord about my future home. And I welcome every opportunity to dialog with others my age who feel the same fascination as I with that incredible place.

An elderly man declared he was homesick for heaven. His granddaughter protested. His answer: "But honey, how can I help being homesick for heaven? After all, at this stage of life I have more friends in heaven than I have on earth!"